Dedication

*To Blair Guilford Camp and Ruth Milner Camp
and all those that came before... and after*

Making Music On Your PC

Victoria Camp

Abacus
www.abacuspub.com

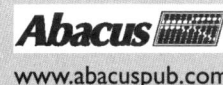

Copyright © 1997   Abacus

5370 52nd Street SE

Grand Rapids, MI 49512

www.abacuspub.com

This book is copyrighted. No part of this book may be reproduced, stored in a retrieval system, or transmitted in any form or by any means, electronic, mechanical, photocopying, recording or otherwise without the prior written permission of Abacus Software.

Every effort has been made to ensure complete and accurate information concerning the material presented in this book. However, Abacus Software can neither guarantee nor be held legally responsible for any mistakes in printing or faulty instructions contained in this book. The authors always appreciate receiving notice of any errors or misprints.

This book contains trade names and trademarks of several companies. Any mention of these names or trademarks in this book are not intended to either convey endorsement or other associations with this book.

Library of Congress Cataloging-in-Publication Data

```
Camp, Victoria.
   Making music on your PC / Victoria Camp.
     p. cm. -- (Creative computing series)
   Includes index.
   ISBN 1-55755-327-0  (pbk.)
   1. Computer sound processing.  I. Title. II. Series
MT723.C36  1997
780'.285'416--dc21                                        97-11569
                                                               CIP
                                                                MN
```

Printed in the U.S.A.

ISBN 1-55755-327-0

10 9 8 7 6 5 4 3 2 1

Contents

1 Introduction To Sound 1-56

Chapter 1. What's On The Companion CD-ROMs 3
Companion CD-ROM Contents 6
  MIDI & WAV programs 7
  CD-ROM audio players 8
  Virtual Web Site 9
  Additional programs 10
  Cakewalk 12
  _MUSIC 12
Voyetra Technologies' Demo 12

Chapter 2. Common Questions And Straight Answers 15
Exercise Assigning System Sounds 27
  Sound schemes 27
  Assigning System Sounds in Windows 95 28
  Assigning System Sounds in Windows 3.x 29

Chapter 3. Simple Sound Facts 31
Do I Really Need To Know This Stuff? 33
How Sound Travels 34
Syntheses And Synthesizers 36
Digitized Sound 37
  Sound conversion 37
  FM Synthesis 38
  Wavetable synthesis 38
  Digital sampling using wavetable synthesis 39

v

Contents

Sound Quality 42
    Direct and indirect recording sources 42
    Recording direct 42
Digital Sampling Rates And Resolution 43
    What affects sound file quality 43
    Digital sampling rate 43

Chapter 4: Music And Sound File Types 47
    WAV—Wave Form Audio File Format 49
    MIDI—Music Instrument Digital Interface 50
Some Other Formats 50
    About DOS file extensions in Windows 95 53
    Changing extension visibility in Windows 95 53
Keeping Those Terms Straight 54
    WAV versus MIDI 54
    Samples versus sampling 55
    Wavetable versus WAV 56

2 Music Hardware   57-166

Chapter 5: Introduction To Music Hardware 59
    If you don't yet have a sound card 62
Music Hardware:: What's Necessary, What's Optional 62
    Sound card 62
    Other basic equipment—headphones or speakers 63
    Electronic keyboard or synthesizer 63
    Microphone 64
    CD-ROM player 64
    Multimedia packages 64
Which Specific Sound Hardware To Buy 65
    A note about drivers 65

Contents

Chapter 6: Building Your Sound System 67

    Know your current system setup 69
    Minimum system requirements 70
    Compatibility issues 71
    Keeping records 71
    Read the manual 72
  How & Where To Shop For Your Sound Card 72
    The "wish list" principle 73
    To buy or not to buy:: Keeping the sound card you have now 73
    Shopping tips—who is the expert here? 74
  Finding The Musical Equipment You Want 75
    Mail order 75
    Shopping the 'Net—online vendors 75
    Go to the source 76
    What's on the web? 76
    Ask questions 77
    I like coffee, you like tea … 78
    Let the (computer) buyer beware ! 78
    Read the box 79
    On-board capabilities—warning, warning! 79
    Compatibility problems with "Sound Blaster Compatibles" 79
    Reputable "Sound-Blaster Type" cards 81
    Old, state of the art or in between? 81
  Summary 84

Chapter 7: Sound Cards 85

    A brief history 88
  Sound Card Features 89
    The basics 89
    Advanced features 89
  Making Choices: What Do You Want To Do? 91
    What will you want right now? 91
  Advanced Sound Card Capabilities 95
    MIDI Capability 95
    Sampling capability 96
    Wavetable synthesis compatibility 96

Contents

Wavetable add-on card 97
Other requirements 98
Letdowns And How To Avoid Them 100
Buy Now Or Later? 101
Will you make a recommendation? 102

Chapter 8: Music Keyboards And MIDI Adapters 103

Keyboard Basics 105
More Is Not Necessarily Better 108
Built-in sounds 108
Modulation wheel 109
Modulation pedal 109
Pitch wheel 110
Key range transposition 110
Channel pressure 110
Acoustic action 111
Multitimbral capability 111
Standalone capability 112
Try Before You Buy 113
Touch 114
Key response 114
Sounds 114
Construction 115
MIDI Adapters 115

Chapter 9: Speakers, Headphones And Microphones 117

Making Sound Decisions On Sound Equipment 119
Built-In speakers 119
Choosing external speakers 120
Your home stereo speakers may be an option 120
Adapters 121
Listening to speakers before you buy 123
Tips On Getting The Best Sound From Your Speakers 125
Room acoustics 125
Positioning speakers for balance 126

Contents

    Check your connections! 126
    Consider headphones 127
Microphones 129

Chapter 10: CD-ROM Drives 131

    Internal vs. external 134
Drive Speed 134
Types Of CD-ROM Drives 135
    CD-ROM playback-only drive 135
    Recordable CD-ROM drive 136
    Multi-disk CD-ROM drive 136
    SCSI 138
    Headphone connection and volume 138
Optimizing Your CD-ROM Player 138

Chapter 11: Hardware Installation & Maintenance 141

Putting It All Together 143
    Making sense of it all 143
    About your system 145
    Computer installation and your kids 146
    Tools and supplies you'll need 147
    Preparing your workspace 150
    Before disconnecting your computer 150
    Cleaning your computer 150
    Collecting your components 151
    Filling out warranties and registration forms 152
    Manuals 153
Installing Your Music Hardware 153
    Installing your sound card 154
    Installing your CD-ROM drive 156
    Installing your speakers and microphone 156
    Connecting your keyboard 157
Guitars And MIDI - The Present & The Future 157

Contents

 Music Software   167-266

Chapter 12: The Windows 95 Sound Utilities 169

Exercise One : Playing WAV Sounds 172
   Windows 95 Sound Recorder 172
Exercise Two: Playing MID or RMI Sound Files 175
   The Windows 95 Media Player 175
   What you need 177
   Adjusting sound quality 177
   The Windows 95 CD Player 178
Exercise Three: Creating An Audio Clip In WAV Format 181
Exercise Four: Creating A Voice Recording In Wav Format 185
   Recording your new vocal WAV sound 186
Exercise Five: Recording WAV Files From A VCR Or Stereo 187
   Your VCR or stereo connection 188
   Your sound card connection 188
Exercise Six: Adding Effects To A Sound File 189
Exercise Seven: Cutting & Snipping: Editing A Sound File 191
Exercise Eight: Insert A Sound File Into A Second Sound File 193
Exercise Nine: Cut And Paste 195
Exercise Ten: Overlaying Sound Files (Mixing) 196
Conclusion 198

Chapter 13: The Fun Continues 199

Advanced Exercise One: Inserting One Sound File Into Another 205
Advanced Exercise Two: How to Overlay Sound Files 208
Advanced Exercise Three: Stereo Recording 210
Advanced Exercise Four: How To Change Sound File Format
   (Audio Codecs) 213
Advanced Exercise Five: How To Convert Sound File Types 217
Advanced Exercise Six: How to Both Overlay and Combine Sound 220

Contents

Polishing and refining your sound files 221
Advanced Exercise Seven: Removing "Dead Air" 221
Advanced Exercise Eight: Get Rid Of Unwanted Noises 223
Advanced Exercise Nine: Fade In, Fade Outs 224
Some Final Tips 226
Throw out the trash 228

Chapter 14: Here's MIDI For You 231

Defining MIDI For The Newcomer 233
EarlyProblems-And The GM Solution 234
System Exclusive — What Is It? 237
What MIDI Means For You 239
Computer Music Education 241
Let's Take A Cakewalk 244
Digital Orchestrator Plus for Windows© 3.1 and 95 by Voyetra 247
DrumTrax for MIDI 247
Harmony Assistant 248
MOZART the Music Processor 248

Chapter 15: How To Use Your Newly Made Sounds 249

Practical Exercise One: Assigning Sounds to System Events 252
Practical Exercise Two: Creating Your Windows 95 System Sound Scheme . 254
Practical Exercise Three: Insert Sound Into A Document 255
Practical Exercise Four: Linking Your Sound File To Your Document 257
What Else Can I Do With My Songs? 259
Looking to promote your songs? 260
More Treats For You 260
Educational software 260
CD Player utilities 262
WAV Managers 263
Extra treats from Syntrillium 264

Contents

 **Music And The Internet**   **267-332**

Chapter 16: An Introduction To The Internet 269

    Internet-wise parenting 272
The Internet And Its Components 272
    The Internet 272
    Newsgroups 274
    Mailing lists 274
    Netiquette 274
    File Transfer Protocol - FTP 277
Connecting To The Internet 277
    Online services 278
    The World Wide Web 278
    Web addresses 279

Chapter 17: Surfing The Web 283

Search Engines 286
Plug-Ins For Your Browser 287
What's On Those Web Pages? 289
    Links 291
    FAQ (Frequently Asked Questions) 293
Downloading And Uploading Files On The Internet 295
Bookmarks - Saving Your Links 301

Chapter 18: The Web For Musicians 303

How To Search The Net: Getting A Quick Start 305
The Companion Bookmark: Following Links And Saving Bookmarks 306
The Webring—A Community Concept 307

xii

Contents

What's Out There For Me? 308
    Magazines, newspapers and journals 308
    Hardware 309
    Software 310
    Software upgrades for products you use 310

Audio And Multimedia—The Music Lover's Plug-ins 313

Audio Video Plug-ins 314
    Apple QuickTime 314
    Real Audio & Video 315
    Crescendo (Plus) By Liveupdate 316
    Yamaha Mid-Plug 317
    Internet Phone by VocalTec 318
    Live3D by Netscape 319
    Shockwave by Macromedia 320
    Koan by SSEYO 321
    AnySearch 322
    Cache Compactor 322
    CYBERsitter 322

Other Types Of Software And Files 323
    Artists 323
    Your own Web page 324
    Sound files 324

Music File Downloading 324

Making Friends On The Internet 325

Quality of Sound Files - Win Some, Lose Some 326
    Research repositories 327
    Going interactive 328

Some Amazing Web Sites 328
    Astounding sites: A bit of everything 331

Appendix A: Glossary 333

Index 343

Introduction

Foreward

Who Should Read This Book

This book was written for beginners. On the subject of music and computing, however, the definition of "beginner" covers a lot of territory!

You may be a computer whiz who knows very little about music, or a musician who's avoided computers. Or, you may already have mastered both music and computers, but you've never put them together. Maybe it's *all* new to you!

Whatever your starting point, this book will build on what you already know and help you learn how to use your computer to create and listen to music and other sounds.

What's In This Book

This book begins by answering simple questions such as "What is sound?" and "What hardware do I need?" Other topics covered include:

   How to store sound and music files on your computer.

   How to best use hardware and software you already have.

   How to enhance your sound system, based on **your** needs.

   How to save money when buying new components.

   How to find and download music and other sound files on the internet.

   How to record, edit, and add audio special effects.

   How to share your creations with others.

Introduction

Although we will sometimes mention particular hardware and software, we will not recommend particular brands and models of components. Instead, we will offer guidance to help you make the best decisions whether your budget is large or small. We will also discuss industry standards for music hardware compatibility, and offer some software for you to experiment with and enjoy.

What's On The CD_ROM?

The companion CD-ROM provides music and sound files for your listening pleasure, as well as programs that will help you work with your CD-ROM player. It includes programs that let you listen to music CDs on your computer, plus others that will enable you to use bits of your favorite music in various ways.

In order to help you master using the sounds, programs and utilities on the CD-ROM, the book offers a series of exercises designed to make your explorations easy and fun.

In addition to the sound-related utilities, instructional programs for those who wish to begin learning piano or guitar are also included.

You Can Do This

With help from this book, even the most novice of computer users can learn to produce enjoyable music.

Regardless of your confidence level or learning style, almost everyone can master the basic information we're providing. This book also points you toward advanced information if you wish to go beyond the basics. If music and sound will be your professional focus, there will be plenty of technical resources to explore once you have a running start.

You may discover new capabilities in yourself, once you learn how to work with sound utilities. Feel free to experiment and be creative!

Music can be an important part of life, but not everyone wants to explore music to the fullest. It can be an enjoyable hobby, used in a business setting, or for amusement between friends.

Introduction

The enjoyment part is the best place to start! Having fun with music and sound is one of the major points of this book. Another is to encourage those who have been frustrated with the amount of computer hardware and software that is on the market today, and who find themselves so overwhelmed that it's difficult to even begin.

Today's "state of the art" in music technology is much different from yesterday's—and tomorrow's! Even with an unlimited budget, the best system you could assemble today may be surpassed by something better (and cheaper) tomorrow. We'll help you make purchase decisions that you can live with.

Families And Learning

Playing with music and other sounds on the computer can turn into a fun family activity. It can be a magnificent way of showing children that learning can be fun. If they already have computer experience, they can probably teach *you* a few tricks in the process!

Parents usually recognize that their children need to acquire computer skills, in preparation for both higher education and for their eventual life's work. At the same time, they may be concerned that computing may get in the way of other activities that parents value, such as reading, interacting with people, outdoor activities and creative expression. But there isn't necessarily a conflict between acquiring computer skills and the traditional developmental steps of a child.

For example, the online world of computing can be a connective and personalizing one. It is easy to locate internet sites where people of all ages share tips and celebrate enjoyment of some mutual interest. Along with music and other creative arts, groups gather to write about handmade paper, camping, rollerblade skating, woodworking, creative writing ... the list is endless. One can readily discover new friends and vast amounts of information! Online services and the internet can be solid and entertaining educational tools.

Even the youngest family members can enjoy music and sounds on the computer. Infants are delighted to hear a computer squawk like a duck! Toddlers enjoy singing along with their favorite nursery rhymes. Older children can learn to play piano or guitar with the accompanying CD-ROM software. And almost everyone is amused to hear their own voice played back.

Introduction

The computer can indeed be a means of sharing and communicating with our children.

Of course, the main goals are to have fun, to learn in an easy way, and to instill confidence in those who thought that it was going to be much harder than it truly is to bring their "computer's voice" to life.

A Word On Creative Ethics
A "Safe Sampling" Overview

New technology creates new choices—and new complications!

Not long ago, there were only two types of sound cards. One would let you listen to sounds in your computer. The other also let you create and play back your own digital recordings.

Choices increased with the popularity of including a CD-ROM unit in new computers. Now you could "sample" and use sounds from favorite composers. Perhaps you'd capture a song's trumpet fanfare to be used as a system sound.

Then MIDI moved from relatively expensive musical instruments to thousands of computer cards. Now it's easy to replace a basic MIDI sound, such as a bass drum, with a different or better bass-drum sound—such as that of a renowned drummer.

There's the rub! The distinctive sound of that renowned drummer—or guitar whiz, or movie theme song—isn't legally yours for the taking, despite how easily it's taken with today's technology.

There has been much artistic, legal and philosophical discussion on whether this practice is right or wrong. As the technology becomes more powerful, affordable and easy to use these issues will become even more pressing. Laws governing this area are still being written, rewritten, interpreted and reinterpreted. Yesterday's copyright laws aren't so easily applied to new technology.

Introduction

Before sampling a sound, remember that someone spent time and money creating that sound—the artist who created the sound should be respected as its owner. One way to show that respect is to give the artist his or her due financially. Sampling professional sounds or compositions and selling them without license is unfair to the person who composed, wrote lyrics, played the instrument, or in any other way created the original sound. If you snag someone else's sound for commercial use, you ought to find out who owns it and arrange for licensing, or you could find yourself in court.

But don't be alarmed! This still leaves open other sampling and sound practices that, so far, remain both fun and safe. Provided it's not a profit-making situation, it's been OK for friends to share "sound bites" from music, movie and television themes, famous people's interviews, and the like. You also won't get in trouble using various sounds on your own system, strictly for your own pleasure. Schools are often given additional leeway to use excerpts from copyright material for educational purposes.

It's beyond the scope of this book to thoroughly discuss copyright law's effect on music technology, and vice versa. If you have a commercial use in mind for someone else's creations, play it safe and do the right thing morally and legally.

With that consideration in mind, let's proceed and learn, among other things, how to "sample and enjoy!"

Acknowledgements

Thanks:

To Ron Hovingh, most beloved confidante and friend. Much appreciation for his own skillfully written contributions to the text of this book. Thanks, too for his fine editing work and patience as mentor and writing teacher. His superb computer knowledge, professional musicianship and irrepressible good humor were graciously offered beyond the call of duty (and gratefully accepted!). Without all facets of his invaluable participation this book would not have come to be. Thanks most of all for his positive influence on my life and growth, both musical and personal.

To his darling daughters, Kathleen Mae Hovingh and Michelle Rose Hovingh, who have put a smile on my face many a time, especially when I needed it most....

To my dear friend Maureen Ward, who believed I could do this book, who made it happen, and who has brought the greatest of joy and warmth into my life by sharing heart, home and family. To her husband Quentin Ward for his never-ending humor and fantastic gourmet meals!!

To Sarah Ward, for her stunning participation—for reading the drafts of this book from cover to cover, and for her great suggestions and ideas. I predict great things for Ms. Sarah in her life, and am so fortunate to have such an amazingly bright, artistic and sensitive young friend.

To Christopher Ward for his great computer skills and testing musical examples with eagerness, intelligence and willingness to help. This young man is the tops in enthusiasm, and I'm glad to be in his life and for the gifts of his smiles and sunny nature.

To Natalie Owen, for bringing life and personality to the "Funky Frog" and for all the years of friendship that we've shared. You go, girl...

To my adored friend-for-life Barbara Segal, who is ever-present in my heart... who has walked the roads of creative growth with me through so very many years, and for so much else that there is no room here to say it all. And to her beloved husband Michael Sears, and sons Jesse and Sean Sears, for just about everything...

To Donna Cornell, for her dear friendship, and for helping me feel really welcome (and teaching me how not to get lost!) in my new home. Thanks especially for kidnapping me to afford me the enjoyable writing breaks and making sure I get a regular dose of great hugs!

To Tom and Cherie Hagen, for their love and musical support, their phenomenal musicianship and their valuable contributions to music in this book. Also, thanks to their fine puppy Ellie, for her contributions of wonderful barks!

To Norma and Bob Williams—Norma for her words of introduction in the preface of this book, and for her support and encouragement in the area of PC Music; Bob for his technical expertise and advice on sound card to stereo connections!

Introduction

To Abacus President Arnie Lee, and all the other wonderful folks at Abacus—Product Development Manager James Oldfield, Jr., whose humor and incredible patience has surely worn him out, but carried me through, Editor Brian "Mad Dog" Howard, who has endured countless questions and revisions, and who always has just the right words at the right time, Editor Scott Slaughter for his creativity and support, Graphic Designer Matt Ridgway, Sales Manager Maureen Ward and the incomparable Julie Snider, who keeps them all in line.

To my brother Neal Guilford Camp for his musical friendship, and to both he and my nephew Erik Guilford Camp, for enduring countless questions and interviews. To my brother, Blair Camp, for urging me to learn computing in the first place, all those years ago.

To my incredible mom, Ruth Camp, for hours of listening and support of my own artistic ambitions.

To my dad, Blair Guilford Camp, who always believed in me and who taught me I could do anything I wanted if I tried.

To my phenomenal, musical, beloved "b," who is everything to me...

To my friends and loved ones, who put up with my unavailability while working on this book, and who believe in me.

Introduction To Sound

SECTION 1

1

What's On The Companion CD-ROM

Inside Chapter 1

Companion CD-ROM Contents 6
    MIDI & WAV programs 7
    CD-ROM audio players 8
    Virtual Web Site 9
    Additional programs 10
    Cakewalk 12
    _MUSIC 12

Voyetra Technologies' Demo 12

What's On The Companion CD-ROM

Welcome to the *Making Music On Your PC* Companion CD-ROM. We have included all the examples and exercises in this book as well as some of the best music and sound utilities on the CD-ROM for you to experiment with. The MENU program is the main screen to access the programs and files on this CD.

To run the CD-ROM in Windows 3.x, select **Run...** from the **File** pull-down menu located at the top left corner of your screen (this is the Windows' Program Manager screen). Type "D:\MENU.EXE" (where "D:" is the letter assigned to your CD-ROM drive) and click [OK]. Click [OK] again and the menu program will be loaded.

To run the CD-ROM in Windows 95, click the [Start] button, select **Run...**, type "D:\MENU.EXE" and click [OK]. This will load the CD's menu program.

What's On The Companion CD-ROM

The Main Menu

Companion CD-ROM Contents

The following lists the directories and their contents on the companion CD ROM. With a little exploration on your part, you'll discover some great tools and techniques to help you enjoy the book.

Abacus	Contains the electronic version of the Abacus Book & Software Catalog.
Cakewalk	Twelve Tone Systems' Cakewalk Software demonstrations.
CDPlayers	Contains various CD utilities.
MIDIWAVP	Several sound, WAV and MIDI utilities.
MOREPRGS	Various sound and music programs.
NR16	Faico's outstanding Web browser—Win 3.1 version.
NR32	Faico's outstanding Web browser—Windows 95 version.
VOYETRA	Voyetra Technologies' Multimedia Catalog and Demos
_MUSIC	Various sound files.

What's On The Companion CD-ROM

The following buttons will take you to the various sub-menus. We have also included several more programs not listed below. Be sure to check the menu for new additions!

MIDI & WAV programs

AWAVe

Awave (© FMJ-Software) reads a veritable host of audio file formats from different platforms, synthesizers and trackers. It presents the instruments contained in a file as a graphical tree with the bank item at the top, instruments as branches and waveforms as leaves.

Cool Edit

Cool Edit (v1.53, © Syntrillium Software) is a digital sound editor for Windows 3.1 and 95. You might think of it as a paint program for audio. Just as a paint program enables you to create images with colors, brush strokes and a variety of special effects, CoolEdit enables you to "paint" with sound: tones, pieces of songs and voices and miscellaneous noises, sine waves and sawtooth waves, noise, or just pure silence. Cool Edit also gives you a wide variety of special effects to "touch up" your sounds: reverberation, noise reduction, echo and delay, flanging, filtering and many others.

Drum Trax

"DrumTrax for MIDI Demo" (© Crit Harmon) is a sampling of "real feel" drum patterns in standard MIDI format. These patterns can be pasted into your own MIDI sequences for modification or used "as is." Musical styles for blues, hip hop, latin and rock are included in this demo version with many patterns for each style. Additional styles and patterns are available in the full commercial version. A special offer for AOL members is included.

What's On The Companion CD-ROM

GoldWave™

GoldWave™ (copyright © 1993-1996 Chris S. Craig) is a comprehensive digital audio editor that allows you to play, record, edit and convert audio on your computer.

Harmony Assistant

Harmony Assistant (© Didier Guillion/Olivier Guillion) is complete easy-to-use software, containing all the tools necessary to discover computer-assisted music. It can be used by beginners as well as experienced composers.

Sound Play

SoundPlay (© hart@netdoor.com) makes it easy to sort large collections of sound files. There are 16 configurable buttons, each of which can represent a directory on your computer. Each button can also be given a name. Then, after selecting a file, a simple press of that button will move or copy the WAV file into that directory. It's that simple.

Wave Audit

This program (© LeapWare, Inc) allows you to select a group of WAV files in a folder, plays them one at a time and prompts you to keep or delete the WAV.

CD-ROM audio players

3D LED

(© Ivan W. Taylor / IMP All Rights Reserved) This is a 3D LED CD audio player. It displays track and track times in its customizable LED displays. This program will run on Windows 95 or Windows NT.

AutoEject for Windows 95

(© Kevin Marty) This is a utility to add the "auto-eject" feature to Windows 95.

What's On The Companion CD-ROM

CD 32-bit

The 32-bit CD Audio Player (v4.0©1996 Ivan W. Taylor / IMP All Rights Reserved) is a 32-bit version of IMP's CD Audio Player. It displays track and track times. Most CD players that I have seen look about the same, but this one has unique Transport Controls and Colors, and you can even change the background colors. There are lots of options to choose from in this program, which runs on Windows 95 or Windows NT.

CD Wizzard

(© 1996 by BFM Software and Brett McDonald) CD Wizzard CD audio player for Windows has all the functions of a home CD player plus many, many more! It saves the disc and tracks names in its database. CD Wizzard has a full 3D look that is totally customizable. In icon mode, the icon is updated with the disc and track time. A full help file describes all the features of CD Wizzard.

Virtual Web Site

NavRoad Web Browser

NavRoad Offline HTML Browser v1.40 (© 1997 by FAICO; GODFREY KO, PO BOX 710, MT GRAVATT 4122, QLD, AUSTRALIA) A small, powerful off-line HTML browser that runs off a floppy and requires no winsock.dll.

To access the Funky Frog Productions' Web site, you will need a Web browser. We have selected to use FAICO's NavRoad Web browser. To load the main file, click the Virtual Web Site button, select **File/Open** and load main.html from the CD-ROM.

This browser lets users view HTML files anytime, anywhere and supports all HTML 2 tags and most HTML 3 tags. It also supports helper applications, image maps, bookmarks and directory buttons. You may export HTML files as plain text (without tags). With its customizable interface and Kiosk mode

What's On The Companion CD-ROM

support this is a fast and easy solution for HTML files distribution. You may register NavRoad on-line with your credit cards (Visa, MasterCard, American Express, Novus brand cards) through REGNET by going to the following web sites:

Single User Licensing
http://www.xmission.com/~wintrnx/regnet/232p.htm

Site Licensing
http://www.xmission.com/~wintrnx/regnet/233p.htm

Royalty Free Licensing
http://www.xmission.com/~wintrnx/regnet/234p.htm

Additional programs

Chords

Music Chord (© Ivan W. Taylor / IMP) will teach you chord inversions and music theory fast. The program also has a built in CD, AVI, MIDI & WAV player.

Ear Power

(Ear Power 2.0 © Nick Baciu) This program has been designed to be used as a daily routine in improving the natural ear for music and much more.

Guitar Workshop

Guitar Workshop (© Oberwerk Corporation) is absolutely the best guitar software on the planet. If you play the guitar, or want to learn—I promise, you want this program. It includes a tutorial, an interactive lesson and some songs to learn. A series of Guitar Workshop song-packs and interactive lessons will be available to registered users. It requires Windows, a sound card, and a fast '486 is recommended. It also supports MIDI synths.

What's On The Companion CD-ROM

Kaleidoscope 95

Kaleidoscope 95 (© Syntrillium Software Corporation) is a colorful and beautiful screen saver for Windows 95 and NT. An infinite variety of striking geometric patterns emerges on your screen as Windows goes to sleep. The program offers a variety of control options that allow you to personalize your favorite kaleidoscopic variations. You can synchronize the program with music coming into your audio card from external sources or from your CD player, and watch the kaleidoscope flow and change with the music. Totally different designs will appear, depending on the style of music being played. This screen saver is an experience you don't want to miss.

Mozart

MOZART (written and © by Dave Webber) is a Music Processor for Windows. Using only the computer keyboard, you can create and edit sheet music. This can be printed with high-quality TrueType symbols on printers supported by Windows and appears on the screen in standard notation as a WYSIWYG display. The primary objective of MOZART is to print parts for musicians, but MIDI files can be exported to provide an "aural preview" on multimedia PCs. Features include: instant transposition, automatic defaultquaver tail groupings, automatic bar-line entry, exporting MIDI files either "straight" or with "swing," and extensive on-line help. MOZART is Shareware.

Music Theory

Basic Music Theory (© Bob Sweet) is a program which will help people learn basic music theory. The program runs on Windows 3.1 or Windows 95. This program tests the user in recognizing notes on the staffs, etc. This is a shareware program with a free 30-day trial period.

Tune It

TUNE!IT (© Volkmer's MusoWare) is a program designed to tune musical instruments by using a microphone or directly connecting your instrument (with a pickup) to the PC's soundcard.

What's On The Companion CD-ROM

Cakewalk

Cakewalk's Home Studio, Professional and Pro Audio are premiere MIDI programs for everyone from the home hobbyist to the multimedia producer. Demonstration versions of each of these programs are in the Cakewalk directory of the companion CD-ROM, each with a complete help file to help you get started. Just run the executable file '.exe' for the program you want to try out and you're well on your way to mastering MIDI with the included tutorials.

_MUSIC

This directory contains sound files for the exercises later in the book and a large collection of miscellaneous sound files that you can install onto your computer as system sounds, embed into documents, trade with friends and otherwise enjoy.

Voyetra Technologies' Demo

The Music & Audio Software Tour

2

Common Questions And Straight Answers

What's On The Companion CD-ROM

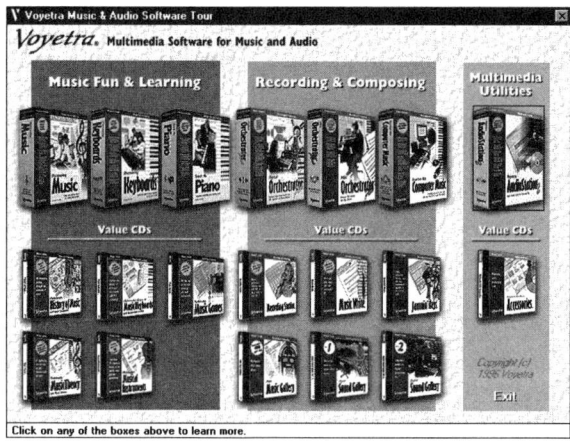

Select a product to preview

You can take a peek at Voyetra's music and audio software and try out their Digital Orchestrator Plus MIDI sequencing program.

Inside Chapter 2

Exercise Assigning System Sounds 27
    Sound schemes 27
    Assigning System Sounds in Windows 95 28
    Assigning System Sounds in Windows 3.x 29

Common Questions And Straight Answers

If you're reading this book, you're probably already a computer user, but you may not be ready to play music on your PC yet. Because there are many different skill levels of computer users, and because music is just one application for which computers can be used, we've collected some of the questions we are frequently asked regarding music, sound and personal computers. If you are experienced and comfortable working with sound files on your computer, you may want to skim this section. Those less familiar with managing PC sounds can use the following questions and answers to get up to speed.

Q What is sound, anyway?

Sound is simply the movement of air created by a source (for example, a baby laughing or a door slamming) and how it is interpreted by the receiver (for example, our ears).

Common Questions And Straight Answers

Q Can computers hear?

Not the same way we do. Sound waves must be converted into the computer's language—strings of numbers! A microphone is the first step toward changing the kind of sounds we hear (sound waves) into numbers (digits) that the computer can store. This is sometimes referred to as "DSP."

Q What is DSP?

One of many acronyms you'll learn, "DSP" stands for "Digital Signal Processing." This is the act of taking signals from a sound source, such as a CD-ROM or microphone, and translating them into digital (numerical) values that the computer understands. It is also known as "digitizing."

Q What is a sound card? How do I tell whether my computer has one?

A sound card is a special circuit board that gives your computer the ability to do more than simply beep. If you've purchased your computer after 1995, it probably has a sound card. Check the documentation that came with your computer to see if a sound card was included. If you have one but are only hearing beeps, the sound card isn't being properly recognized by Windows 95. Look for "Sound cards" in section two of this book for help configuring your sound card to achieve its potential.

Q If I don't have a sound card, why do I still hear sounds from my computer?

PC computers almost always have a small, built-in speaker (the PC speaker). It is limited to producing tinny chimes, error beeps and the like. This "beep" speaker will be present even if you also have a pair of larger, more functional speakers, which may be accessories or built-in.

Common Questions And Straight Answers

Q **Is that pathetic little built-in speaker any good for music?**

It is possible to create and play music by changing the tones of the beeps that the speaker plays. However, it's not easy to do and the music is basic. You have to use an elementary set of DOS programming commands, and the work involved is tedious.

A small Windows program called "speak.exe" makes listening to WAV files much easier for those with no sound card. This program usually works just fine with Windows 95's Sound Recorder. The music won't sound as good as it would with a sound card installed, but at least you'll hear it.

We'll show you how to set this up in the Software section of this book.

Q **What other hardware might I need besides a sound card?**

If you only want to listen to sounds and music on your computer, all you need is a sound card and a set of speakers (or headphones). If you want to get more involved, there are many other audio components to consider, including microphones, piano keyboards, CD burners, stereo amplifiers, etc.

Q **What software do I need in order to use my sound card?**

The sound card package includes device drivers and other software needed by the sound card. The most common sound files can be played with Windows 95's Sound Recorder or Media Player. However, some sound techniques and file formats require software that does not come with Windows 95. This book's companion CD-ROM has utilities that will play most of these for you. See the CD-ROM chapter for details on installing and using these programs.

Common Questions And Straight Answers

Q What are multimedia files? Can I use them?

Multimedia files are audio-visual files that usually contain video clips with music or other sounds. CD-ROMs are often used to store high-resolution multimedia files, which are too big to store on floppy disks. Most of these will run quicker and smoother from the hard drive than the CD, but be aware: even relatively short clips, ones that last less than 30 seconds, can gobble up 6 megabytes or more of hard-drive space!

Like audio CDs that you purchase, these small movie-type clips are most often professionally prepared.

Q How can I play multimedia files?

The Windows 95 Media Player is one of the software programs that will play multimedia files, as well as other file types, such as WAV and MID sounds.

Q I want to try this! Where can I find sounds and music files right now on my computer?

You are only five double-clicks away from playing a sound! Here's your path:

For Windows 95:

- Double-click on your "My Computer" icon. You will see a list of drives, then …

- Double-click on the icon above the "(C:)," which represents your hard drive.

- Double-click on the folder entitled "Windows." (You may need to scroll down to reach it.) You'll see other folders inside the Windows folder.

- Double-click on the folder called "Media."

Common Questions And Straight Answers

♪ Do you see files with little musical notes or speakers on them? Double-click one to hear it!

Remember this location. It's a good place to put sound files you want to keep handy. It's also where Windows 95 expects to find them!

If the Media folder is empty or missing, someone must have either skipped this part of installation or removed the sound files. Follow these steps to reinstall them:

♪ Put your Windows 95 CD-ROM in your CD-ROM drive.

♪ Double-click on "My Computer" and locate the Control Panel icon.

♪ Double-click on the "Control Panel" icon, then on "Add/Remove Programs."

♪ Click on the "Windows Setup" tab. A list box of choices will appear.

♪ Locate the item in the list box called "Multimedia."

♪ Highlight "Multimedia" and click on "Details." A list box will appear.

♪ Locate "Sample Sounds" in the list box and click on the checkbox to the left of that. Click "OK."

♪ Now click on "Have Disk."

Windows 95 does the rest!

For Windows 3.x:

In Windows 3.x, the WAV and MID sounds that come with the installation program are usually located in your Windows directory. Presuming you have installed to a single hard drive, that directory would be "C:\Windows."

Common Questions And Straight Answers

To listen to sounds in Windows 3.X, do the following:

♪ Double Click on the group entitled "Main."

♪ Inside the Main group you will see an icon entitled "File Manager." Double-click on it.

♪ In the panel that appears, locate the directory called "C:\Windows."

♪ Highlight "C:\Windows" and double-click to open it.

♪ Search for a file entitled "ding.wav."

♪ Highlight "ding.wav" and double-click it.

♪ The Sound Recorder will appear. Click the > button to play the file.

♪ Close the Sound Recorder.

> If you cannot locate ding.wav, go to the "WAVS" directory on the companion CD-ROM and copy any sound file from that directory to C:\Windows. Then follow the instructions above.

Q That was neat! Can I try some more right away?

Yes! There is a selection of WAV and MID files on the CD-ROM included with this book. See Chapter 1 ("What's On The Companion CD-ROM") for instructions on where to find those files and how to install them on your hard drive.

Q Can I put my own voice on my computer, too?

Yes, if you have a microphone and sound card. Windows 95 includes the software for recording through a microphone. You can even use special effects to alter your voice! Section 3 will explain how to do this.

22

Common Questions And Straight Answers

Q: Can I add other new sounds to my computer?

Yes, in several ways. Besides the microphone, you can download sounds through a modem. You may also be able to capture them from a CD-ROM, tape player, VCR or other source.

Q: Download? What's that?

Downloading is bringing information from an on-line source into your computer through a modem. You can connect with sound libraries located on the internet or various online services, such as America Online. We'll show you how to download and install sounds in a later chapter.

Q: What is a conversion program?

In this case, a conversion program is software that translates sounds from one file format to another, so they can be played and edited with other types of computers or software. For example, to use a Macintosh SND sound file on a typical PC, you first need to convert it to a Windows WAV file.

Q: What else can I do with sound files I have?

You can learn to change those sounds as well, by using "effects." Effects alter the sound file so that is not the same as when you first played it. Some simple effects alter the volume or change the pitch.

Reverberation, commonly referred to as "reverb," adds an echo-like effect to the sound. In fact, The Sound Recorder even calls the "reverb" effect "echo" in the "Effects" menu of the Sound Recorder.

You can try playing or altering a sound file right now, by referring to the Software section of this book.

Common Questions And Straight Answers

Q How will I know which files are music files?

A sound file can be one of several different types. In Windows 3.x it can usually be identified by its file extension. This refers to the three letters after the dot (or period) in the names of files on your PC. For example, you will be dealing mainly with WAV files, so they have names such as QUACK.*WAV* or TRUMPET.*WAV*.

Windows 95, depending on the setup of your Windows Explorer, may or may not show those extensions.

Q What if I don't see those extensions on my Windows 95 computer?

The sound files will work the same way, whether you have Windows 95 set up to show—or *not* show—the file extensions. The default Windows 95 settings will *not* display file extensions. QUACK.WAV would show up in lists as simply QUACK.

Either way, Windows 95 knows what type of files they are, and starts up the proper program to play them, either the Sound Recorder or the Windows Media Player.

Q How else can I identify a sound file?

You can select a file with the mouse and choose "Properties" from the File menu to display information about the file; but there's an easier way—icons!

Here's a look at the two icons you'll see most often for PC sound files.

These icons indicate that the associated file is in WAV or MID format, respectively

24

Common Questions And Straight Answers

Q Should I worry about hard-disk space?

Yes! Keeping an eye on your hard-drive capacity is very important, because some music files, especially WAV files, can take up huge amounts of space on your hard drive.

Newer sound cards have the ability to record more accurate representations of the sound source you might be recording from, providing higher quality recordings. But that gain has a trade-off. The higher the quality of the recorded file, the larger it is.

Therefore, quality WAVs will occupy more space on your hard drive. A simple WAV file 30 seconds in length can eat up 5 megabytes or more of your hard drive space!

Parents have been known to find their hard disk suddenly full to overflowing with home-made WAV files, courtesy of their talented children! This can certainly complicate things—not leaving enough room for downloading or saving changes to your work files. A hard disk that is less than 350 megabytes is certainly not suited for tons of "wave making!" If you get into multimedia production, your space needs will multiply.

In contrast, a MID file takes less room on your hard disk. MID files require some compositional technique, and are therefore not as simple to create as a WAV file you may have made by recording small musical segments from your favorite CD.

Q Do I have to compose MID files or create WAV files in order to have new ones?

Not at all! There are thousands upon thousands of downloadable sound files in many different formats available on the internet, as well as those sound files we have included on the CD-ROM.

Common Questions And Straight Answers

Q: What can I use sounds for?

Sound files can be used for, among other things, entertainment, education and business presentations. Here are some of the fun things you can learn to do in the following pages:

- ♪ Listen to sounds and music
- ♪ Record sounds to entertain yourself, or to trade with friends
- ♪ Customize your computer system
- ♪ Embed sounds in documents for business or school presentations
- ♪ Learn to compose and write music
- ♪ Play an instrument using sound software and hardware

Q: One easy thing you can learn quickly, besides just listening to sounds, is assigning various sound files to your PC System.

What are PC Systems Sounds?

PC Systems Sounds are those sounds that you assign to various "events" that take place on your computer.

Major actions performed on the computer (by Windows 95, other programs or you) are called "events." Examples of events include starting or shutting down Windows, launching a program or closing a window. Windows can be configured to alert you with a sound when one of these events occurs. If you don't have a sound card this notification is limited to a system alert beep. With a sound card, you can select any sound file to play when an event occurs, from a duck's quack to a few bars of your favorite song.

Common Questions And Straight Answers

Q **How can I assign sounds to my computer's system events?**

In both Windows 3.x and Windows 95, it is possible to assign system sounds to various Windows functions. For example, you may change or add a sound that occurs when you enter or exit Windows, when an error occurs, when a file is opened, and so forth. Here's your first exercise to try!

Exercise Assigning System Sounds

Sound schemes

Windows 95 gives you the capacity to assign sounds to a group of PC System events, and save that scheme with a name you choose.

The Windows CD-ROM comes with four ready-made sound schemes, titled "Jungle," "Musica," "Robotz" and "Utopia." By default, not all sound schemes are installed during Windows Setup.

Here's how to install one or all of the sound schemes on your Windows 95 CD-ROM.

♪ Place your Windows 95 CD-ROM in your CD-ROM drive.

♪ Double-click on "My Computer" and locate the Control Panel icon.

♪ Double-click the Control Panel icon, then on "Add/Remove Programs."

♪ Click on the "Windows Setup" tab. A list box of choices will appear.

♪ Locate "Multimedia" in the list box.

♪ Highlight "Multimedia" and click on "Details." A list box will appear.

27

Common Questions And Straight Answers

♪ Locate "Jungle Sound Scheme" in the list box and click on the checkbox to the left of that.

♪ Click on the "Musica," "Robotz" and "Utopia" Sound Schemes.

♪ Click "Have Disk."

You can also use the sounds we have provided on the companion CD-ROM.

Assigning System Sounds in Windows 95

In Windows 95, double-click on the following folders: "My Computer," then "Control Panel," then "Sounds." You will see a dialog box that looks like this:

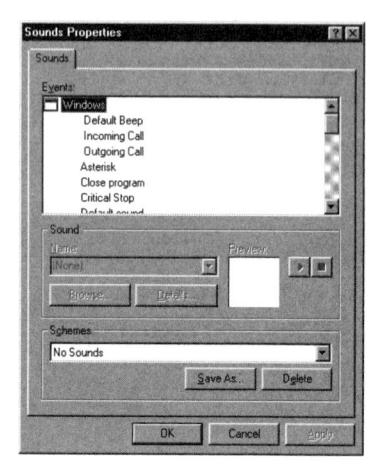

In the Events list, click the event for which you want to assign a sound.

In the Name list, select the sound you want Windows to play whenever the selected event occurs. If the file you want to use isn't listed, click the Browse... button to locate it.

To test a sound, click its name, and then click the Right Arrow (">") button.

Common Questions And Straight Answers

You can assign different sounds to different events so that each has its own sound, or use one sound for a number of events.

After you've assigned a sound to the events, you can save the entire group of sound settings as a "Scheme" by clicking "Save As" and then naming the sound scheme you've created. This will tell Windows 95 to recall all of the settings for every event for which you have added a sound file. That name will appear in the Schemes list, so you can easily change or restore these settings, or create more than one sound scheme.

Assigning System Sounds in Windows 3.x

♪ Double-click the "Main" icon.

♪ Double-click "Control Panel."

♪ Double-click "Sound."

♪ Highlight an event in the list box on the left.

♪ Select a sound you think you might like in the list box on the right.

♪ Click "Test" to hear the sound.

♪ Select other events and add sounds.

♪ Close the box by clicking on "OK."

No Sound Schemes are available in Windows 3.x

Q Is this a permanent change?

Only until you change the settings. Once you've added new sounds, you may want to alter the sounds in your existing schemes, or create new sound schemes. You can do that any time you wish by repeating the above procedure.

Common Questions And Straight Answers

Q What else do I need to know about sound?

Some simple facts on how sound works will make learning about music on the computer lots easier. The remaining two chapters in section one discuss the terms, materials and processes you'll need to know to create quality original music and work with existing sound files on your PC.

Ready? Here we go!

3

Simple Sound Facts

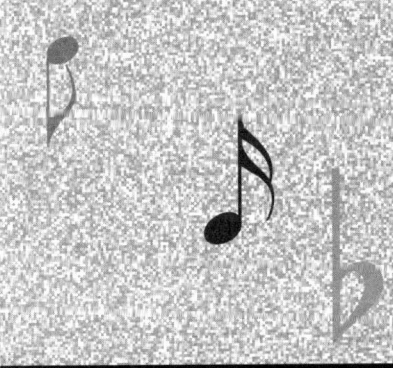

Inside Chapter 3

Do I Really Need To Know This Stuff? 33
How Sound Travels 34
Syntheses And Synthesizers 36
Digitized Sound 37

    Sound conversion 37
    FM Synthesis 38
    Wavetable synthesis 38
    Digital sampling using wavetable synthesis 39

Sound Quality 42

    Direct and indirect recording sources 42
    Recording direct 42

Digital Sampling Rates And Resolution 43

    What affects sound file quality 43
    Digital sampling rate 43

Simple Sound Facts

Do I *Really* Need To Know This Stuff?

Learning about sound is easier than you might think, though it's probably a temptation skip over this section.

So we have designed the exercises in this book so that you really can do them without having a clue how sound works. But learning *why* these exercises work is just as important as *how* to do them. It will set your feet firmly on the road to exploring your own creativity rather than just imitating the steps we have given you here.

It's probably not going to sink in all at once. That's okay, too. Don't worry about memorizing anything—there won't be a pop quiz in the morning!

If this section seems overwhelming, try skimming this information (unless, of course, it is something you have always wanted to recite at parties). Come back later and read it again when you have a question about the basics of sound.

3 Simple Sound Facts

This section is a reference for concepts that occur throughout this book. You will find them useful in doing the recording and editing exercises that use these terms and ideas. Don't despair if not all of it makes sense right now. It will!

How Sound Travels

Sound travels in waves. Think of the ripples created in a pond when you toss in a rock. Those ripples disturb the calm, clear surface of the pond. The ripples travel in all directions from the place where the rock hit the water. The ripples each create a roughly defined circle.

Sound travels the same way, creating a disturbance in the air in all directions from the source that produced it.

At the same time the ripples are traveling through the water, the splashing sound of the rock impacting the water is traveling through the air in all directions, too!

How we hear

Sound creates changes in the air pressure. We sense that change of air pressure in our eardrums, which are always in action. Our eardrums pass that information to the brain. The brain interprets that information and tells us a sound is being made.

Simple Sound Facts

How we "see" sound

You've probably seen a sound wave drawn on a graph like the one below. This graph depicts a simple sound wave called a "sine wave."

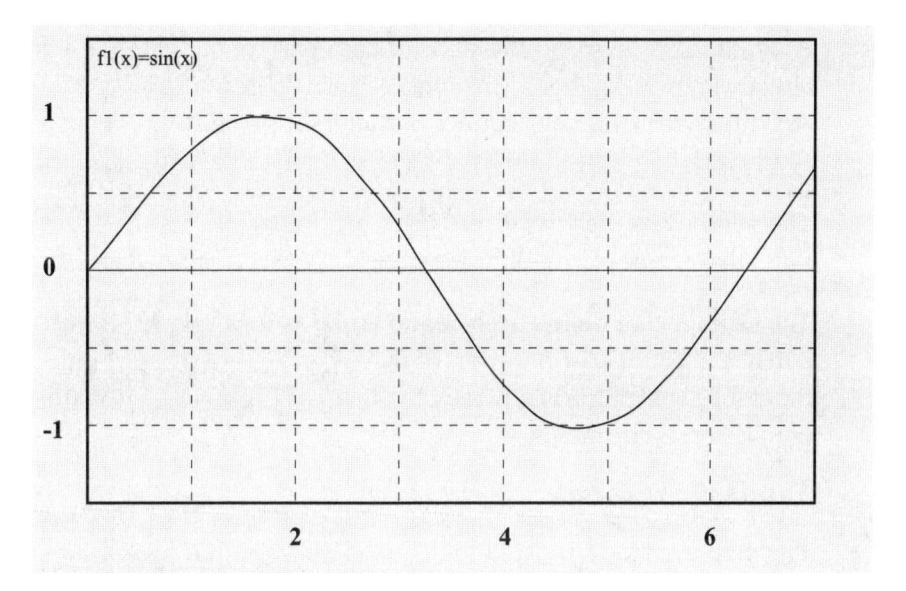

How sound is measured

A Hertz (Hz) is the unit of measure for sound waves. Hertz values that we will refer to are kilohertz (kHz) and megahertz (mHz), for units of a thousand and a million, respectively.

Simple Sound Facts

Syntheses And Synthesizers

Synthesis uses digital (numerical) methods to create (and alter) sound.

A synthesizer is an electronic musical instrument. The one you probably already know of is a keyboard synthesizer. (There is also a guitar synthesizer!) A synthesizer generates sound and alters it using digital instructions. One synthesizer may use a different process than another to create those sounds.

The synthesizer hardware provides a number of "voices" (the number of notes that can be played simultaneously). Most offer between 6 and 20 voices.

The settings that define each sound (such as tone, pitch, etc.) are saved as a **patch**. Collections, or libraries, of these patches are stored on disk as "patch files." Each patch file is typically made up of 128 melodic instruments and 47 percussion instruments.

Types of synthesis

The two methods most widely used with sound cards are **Frequency Modulation (FM) Synthesis** and **Wavetable Synthesis**. FM synthesis manipulates artificial sound waves that it digitizes and sends to the computer. Wavetable Synthesis captures real instrument sounds to be digitized and transferred to the computer.

We will be talking more about those two methods because they apply directly to what we will be doing. First, let's talk a bit about how sound gets transferred to the computer.

Simple Sound Facts

Digitized Sound

Sound must be stored in the computer in a way that the PC understands. Computers read information in a numerical format known as the binary system. Translating sound to binary code is known as "digitizing" sound. These digitized sounds are stored in the computer as a file of sequential ones and zeros which the sound card can translate back into sounds.

One might, therefore, think of digitized sounds as the computer equivalent of a tape recording of real or artificial sounds!

Sound conversion

Our ears process sound as **analog** information. Computers work with sound in a **digital** form. For sound information to be shared between computers and our ears, it must be converted between these two forms of data. Digital to Analog Conversion (DAC) is the process of converting digital sounds–the kind stored on your computer, into analog sound—the kind your ears can hear. The sound card has a component called a Digital to Analog Converter (DAC) that does this job.

Translating sound waveforms as we hear them into the numbers the computer needs requires the reverse: an Analog to Digital converter (ADC). Most sound cards also come with an Analog to Digital Converter as one of their standard components.

Low end sound cards typically have 8-bit (slower) DAC and ADC converters. High-end sound cards are 16-bit yet, as with every computer component, some are more precise than others.

Simple Sound Facts

Most sound cards on the market today are capable of FM synthesis and perform two basic functions: sound playback (such as WAV files) and playing music scores that use the sound of actual instruments (such as MID files). Many are also capable of wavetable synthesis, either out of the box or with an additional wavetable upgrade card.

FM Synthesis

Until the early 1990's, sound cards used only FM synthesis for MIDI playback. It is relatively inexpensive and uses only a few components to create complex sounds.

FM synthesis mimics musical instruments and special effects. It modifies sound wave forms using mathematical procedures that manipulate those waves. (Remember, computers need numbers to translate sound!)

Trying to get instrument-quality sounds using FM Synthesis can be very disappointing. FM sound waveforms can only approximate the sounds we hear. Subtle factors, such as how a sound begins (attack) and how it fades out (decay), are even harder to imitate than the tone of the instrument itself.

While state-of-the-art music systems have moved to another method known as digital sampling, many still include FM synthesis for backward compatibility.

Wavetable synthesis

Wavetable synthesis is this state of the art for sound cards. It allows digitally sampled instrument sounds, also called "voices," to be downloaded into the sound card's memory by the user. Because these realistic sounds contain information recorded from actual instruments, these cards require more on-board memory than cards that simulate the instrument sounds.

Simple Sound Facts

The sound card provides the user with the capability of modifying to varying degrees these sound samples by playing notes on the musical instrument connected to the sound card.

Rather than manipulate sine waves (as FM Synthesis does), wavetable synthesis uses digitally recorded samples, (or "chunks" of a particular real instrument's sound) as a basis for creating sounds for the computer. That quality and use of the real instrument as a source results in a sound that is much richer, truer and more realistic than an FM synthesized sound.

Wavetable synthesis techniques are not always completely compatible with older sound cards, although sound cards that support it can easily simulate FM Synthesis.

The hardware components and methods used to create wavetable synthesis are more complex and more expensive than FM Synthesis. As popularity increases though, the cost has been dropping!

Digital sampling using wavetable synthesis

How are these realistic sounds created? The process of capturing and properly synthesizing real musical instrument sounds from bits of those sounds is known as **digital sampling**, or "sampling" for short.

The use of real instrument sounds is a delightful improvement for the musical artist!

Imagine laboring over your music composition only to be disappointed by fake-sounding imitations of the real thing; tinny violin lines sounding like a swarm of stressed-out bumblebees and drums that sound like Junior pounding on kitchen utensils do not a musical composition make! Digital sampling has changed all that.

Simple Sound Facts

When you record a digital sound, it is as clean as if you were recording directly from a CD. But instead sending the digital signals from a CD to the sound card, you send them from a music keyboard. The sound card plays the instruments via those signals and sends them to the software on your hard drive as you play. Once you save the file you've created, it is recorded.

When played back, the computer reads the musical data from the file on your hard drive, and sends instructions to the sound card that tell it what instruments and notes to produce. Thus, the data from the file on your hard drive is funneled straight through the sound card to the speakers, as though it were being played by a CD-ROM.

Of course, computer musicians still have complaints! Instrument sounds are hard to capture. The sounds of acoustic instruments, like piano or guitar, are especially difficult to reproduce.

Musicians and composers seek satisfying sounds for their compositions, and digital sampling provides the best technology we know of today. Undoubtedly, as time goes on there will be new discoveries in this area of sound reproduction.

Some people prefer not to create their own samples. A small industry of professionals and amateurs has grown up supplying digital samples to aspiring musicians. Some of these commercial or shareware samples are created by true artists of digitized music—others are not so good.

If you prefer to use other people's sounds to replace the ones in your own compositions, we will guide you to resources where you can obtain these patches.

It is also possible to replace one sound on your computer with another. If you've finally found that sweet French Horn sound you've been dying for, you can use it to replace the old one. In addition to real instrument sounds, digital sampling allows the use of speech and a wide range of "artificially produced" sounds.

Simple Sound Facts

A sample may not be an entire note. The person editing the sound may be looking for qualities of sound that the instrument has which set it apart from another; a violin sounds drastically different from a trumpet!

So, a refinement of our earlier comments about real instruments is necessary. Each note played on an instrument sounds slightly different—not just the pitch (name) of the note itself, but also how each note is played. A trumpet can have a breathy, quiet sound of long duration or a bright, sharp attack. Every instrument is capable of a range of sounds. But no matter how hard it tries, a trumpet cannot imitate a violin (at least not without the help of some complicated electronic devices)!

So, those who create instrument patches often strive to create sounds that will be useful no matter how that note is played. A finished sample may be restricted to a particular aspect of that trumpet, or it may be enhanced in such a way that the trumpet sound can be used for a broad range of purposes.

It is an art form to know which chunks of musical sound to select and store, how to store them, and how to electronically manipulate them to resemble the real thing. As with any artistic medium, the quality of the sound patch depends on the abilities of the person who created them.

It is unrealistic to expect to be able to learn the techniques of instrument sampling overnight. It's beyond the scope of this book, as well! If your interest points in that direction, you will need more sophisticated equipment than exists in the inexpensive to middle range of the sound equipment available for today's computers.

Simple Sound Facts

Sound Quality

Direct and indirect recording sources

Sounds recorded directly from an original source (for example, a CD-ROM connected to the sound card) are known as "direct" recordings, because the source, such as the "audio-out" of the CD-ROM, is connected *directly* to the "audio-in" on the PC sound card. Another example of a direct recording would be a first generation cassette/VHS recording (such as a purchased movie or music video) recorded from a VCR which is plugged directly into the sound card.

Some examples of indirect recordings would be sounds, music, or spoken words recorded using a microphone in between the sound card and a speaker, guitar or other instrument.

Recording direct

A WAV sound, for example, recorded at a frequency level of 44kHz directly from the source (such as the CD-ROM player in your computer) without using a microphone or other recording device are likely to be of the best quality.

Although it is also possible to connect the "audio out" on the back of your VCR or tape deck directly to the computer, this may not be possible due to location or lack of proper cables or connectors.

Indirect recordings—Recording with a microphone

You might, instead, use a microphone to tape the sound or music from your TV or VCR, a CD playing on your stereo system (not the one in your computer!) or your own voice or guitar.

Simple Sound Facts

To record music using a microphone connected to your sound card, one needs to place a microphone next to the source (your voice, TV or Tape deck speakers) and record via that microphone onto the computer.

Recording using a microphone connected to your sound card will not produce sound as clear and high-quality as a direct recording. The more "interference" between the source of sound and your recording, the more opportunity there is for noise to infiltrate the recording.

Still, this is one of the easiest ways to record a quote from your favorite TV personality, and most certainly the easiest to record your voice! Often, a spoken phrase or word can be recorded at a lesser translation rate without much noticeable loss of quality. You can only discover by trying!

Digital Sampling Rates And Resolution

What affects sound file quality

The files you may download from the internet will vary in quality, depending on many things:

- Quality of the recording equipment
- Quality of the material being recorded
- Rate at which the sound information is translated from the source to the recording equipment.

Digital sampling rate

Sampling rate, in simple terms, is the rate of speed at which the sample is recorded. Other terms used in conjunction with this concept are **frequency level** and **translation rate**.

Simple Sound Facts

Frequency levels are measured in kilohertz, abbreviated as "kHz." The rates typically used with sound cards are, at the slow end, eleven thousand times per second (11 kilohertz), and forty-four thousand one hundred times per second (44.1 kilohertz) at the upper practical limit, with 22 kilohertz being a common and comfortable compromise.

The slower the speed, the less accurately the information is recorded. Therefore, the quality of a sample recorded at 11 kilohertz will be drastically less than one recorded at 44.1 kilohertz. However, the 11kHz file will also be much smaller than the higher quality file.

As a guideline, recording an indirect sound at 44kHz would be roughly equivalent in quality to recording a direct sound at 22kHz. As the rate drops to an 11kHz direct recording, the quality lessens accordingly. Anything less than that is likely to be so poor that it would be nearly useless.

The better the translation rate, or the rate at which the information is sent from the source to the recording, the better the quality of the recording and the larger the file size.

Digital sampling resolution: Bits and bytes—oh, now what?

Sampling resolution has to do with how much of the computer's memory is assigned to doing a particular task. You'll see sound cards and other peripherals being offered as 8-bit and 16-bit. What's that mean?

Computers store information in units called bytes, each of which has eight segments called "bits."

8-bit cards use just 8 bits of computer memory per note. 16-bit cards use 16 bits for each note, and more memory means better sound!

Just how much better? For our purposes, it's easy enough to remember this: when a computer peripheral offers 16-bit memory storage, it's offering you 256 times more storage than an 8-bit card affords.

Simple Sound Facts

That's a lot of difference! Will you be able to hear that difference? You bet! A sixteen-bit sound card will offer you a lot more in terms of sound quality.

It's not important to memorize all this data right now. If you're a beginner, you'll be much more successful learning about PC music one bite at a time, adding another term or method to your repertoire when you are ready, rather than trying to swallow it all at once. You can always refer back to this chapter to refresh your memory.

The next chapter will introduce the computer file formats that are capable of playing and storing sound data, explaining the pros and cons of each.

4

Music And Sound File Types

Inside Chapter 4

WAV—Wave Form Audio File Format 49
MIDI—Music Instrument Digital Interface 50

Some Other Formats 50

About DOS file extensions in Windows 95 53
Changing extension visibility in Windows 95 53

Keeping Those Terms Straight 54

WAV versus MIDI 54
Samples versus sampling 55
Wavetable versus WAV 56

Music And Sound File

The main file formats we will be using in this book are WAV and MID. Both MID and WAV files, as well as the other sound formats, contain numerically translated (digitized) sound information that the computer can understand and translate back into a form you will interpret as sound. Microsoft's WAV format can even be played under DOS, with the help of some DOS software!

WAV—Wave Form Audio File Format

WAV is a Microsoft Windows sound standard, and can be played by using the Windows 3.x Media Player or in Windows 95, either the Sound Recorder or the Media Player. Because it is the Microsoft audio file standard, WAV files can be read by almost all sound software—freeware, shareware and retail—including the WAV recording and editing program on the companion CD-ROM.

The extension for WAV files is ".wav." A sound created on your computer entitled "Sunset," for example, would appear on your hard drive as the following (or as the icon on the right).

```
sunset.wav
```

sunset.wav

4 Music And Sound File Types

MIDI—Music Instrument Digital Interface

This is one of the two most popular digital musical formats, and the less simple of those two to learn to use. The MIDI concept was developed in the early 1980s, and is still one of the most widely accepted standards for passing musical information between instruments and electronic equipment (as between a synthesizer keyboard and a computer).

While WAV files are digitized sounds, MIDI files are closer to digitized sheet music. These files use sound definitions (notes) and sequence control commands (rhythm) to tell a MIDI device (your sound card, for instance) not only which instruments to play, but when, for how long and with what settings. It contains information about what key the piece is in, what instruments are used, the length of each note, and how loud or soft, fast or slow each is played.

There's a lot of software available for playing and composing MIDI music. MIDI music files can be played using the Windows Media Player or any other MIDI file player or MIDI sequencing program.

The primary extension for MIDI files is ".mid" for pre-Windows 95 configurations. Windows 95 uses ".rmi" to denote some MIDI files. For example, a MIDI song titled "Sunrise" would appear on your computer as

```
sunrise.mid or sunrise.rmi
```
or as one of the icons on the right.

Some Other Formats

MOD

The primary file extension for MOD files is ".mod."

50

Music And Sound File Types

MODs (modules) are digital music files compiled using samples of instruments. Created with a variety of different software trackers and/or editors, MODs come in a number of different types, and may have other file extensions depending on the software used to create them.

These files are fun to listen to, and youngsters seem to enjoy working with them. However, these aren't as easy to work with as WAV files.

ULAW

The primary file extension for ULAW is ".au."

If you're new to computers you probably don't remember NeXt. Appearing in the late '80s, NeXt was heralded as the latest and greatest, but never achieved widespread acceptance. .Au files are the NeXt Computer's standard audio files, storing digitized sound data much like WAV files. ULAW files will require an .au file player to be played on a PC.

VOC

The primary file extension for VOC is ".voc."

The VOC format was an early standard for PC sound files, and was created by Creative Labs for their Sound Blaster sound boards. Sound Blasters still come with DOS software that allow you to play these files.

These Sound Blaster VOC files produce sound similar, but not equal, to the WAV files. These files will require a VOC file player, or can be translated to WAV files using a conversion program.

We have included playback and conversion software on the CD-ROM which will allow you to use VOC files with your computer.

Music And Sound File Types

> If you are acquiring audio files and can find a clip from one of your favorite bands only in VOC format, you can convert it to a WAV so you can play it. But, if you locate the same sound in both WAV and VOC formats, it's better to choose the WAV file! The quality will be much better. A VOC file translated to WAV format will only be as good as it was in VOC format; sounds recorded in WAV format sound much better to begin with.

CMF

The primary extension for CMF files is ".cmf." CMF files are music files that can be played using a CMF file player. This, too, was an early Sound Blaster file format, and can be translated into other formats.

MPEG—Moving Pictures Experts Group

The extensions for MPEG files are ".mp2" or ".mpa."

MPEG is an international multimedia file standard. MPEG derives its name from the organization that structures its requirements, and sets the standards for compression of this type of file, which contains both moving pictures and sound. Due to the enhanced compression techniques, MPEG audio files are smaller than comparable WAV files without sacrificing any quality.

ROL

The primary extension for ROL files is ".rol." These are sounds that were first created for the AdLib sound card and can be played by any software program that includes capabilities for playing ROL files.

SND

The primary extension for SND files is ".snd." These are Apple Macintosh sound files. There are many interesting and well-made sound files available for the Apple Macintosh computer, and not having access to them on a PC would be ignoring a huge amount of good sound and music material.

Music And Sound File Types

Although SND files cannot be used "as is" directly from the Macintosh, these great sounds can be used on a PC with a simple conversion program which translates the Macintosh sound information into a format that your PC can understand.

About DOS file extensions in Windows 95

As we mentioned, Windows 95 does not ordinarily display the three-letter extension for some file types, primarily system files (files that Windows 95 needs to run programs and execute actions) and file types that are registered.

Registered files are those that the Windows 95 Registry knows are to be executed by a particular program or utility. For example, Windows knows to launch the Sound Recorder (once installed) to execute WAV files. As you add new programs to Windows 95, many of them, upon installation, let Windows 95 know that certain file extensions "belong" to that program.

This can be confusing if you're using Windows 95 for the first time. Some people feel more comfortable being able to see the file extensions. Viewing the file extensions can help you identify your files by their type, which is particularly useful when files belonging to a program are given the same or similar names. When this happens, the extension is the only way to tell them apart.

Changing extension visibility in Windows 95

If you wish, you can change the way Windows 95 shows you the filenames, until you get accustomed to the extensions that each program uses.

To do so:

- Click the "Start" button on the Windows 95 Taskbar.
- Click "Program" and select "Windows Explorer."
- Click "View" on the Windows Explorer Menu bar.

4 Music And Sound File Types

♪ Select "Options."

♪ **OPTIONAL**: If you wish to see your System Files as well, make sure the radio button "Show all files" has been selected.

♪ Make sure the box next to "Hide MS-DOS file extensions for file types that are registered" is unchecked.

♪ Click [Apply] to save the settings and [OK] to exit.

Now your files will be displayed with their file-type suffixes.

Keeping Those Terms Straight

With all this new terminology, it's easy to confuse terms. Here are three that occur constantly when speaking of music and computing. Knowing the differences is important when deciding what sound card you want.

WAV versus MIDI

WAV files and MIDI files are as different as night and day. WAVs are used mainly for simple enjoyment. They can range from small clips of your favorite band to humorous words, sounds, or comments made by your favorite TV or movie personality. You can use WAVs for system sounds, fun and games in internet chat rooms, and more.

The main drawback of WAV files is that they are usually quite large, and the better the sound quality, the larger the file. It's impractical to store your favorite audio CD on your hard disk. One 60 minute CD recorded at high quality could easily fill your disk!

MIDI files are much smaller than WAV files! At their most basic they can also be used for games and other entertainment. However, they are much more sophisticated in construction, and professional musicians use them for both audio and multimedia (combined audio and video) scoring.

Music And Sound File Types

To exemplify the differences between the two, think of a recording studio. Sixteen musicians have arrived to record a song. They play their parts, which are put on separate tracks. The engineer "mixes" that sound so it is balanced. That means the violin that belongs in the background isn't shrieking, squawking and drowning out your favorite singer!

A WAV file delivers that "mix" to you. The engineer has blended all those tracks, combining the instruments so that they now all exist on one (mono) or two (stereo) tracks. You can alter WAV files with software, but you cannot go back and find that violin, and cause it to drown out that singer by raising its volume. If you raise, lower, or add effects to one instrument, you affect them all.

A MIDI file is also "mixed" when you hear the final result, but there's a big difference: its separate tracks still exist on your computer. With the proper software, you can go back and raise or lower the level of that violin without affecting any other instrument. You can do the same with any other instrument, as well.

Another way to remember is that with a WAV file, you're primarily the audience; you can control some basic things, like raising and lowering the volume, or adding echo. However, any change you make affects all of the instruments. With a MIDI file, you can be the conductor, telling each separate instrument what to do and when to do it!

Samples versus sampling

In the previous chapter we define "sampling" as a process of extracting real instrument sounds for use on your computer. That kind of sampling is very sophisticated, and is usually associated with MID files.

The word "sampling" can indicate another function: collecting clips of favorite sound effects, spoken phrases or music and storing them on your computer to use. That kind of sampling is associated with WAV files, for the purposes we've suggested above, such as snipping bits of your favorite band

Music And Sound File Types

for your own enjoyment. It might be better to think of this activity as "sound clipping" rather than "sampling," but the two are closely related. The term "sampling" applies to both because, in essence, it refers to how computers store sound, by taking samples of that sound and storing them as digital information.

Wavetable versus WAV

No, they're not associated. Wavetable Synthesis is a format used in newer sound cards that allows more realistic instrument sounds, versus the older FM Synthesis.

WAVs are a file type.

You can listen to and create WAVs and other file types using a sound card whether you have an older card using FM synthesis (artificially created), or a newer one that allows for wavetable synthesis (real instrument sound).

Each of these filetypes has its own advantages and disadvantages. Which you choose to work with depends on how you will be applying the files and what materials you have with which to work. WAV and MID will probably be your choices, since they are versatile and widespread, allowing many users to play them for many applications.

The next section details the equipment you will need to work with these files, from the basic PC speaker to advanced MIDI keyboard controllers, and how to attach each to your computer.

Music Hardware

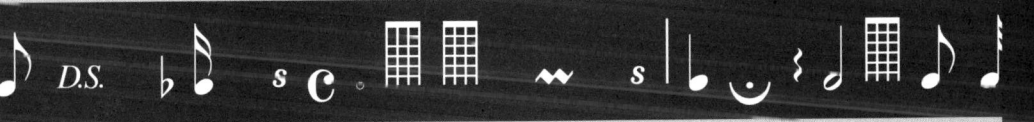

SECTION 2

5
Introduction To Music Hardware

Inside Chapter 5

If you don't yet have a sound card 62

Music Hardware:: What's Necessary, What's Optional ... 62

Sound card 62
Other basic equipment—headphones or speakers 63
Electronic keyboard or synthesizer 63
Microphone 64
CD-ROM player 64
Multimedia packages 64

Which Specific Sound Hardware To Buy 65

A note about drivers 65

Introduction To Music Hardware

With a wide range of music and multimedia components on the market, it's difficult for beginners to know where to begin. In this section we will explore what components are available and help you make decisions on how to set up your music system. This overview of the chapters in this section will summarize the components that are useful and/or necessary to create music on your PC.

Our aims in discussing music hardware for your system:

- ♪ Help you decide what you want to do with music

- ♪ Help you make reasonable hardware decisions based on what you want to do

- ♪ Provide tips on hardware that won't be immediately obsolete

- ♪ Arm you with information to avoid common purchase pitfalls

- ♪ Suggest alternate means of acquiring hardware

Introduction To Music Hardware

If you don't yet have a sound card

The very small speaker inside virtually all PC computers is called the "PC speaker." It allows you to hear the beep tones that a computer plays when it boots, and more importantly the error beep that indicates something is awry. For example, you may hear a beep tone when the typing keyboard is not properly connected.

A small Windows 3.x program called "speak.exe" allows you to hear WAV files through that PC speaker. If you don't have a sound card, we have included speak.exe on the companion CD-ROM so you may enjoy WAV files and follow some of the examples in this book.

Although you can play sounds on your computer without a sound card or stereo speakers, your ability to create, edit, play and enjoy sound files will be practically non-existent.

Music Hardware: What's Necessary, What's Optional

Sound card

In order to truly work with music and sound files on your computer, the very minimum requirement is a sound card. Chapter six will explain sound cards in detail.

> We are assuming that your computer already has standard peripherals, like a computer keyboard, monitor and mouse.

62

Introduction To Music Hardware

Other basic equipment—headphones or speakers

You also need either headphones or speakers other than the tiny PC speaker inside your computer.

For more professional applications of listening to, creating, and editing sounds, headphones will come in very handy, even if you already have speakers. Chapter eight has more information on audio output devices.

Electronic keyboard or synthesizer

Some basic music software assigns musical notes to the letter keys on a standard computer keyboard. This allows you to try composing without buying a music keyboard, such as a synthesizer.

> Modern computers often come with built in stereophonic audio speakers! Read the documentation on your particular computer if you're not sure what you have.

Other music programs create a piano-style keyboard on your screen, which allows you to use either your mouse or computer keyboard to compose music using your sound card.

These alternatives to a music keyboard can be tolerable, but they are awkward and limited. Your musical goals will be better achieved by purchasing a synthesizer-type keyboard that can attach to your sound card.

A music keyboard requires an adapter and/or set of cables that run between it and the sound card. Called "MIDI cables," these are supplied with some sound cards. Otherwise you must purchase the cables separately. Chapter seven provides the low-down on PC-ready music keyboards.

Introduction To Music Hardware

Microphone

A microphone is useful for recording your voice or other sound sources that cannot connect directly to your sound card. If your sound card didn't come with a microphone, most computer and electronics stores carry them separately.

CD-ROM player

A CD-ROM player affords you the pleasure of listening to your audio CDs while you work, as well as using CD-ROMs that contain software programs or educational data. Wonderful games are available on CD-ROM, too!

A recent development is the recordable CD-ROM, which allows you to record data and music, as well as archive or back up your files. The CD-ROM chapter (chapter nine) will help you select and use CD-ROM drives.

Multimedia packages

Some manufacturers offer a "Multimedia Package," which may include some or all of the following:

- ♪ CD-ROM player
- ♪ Sound card
- ♪ Microphone
- ♪ MIDI Cable (for game joysticks and musical instruments)
- ♪ Speakers

Introduction To Music Hardware

Though this package is a quick solution to putting a sound system into your computer, you may find that buying these pieces separately will result in a better system (and maybe a better price). If you do decide to purchase a package, watch out for lower-speed CD-ROM drives with slow access rates and low-quality speakers and microphones.

Which Specific Sound Hardware To Buy

Although we have mentioned some manufacturers, we have stopped short of recommending particular hardware. Technology is in constant change, but is at present fairly stable in the realm of sound equipment. Sound equipment that uses today's technology will likely be more than adequate for a year or two, which is a long stretch in techno-time!

A note about drivers

Every sound card depends on the most current versions of its own configuration software to run well. There are software *drivers* and other resource files that manufacturers update from time to time. It's a good idea to know where to go to check for those drivers.

Drivers do exactly what the name indicates! They tell Windows 95 or DOS how to "drive" your system hardware. Driver files contain specific information about your hardware that Windows needs in order to run that component smoothly. Sometimes the software drivers initially supplied with your hardware must be revised for smoother operation and compatibility.

We will show you how to obtain the most updated drivers and other software for your system hardware via online services and the World Wide Web.

Introduction To Music Hardware

Before we begin discussing each component at length, here's something to think about. Prices will go down as technology develops; CD-ROMs get faster, recordable CD-ROMs become more popular and wavetable synthesis is included on newer, faster, cleaner sound cards. This is already happening. It's not a bad idea to wait a bit, shop, and make plans using the suggestions we'll be mentioning here—with strategic shopping you can save money and still build a superb, contemporary sound system!

6

Building Your Sound System

Inside Chapter 6

Know your current system setup 69
Minimum system requirements 70
Compatibility issues 71
Keeping records 71
Read the manual 72

How & Where To Shop For Your Sound Card 72

The "wish list" principle 73
To buy or not to buy:: Keeping the sound card you have now 73
Shopping tips—who is the expert here? 74

Finding The Musical Equipment You Want 75

Mail order 75
Shopping the 'Net—online vendors 75
Go to the source 76
What's on the web? 76
Ask questions 77
I like coffee, you like tea … 78
Let the (computer) buyer beware ! 78
Read the box 79
On-board capabilities—warning, warning! 79
Compatibility problems with "Sound Blaster Compatibles" 79
Reputable "Sound-Blaster Type" cards 81
Old, state of the art or in between? 81

Summary 84

Building Your Sound System

In order to know what you need to buy, you need to know what you already have!

Know your current system setup

When you call a manufacturer, vendor or technical-support person for trouble-shooting instructions or product information, they'll ask for specific details about your computer and how it's set up.

Accurate information about your system will make it more likely that you'll get proper advice. Technical-support providers are usually familiar with "weak links" between components or peculiarities that may require special instructions. You might hear statements such as: "Aha, so you have the Gizmo Model 909 and only 4Mb of RAM? In that case, here's what we need to do..."

In order to buy enhancements wisely for your computer, it's important to know what's already in your system. We have suggestions below on record-keeping techniques.

Building Your Sound System

Minimum system requirements

Here are guidelines on minimum hardware needed for handling music and other sounds with either Windows 95 or Windows 3.x:

Windows 95

- 486 computer processor
- 8 Mb RAM
- 40-60 Mb hard-disk space
- 350 Mb or larger hard disk

Windows 3.x

- 386 computer processor
- 4-8 Mb RAM
- 40-60 Mb hard-disk space
- 250 Mb or larger hard disk

These figures may be higher than you've seen elsewhere, due to the special circumstances surrounding music and sound:

- The WAV files you download and create have a way of eating up hard-disk space in a hurry. Those who are new to WAV files tend to get carried away, keeping every sound they download or create. Eventually, you will probably pare it down to a few dozen favorites—but you will always be adding new ones, too!

- Anything less than a 486 processor and 8 megabytes of RAM in Windows 95 is nearly crippling. It will quickly grow tiresome when you are trying to edit and compose music as you wait for those files to load and save. Most of the software written for Windows 95 carry these minimums, and will also need hard-disk space of its own.

Building Your Sound System

Compatibility issues

You need to know whether a particular sound card and related music peripherals will work with your system. While most sound cards support DOS and Windows 3.x, you may run into a number of problems with Windows 95. If you don't have the appropriate drivers and software for Windows 95, it's not always easy to run older hardware.

Windows 95 is usually tolerant of hardware and software designed for Windows 3.x, but there may be unanticipated complications. Sound cards are no exception.

Also, bear in mind that Plug-and-Play hardware is designed for Windows 95. Windows 3.x will probably not respond to Plug-and-Play setups. Usually, if adaptation is possible, printed documentation will show you how to adjust Plug-and-Play capabilities for use with Windows 3.x. In other instances, Windows 3.x will not be compatible with a card designed only for Plug-and-Play.

Keeping records

A three-ring binder with pockets for holding manufacturers' documentation will save you hours of heartache if you ever need to reinstall your system software or reconfigure the hardware.

It's good to keep a record of what you already have in your system, including the model numbers and manufacturers. In addition, if you've had to make any system adjustments, write those down. If you don't know what you have, you might find that information in the "readme" files on diskettes that came with your new hardware. (These are sometimes installed on your hard drive.)

Each time you make a change to your system hardware, write it down! Some items to include in this record are:

Building Your Sound System

♪ The type and model of installed hardware

♪ The date you installed it

♪ Installation instructions

♪ Any additional documentation that came with your hardware

♪ Any advice offered via e-mail or telephone from Technical Support

♪ Any changes you have made to your system configuration, including IRQ, DMA and Com Port settings

If you're not sure what we mean by IRQ settings, refer to the manual that came with your computer.

Read the manual

Reading the manual can help you avoid a lot of wasted time and frustration. Manuals or "readme" files often tell you the best way to obtain technical support or solve your problem before you call it in.

Even if the manual is vague or confusing, then at least you are able to say to a technical support specialist: "Your manual says this—could you please explain that?" People are usually more patient when they see you've already tried to figure it out on your own.

How & Where To Shop For Your Sound Card

Now that you've determined what you have, here are some hints on obtaining what you'll need to build your PC music system.

Building Your Sound System

The "wish list" principle

As you plan your sound system, begin to make a list. We'll refer to this as your "wish list."

In the chapters that follow, we will be discussing the components of a sound system. As you read each chapter, and learn about what these components can do, start a list that itemizes 1) which functions you want your equipment to perform, both now and later, and 2) which features of each component are most important to you for the present. We will help you break this down, explaining which features provide which functions.

This "Wish list principle" can be applied to shopping for just about anything you can purchase for a computer. We'll show you how to make a wish list to take along when you shop for your sound card. You can adapt that list and the strategies discussed when shopping for other components in your sound system.

To buy or not to buy:
Keeping the sound card you have now

Before you buy, investigate what you already have. Sound cards that come bundled with PCs are usually inexpensive and basic, so replacing your sound card may bring you better performance and more features.

On the other hand, the card you already have may perform as well as you will need it to. At the low end, many older cards will still be quite adequate for simply hearing sounds on your computer. Once you've completed the chapter on sound cards, you will be better able to determine your needs—so it's still not a bad thing to make a wish list!

If you already have an older sound card, you may be able to improve it. Knowing what components you need for each function will allow you to intelligently discuss upgrading with the manufacturer. Some older cards allow you to add extra memory and other upgrade components.

Building Your Sound System

Check the documentation to see what "extras" your card permits. Also, check with the manufacturer before you consider buying another. They may have the additional equipment you need, or may be able to recommend add-ons from another manufacturer that they know work best with their cards.

Also, ask the manufacturer about exchanging your sound card for their newer models. Some companies whose old models do not work with Windows 95 will offer trade-ups to existing customers.

If you decide that a new card is the way to go, here are some tips on how to shop.

Shopping tips—who is the expert here?

It's good to have your wish list completed before you head out to shop for sound equipment. That way, you have common ground on which you and the vendor can begin discussing which models will meet your needs.

Shopping for a sound card is easier if you know what you want to do with one, since many cards perform specialized functions. Keep in mind that once you buy, you'll likely not be replacing it for a two years or more. That is, unless you become a musical techno-whiz overnight, and find you suddenly need the ultimate in sound capabilities! So consider both your present needs and what you may want to do later.

It may seem an overwhelming challenge to read reviews, wade through advertising claims and package blurbs, and talk to vendors and manufacturers. Focusing on your sound card needs is a worthwhile exercise, though. How disappointing it would be to find out your sound card cannot use MIDI composing software, if this is what you had your heart set on doing! Likewise, it would be foolish to spend money on a super-deluxe card that performs tasks you'll never use.

Building Your Sound System

There is a wide range of cards to suit every need and budget. More often than not, what you get in the way of computer equipment is equal to time plus care plus the financial investment you make.

Finding The Musical Equipment You Want

Not all stores will carry all lines of sound equipment. You may find only low-end sound cards from one manufacturer, or one or two brands of sound card ranging from the low to mid-range series.

It is possible that a store may deal primarily with one brand of sound cards, ranging from the simple (and less expensive) to that vendor's "top of the line" card.

However, if you already know what you want, many retailers will be happy to special-order a particular item for you.

Mail order

If you still cannot locate that card you're longing for, there are other sources from which to acquire a sound card than your local computer store. Mail-order computer companies, especially ones that specialize in sound and music equipment, are a good solution.

Many mail-order vendors have the same equipment, and more, as you'll find locally and it will often be at far lower prices than a local store!

Shopping the 'Net—online vendors

Another means for determining price and functionality is the internet. There are vendors available, ranging from factory-direct to wholesale internet vendors, who offer better prices and specials than can be found even in some computer super-stores.

Building Your Sound System

Go to the source

There's a fourth shopping idea that few people consider! Go directly to the source—the manufacturer of the sound card.

Not all manufacturers sell direct, but most do, via the internet or by telephone. At the very least, they can provide you with helpful answers to your questions, and in this manner you will be able to eliminate sound cards and equipment that are beyond or beneath your needs, incompatible with your system, or too expensive for your budget.

They can also advise you of upcoming releases of new hardware, and give you the specifics on new items of which you may not have been aware!

And they can also steer you towards a local vendor, if they do not sell directly to the public.

What's on the web?

Many sound card companies now have World Wide Web pages on the internet. These pages provide information on cards they are currently offering—probably a lot more information than you could get at a local store.

Some Web pages are stunningly good; we will point you toward those pages later in this book. Most manufacturers have organized their Web pages so you can quickly find what you need. Several manufacturers post lists of compatible systems. Some contain a virtual wealth of related information!

Most web pages contain information on the manufacturer's most current products, e-mail addresses for technical support and sales, and more.

Make note of the manufacturers to whom you speak or write. If your e-mail is not answered, or the information given you is vague, this gives you vital information on that company's consumer operations. It's fair to assume that the technical support you receive from that company is going to be equally unhelpful. Technical support can range from initial purchasing decision-

Building Your Sound System

making to answers on installation and software questions that arise as you begin to explore the capabilities of your card. A manufacturer interested in keeping you as a customer, and who treats you accordingly, is likely to be available when you have questions.

Because there are so many combinations of PC equipment, it is likely that the company that manufactures the sound card has tested it with many combinations of computer setups. After all, sales won't be profitable if their card only works with one brand of computer!

If, after reading the information they have provided, you find yourself still confused, write or phone them directly. This is a sure-fire way to find the information you need. Knowing your system will pay off here because it's important to know what questions to ask once you get someone on the line.

Ask questions

Armed with your wish list and the information you've obtained from this book, product reviews and Web sites, you'll be ready to ask key questions of manufacturers and vendors. Careful shopping will minimize the chance for regrets when you've unpacked and installed your sound card.

Sometimes, when questioning a computer salesperson about the features of sound equipment, you may find he or she does not know as much as *you* have learned! Sales people, especially in super-stores, have a lot of equipment and software to learn about, with changes being made daily. Unless their personal interest leans toward something you need to know, the sales personnel may not be as informed as they should be. Even when you are pointed towards the "music expert" in a store, that "expert" may not be able to help you in more than a vague way.

Building Your Sound System

In stores that deal with a wide range of computers and peripherals, there is often a general assumption that the average buyer wants average equipment. One who professes little or no knowledge of music is judged to be interested only in basic sound card functions. That buyer is thereby pointed by the vendor towards the lowest end of the sound card range.

I like coffee, you like tea ...

Don't automatically accept the word of vendors, co-workers or friends who tell you "this is the *best* card on the market!" Everyone has an opinion, and many fancy themselves experts, especially when it comes to musical equipment. The vendor may simply be repeating what he or she has been told, perhaps due to the profit mark-up on a certain brand or model. Your co-worker may love the way one particular sound card plays game sounds—but you want to do MIDI composing. Your best friend may have dashed out to buy that "best" sound card only because someone *else* said it was the one to have.

Knowing what you want before you go shopping for a sound card prevents an over-eager, under-informed salesperson from deciding for you. That's dangerous!

This is not to say that all vendors are uninformed! Even the best salesperson can't help you if he or she doesn't know what you have in mind because you haven't given it enough thought beforehand.

Let the (computer) buyer beware !

A store may offer what seems to be a terrific sale on discontinued sound cards. However, as we've noted, the cost advantage of older cards may be outweighed by compatibility headaches and limited features. Sometimes the savings aren't that great; you might, for instance, notice a 4x (speed) CD-ROM package for $129 sitting right next to a faster 8x CD-ROM package from the same manufacturer for $139—only $10 more!

Building Your Sound System

Some vendors depend on consumer bewilderment for unloading older equipment from their inventory. "Let the buyer beware" is not a casual comment in the world of computing.

Read the box

Sound cards usually come in boxes that carry lots of information about the card, its features, and its compatibility traits. Watch for indications on system compatibility, as well as minimum system and software requirements. If you know your system, then you know what you already have, or must acquire, in order to use new peripherals.

On-board capabilities—warning, warning!

On-board means that the particular feature can be contained on the card itself. A card with on-board memory, e.g., has its memory chips installed as part of itself.

Extra on-board features may have been installed by the manufacturer prior to shipping. Other cards support on-board features that may not yet have been installed. If the card is labeled "capable" of one special feature or another, it does not necessarily mean that the card comes equipped with that feature. It can (and often does) mean that you will have to spend extra money to acquire that feature.

Compatibility problems with "Sound Blaster Compatibles"

The Sound Blaster series of cards, created by Creative Labs, has become the *de facto* sound card standard. Many software publishers test their products for Sound Blaster compatibility exclusively. Sometimes, other manufacturers claim that their cards are "Sound Blaster compatible." While this is possible, some "no-name brand" cards have been known to cause problems, due to proprietary "features" that do not exist on Sound Blaster cards, or Sound Blaster features that are missing on the clones.

Building Your Sound System

One problem that can arise is that sound card drivers intended only for the Sound Blaster series may recognize the clone card as being somewhat compatible, but will only work intermittently. Other times, the driver may not recognize or allow the card to work at all.

If a Sound Blaster clone is compatible for the most part, the card may start up (initialize) correctly, then freeze in the middle of a session due to hardware commands that the software does not recognize.

If this is your case, your introduction to music on the computer quickly becomes "Reboot, tweak, reboot, tweak, reboot…" accompanied by the sound of gnashing teeth. It's enough to make anyone quit before they play a note!

In some cases, "compatibility" indicates only that the card is capable of performing some of the functions that the Creative Labs Sound Blaster does. For example, they may play back Sound Blaster-created sound files, but not allow editing of these sound files or any other function.

These problems may often be easily solved by ensuring that the proper drivers are installed. Software that comes with these clone cards differ from the software drivers offered for the original Sound Blasters; a card's proprietary drivers and other utilities should be included in any sound card package.

Opting for a cheaper card is a "try at your own risk" situation if you are unfamiliar with the manufacturer. Even cards claiming 100% compatibility won't be the same as a genuine Sound Blaster card (not without impinging Creative Labs's patent). If your main concern is compatibility, look seriously at real Sound Blaster cards. However, some reputable companies do offer Sound Blaster compatibility at the 100% rate, and it is likely quite safe to anticipate that these cards will work just fine.

In short, be wary of "no-name" brands.

Reputable "Sound-Blaster Type" cards

Lest you be concerned, reputable manufacturers stand behind their products, and should not be a worry. Some major manufacturers have recently begun to produce "Sound-Blaster compatible" cards to capture their share of that particular market. Their specialty has been in other types of cards, particularly high-end cards for professionals, and they have decided to expand their customer base. These cards are generally just fine!

Old, state of the art or in between?

Out with the old...

It is, in general, not a good practice to purchase old or used computer equipment. Last year's "state of the art" carries a higher risk of incompatibility with your current and future components.

Manufacturers of some older sound cards and other peripherals are no longer in business. If there is no upgrade or technical support for your card, you may run into some frustrating dead-ends!

It may be difficult to find an older type of sound card for sale today—unless the local discount store has a few leftovers to unload. You are more likely to get used ones from people who've upgraded. But don't expect older cards to perform all the functions that today's software allows. Three years ago, most of that software wasn't even created!

Another consideration: older cards were monaural (mono) versus today's stereo. Though you can still buy sound cards that are compatible with the original mono Sound Blaster setup, the most exciting and interesting new cards are stereo. It is unlikely that you will find a new monaural sound card. Monaural cards cannot be upgraded to stereo.

Building Your Sound System

Those devoted to Windows and DOS games may, for a time, find these older cards work just fine. However, games continue to increase in complexity and sophistication. These older cards may eventually prove to be more hassle than is justified by the cost-saving angle. Eventually all will be rendered entirely useless.

If, after reading the above, you still desire to buy a used card, be sure that you read its documentation to see whether it will work with your system. Also be sure to check whether or not the manufacturer is still in business.

If that card was built so long ago that Windows 95 had not been released, you may be in big trouble. Find out whether new drivers are available for Windows 95 systems. Some older cards will not operate properly with Windows 95, simply because the company is out of business and nobody else has created drivers that are Windows 95 compatible.

State of the art...

Buying today's popular flavor of state-of-the-art equipment is not without risks either. Although manufacturers usually run components through test after test, consumer use is the only proof of how new software or hardware works in the real world.

If you're among the first to buy this equipment, you may be the first to discover annoyances and problems; some easily corrected, others that may require you returning the card to the manufacturer for a "fix." Some never really do work properly, despite all valiant efforts to the contrary.

If you really *must* have that newest sound card or other gizmo, at the very least wait a few weeks until reviews are available, or until you've read what other consumers have to say!

Building Your Sound System

In between ...

It's a good choice to aim for mainstream hardware that has proven its worth in the consumer arena. Even if that hardware is replaced by something newer, faster and flashier in a matter of months or a year, your equipment will be supported by a reputable manufacturer for a good amount of time beyond that. By the time your equipment is hopelessly out of date, two or three more cycles of computer technology may have passed!

Just as some video cards created for Windows 3.x systems were the "speed demons" of the Windows 3.x era, so some sound cards were the Windows 3.x "screamers." Though many people still use Windows 3.x, the day will soon come when newer, faster equipment and software preclude the use of older equipment and software.

However, much of that equipment works quite nicely with Windows 95! The manufacturers of such equipment have sometimes put enormous effort into compatibility issues, especially if the particular hardware involved was the very best. People are reluctant to surrender equipment that produces great results. Competent manufacturers know that, and try to look ahead as best they can.

Visit Web sites, read reviews and benchmarks in PC magazines, and make your wish list. In this way, you'll make a solid choice of equipment that will work now and many miles down the road.

Building Your Sound System

Summary

The four main factors in purchasing a sound card:

- ♪ Know what tasks sound cards can perform
- ♪ Decide what you want to use your sound card for
- ♪ Know what hardware suits your tasks, now and later
- ♪ Make sure your system supports the card you want to buy

7

Sound Cards

Inside Chapter 7

A brief history	88
Sound Card Features	**89**
The basics	89
Advanced features	89
Making Choices: What Do You Want To Do?	**91**
What will you want right now?	91
Advanced Sound Card Capabilities	**95**
MIDI Capability	95
Sampling capability	96
Wavetable synthesis compatibility	96
Wavetable add-on card	97
Other requirements	98
Letdowns And How To Avoid Them	**100**
Buy Now Or Later?	**101**
Will you make a recommendation?	102

Sound Cards

A decent sound card is standard equipment on most new computers. Manufacturers include sound cards as automatically as they do a video card or hard disk drive. There's a lot to hear out there, and people want to hear it!

A great deal of today's software assumes the presence of a sound card in one way or another. People who don't have sound cards will not be able to enjoy the increasing role of sound in entertainment and educational programs. The biggest uses are still in gaming and music—two areas that helped make sounds popular on computers—but sound applications are growing daily, including placing sound in multimedia presentations and listening to radio broadcasts or music on the internet.

In order to help you choose the sound card that will work best for you, we begin by letting you know what sound cards will allow you to do. After that, we will present you with a list of questions to ask yourself that will help you plan ahead, determining what you want to do now and later. Finally, we'll let you know which features perform the tasks you require. In this way, we hope to help guide you towards the card that's right for you!

Sound Cards

We will consider two crucial factors: 1) capabilities of sound cards and 2) what you want to do with those abilities, both now and later.

A brief history

Just a few years ago the selection of sound cards was limited. There were only two or three manufacturers. They made 8-bit cards with mono (one-channel) sound and limited recording and playback capabilities via FM synthesis—a relatively limited technology.

Creative Labs's early Sound Blaster series brought us FM synthesis techniques. FM synthesis handled all the music and sound functions those early cards supported and was a huge improvement over the weak sounds produced by the PC speaker. FM synthesis is supported by practically all software. Sound cards that advertise "Sound Blaster compatibility" are indicating that they, too, support these sound formats and FM synthesis.

Refer back to Simple Sound Facts (chapter two) of this book for more information on FM synthesis and the more contemporary alternative, wavetable synthesis. Today's standard is 16-bit (per note), stereo (two-channel), CD-quality sound. Many cards also include a MIDI interface for attaching a joystick, music keyboard, or other music sources to your sound card.

With so many more sound cards on the market today, deciding which one to buy isn't so simple anymore. Cards range from under $50, which will buy an older type card with older FM synthesis and no extra memory for sampling, to more than $700 for one with all the "bells and whistles." Many good sound cards are available for less than $250.

Sound Cards

Sound Card Features

Sound cards can help you accomplish a number of tasks, either alone or in combination with other music hardware and software.

The basics

Here is a list of basic features that most elementary sound cards offer:

- Generate artificially created musical sound from an internal FM synthesizer

- Play digitized sounds, such as WAV files

- Play music scores, such as MID files

- Control volume (loudness) via hardware or software

- Control tone (treble/bass) via hardware or software

- Run various musical software, such as piano- and guitar-instruction programs

Advanced features

Below are some additional sound card features. Not all cards will perform all the functions (or include all the features) listed below.

- Play music from audio-input devices, such as your computer's CD-ROM player

Sound Cards

- ♪ Generate real instrument sounds from an internal wavetable synthesizer

- ♪ Play games through a joystick interface to hear the game's sound effects

- ♪ Control external MIDI devices, such as electronic piano keyboards

- ♪ Run music-composition software to create your own MIDI songs

- ♪ Record sounds from MIDI-capable music instruments.

- ♪ Record sounds from external sources, such as a radio, television or microphone

- ♪ Create your own audio recordings from internal and external sources

- ♪ Generate CD-quality sound files

- ♪ Produce special effects, like 3D and surround sound

- ♪ Install easily with Windows 95 Plug-and-Play

The most simple and inexpensive sound cards may be adequate if games are your thing, or you don't think you want to go much further than listening to sounds and music files which you've downloaded through your modem.

There are many mid-priced cards that will perform the major functions of music applications in addition to playing game and sound files.

A professional musician may opt to buy a high-end sound card to use for sophisticated audio and video production.

Sound Cards

Remember that it is important to research several different sound cards, because some offer features that others do not. Deciding which features are for you is very important!

Making Choices: What Do You Want To Do?

What will you want right now?

In order to help you decide what you want to use your sound card for, we've presented some things to think about for your wish list. Remember, not all cards perform all the functions.

You've seen the range of functions of various sound cards. Ask yourself which of these you'd like to do! Your choice of sound cards should relate directly to the type of activities you want to accomplish and the features that will allow you to do so. Some cards have an enormous number of features, and usually the price goes up as the list of abilities gets longer.

First, consider whether you intend to go beyond the basic activities. Decide which of these features is most important to you for the present; then, what is important for the future. Keep "now" and "future" separate on your list.

Here is what most basic sound cards will allow you to do:

- ♪ Listen to WAV and MIDI files that come with Windows 95
- ♪ Add new sound files to your collection
- ♪ Use sound files as system sounds
- ♪ Hear sounds that play for you in the background from an internet site

Sound Cards

♪ Hear sounds that are contained in multimedia files

♪ Enjoy audio CDs in your computer's CD-ROM player

♪ Play games with a joystick attached to the sound card to hear the games' sounds in all their sonic splendor

Now that you know what a basic card does, consider what advanced features will allow you to do. These are some more items you must decide on before shopping for your card.

Would you like to:

♪ Attach a piano keyboard to your sound card?

♪ Compose and edit your own multi-voiced MIDI compositions?

♪ Use a microphone to record TV, radio, phonograph, VCR or voice?

♪ Have real instrument sounds, rather than artificially created ones?

♪ Sample sounds from your favorite audio CD-ROMs?

♪ Enjoy monaural or stereo sound?

♪ Have a guarantee of long-term vendor support?

♪ Learn about multimedia production, which involves both audio and video?

Sound Cards

That's not all, though! We have some more questions for you. These questions relate to the more advanced features on sound cards we mentioned above. You may want to include them on the "now" part of your list.

- How many people in your immediate home have an interest in music? Might they want to use a music keyboard to take piano lessons?

- Do you or another family member wish to learn to compose music?

- Is there a child in your home who is either taking music lessons, or who will soon be old enough to develop an interest in an instrument?

- Is your child learning about sound and music at school? (It may be good to reinforce that at home.)

- Do you want to learn how to incorporate sound and video?

- Is there a baby on the way? Babies are just tickled by sounds, music and voices as soon as they are old enough to sit on your lap and listen. Quacking ducks and mooing cows are sparks for spending lots of time listening together!

- Are you working on your family history? Would you like to have snippets of your family's voices to attach to their history pages with their photos?

- Do you want to use narration or sound effects in your business presentations?

- Do you have access to a computer or laptop at school? If so, would you like to include your voice or other sounds in school reports or projects?

Sound Cards

♪ Would you like to replace those boring system sounds on your computer with fun ones of your own design?

♪ Is learning about music files a means to an end? Will you want to explore multimedia files (combined sound and video) later on?

If you think some of these considerations apply to you, and that you want to dive into these things immediately, it's good to consider a card that has all of the finer capabilities now. Growing children may develop a burning interest in composing and editing. Your old card may not handle all of these features.

You may also want to look through the activities and exercises in the software section of this book to get an idea of what other fun you can have with these additional features.

Once you've got your present goals on your list it's time to think about what you may want to do later on. Determining as best you can the immediate and future plans you have for using your sound card will help determine what to buy now so you don't have to upgrade later. If there are any items above that you omitted from your list but will want later on, add them now.

If you are more cautious, and want to see how your interest develops, it's sensible to consider a sound card that will provide you added capabilities with the addition of a daughter board or extra memory later on.

Check the price of upgrade components before you buy a basic, upgradeable card. Compare that to the price of the entire (already upgraded) package. You may save more by planning ahead and buying the whole package now, rather than buying now and adding on.

Sound Cards

Advanced Sound Card Capabilities

The following is a list of advanced features found on some sound cards. At the end of each section, we've included a list of some of the activities these features allow.

MIDI Capability

MIDI capability indicates that your sound card can relay digital sound information from a MIDI-capable music instrument to your computer. The plug on these instruments is a 5-prong, circular plug that must connect to a sound card. You'll need a MIDI cable for this.

Both your sound card and your music keyboard (also called a "controller" keyboard), must be MIDI-capable. This means that the sound card comes with a MIDI-type plug which allows a MIDI cable to join instruments, such as an external electronic keyboard, directly to the card. It is possible that a middle-of-the-road card simply will not perform all of the functions necessary for MIDI.

The good news is even if you have a sound card that is not MIDI capable, or does not allow for sampling, there are additions which might be able to enhance hardware that you already own that can be purchased more inexpensively than rushing out to buy a brand-new sound card.

You need MIDI capability and a MIDI adapter cable for: connecting your sound card to and recording sounds via MIDI-capable instruments, such as a keyboard, game joystick, or other MIDI instrument.

Sound Cards

Sampling capability

A sound card with sampling capability allows you to "sample" audio CD-ROM bits to use on your computer. Sampling allows you to capture your own favorite sounds and use them in any number of ways; to share and trade with friends, to replace your current system sounds, to include in school demonstrations, reports, and projects and in business presentations.

> You need sampling capability (and the extra memory required to run it) for: capturing sounds directly from your computer's CD-ROM player.

Sampling requires a good deal of memory and some cards do not come directly from the factory with the necessary amount on-board. A sound card is technically "non-sampling" until that extra memory is installed. Adding this memory is all that's needed to enhance the card so that it is capable of sampling music.

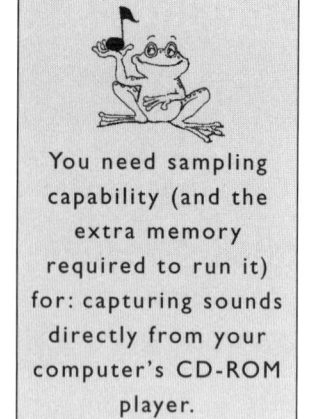

Sound cards purchased today should allow for 44 kHz sampling rates. 22kHz is good for general-purpose sampling, but there will be times when you'll want the high quality that 44kHz furnishes.

Wavetable synthesis compatibility

Today's better sound cards will still include FM synthesis, which only imitates real sound via synthesizer chips. This ensures compatibility with older hardware and software. But their main feature is wavetable synthesis. At present, this technology is more expensive than the less complicated FM synthesis. If you will only be using your card for the basics and your budget is limited, you may be better off buying a card that does not have this added feature.

> You need wavetable synthesis for: sound quality; state-of-the-art real instrument sound in playback of sound files and using music lesson, recording, composing and editing software.

Sound Cards

A wavetable sound card must have on-board memory where those real-instrument sound samples can be stored. Data derived from digital recordings of live instruments are put into memory and played back when you request the computer to use it.

If you like high-quality music, one of the main disappointments in purchasing a sound card is discovering that the card is incapable of addressing wavetable synthesis. This can limit one's ability to compose and edit music files in various formats, and does not allow for "real instrument" sound!

Wavetable add-on card

Many cards today can handle wavetable synthesis. A card that does not allow for the state of the art wavetable synthesis will often allow you to add a "daughter card" that will make your card capable of this. **Wavetable add-on cards**, sometimes referred to as **wavetable daughter cards** or **wavetable upgrade cards**, enable wavetable synthesis for sound cards that are otherwise not capable of handling it. This synthesis, as we've said, is state of the art, and most new mid-range and high quality sound cards support it.

As we've mentioned, wavetable synthesis is more capable of producing near-real or real sounds of actual music instruments and other effects. Some sound cards, especially those that were manufactured earlier than 1994, are not equipped to handle this kind of information.

A wavetable upgrade card is a "daughter card" (a card which is attached to a sound card not capable of wavetable synthesis on its own) which will enable this type of sound creation, composition and editing.

Most reputable sound card companies offer PC-compatible sound cards that have sampling capabilities, MIDI interface and either true digital sample playback (wavetable) synthesizers or the capability for a wavetable upgrade. That does not mean they necessarily include these features in the basic package!

Sound Cards

It is important to determine whether the card you buy is capable of that "as is," or whether it will require the addition of a "daughter card" to add this capability. In addition to daughter cards, there are "stand-alone" products that will provide you with wavetable capabilities.

> You need a wavetable add-on card for: upgrading a current sound card that does not allow for wavetable synthesis (real instrument sound).

Other requirements

Here are the additional sound card features, and some of the tasks for which they are needed.

System compatibility

What if you buy all that great new hardware, then find out that it won't work with the system you already have? It's important to know that all of your computer's components will work together smoothly.

Unlike video cards, sound cards do not need to have PCI capability to work in a Pentium environment. That specific compatibility element is not part of a sound card's design.

Those cards created to work specifically with Windows 95 are generally 16-bit, thus faster, "cleaner" in sound quality and more efficient. More "extras" have usually been added to these cards, such as true on-board digital sample playback (wavetable) synthesizers, CD-quality sound, MIDI interface, FM synthesizer and a built-in sampler with expandable memory.

The other compatibility feature you may wish to consider is the Windows 95 Plug-and-Play configuration. If your sound card is labeled "Plug-and-Play," chances are that it will be automatically recognized by Windows 95 upon installation, and properly configured with the software included in your sound card package.

Windows 3.x does not usually recognize Plug-and-Play configurations. Make sure, if you are still running Windows 3.x, that any Plug-and-Play card you buy also supports Windows 3.x. For multimedia production your sound card needs to be compatible with your video card, CD-ROM drive, and any

Sound Cards

software you use. You need system compatibility for multimedia (audio/video) production, ease of use and proper interaction with other music components such as headphones, speakers and CD-ROM player

Speaker input
You need speaker input to attach external speakers or headphones to your sound card.

CD-ROM input and adapter cord
This is needed for attaching your computer's CD-ROM player directly to your sound card. You'll need to do this so you can enjoy your audio CD-ROMs through your computer's speakers, and to record (sample) sounds from your CD-ROM player. Be sure a CD-ROM adapter comes with your sound card; if it doesn't, you'll have to obtain one!

> By external speakers, we are also referring to those stereo speakers that may have been included with and are attached to your computer. We are NOT referring to the PC's internal "error beep" speaker.

Auxiliary input
To create audio recordings **directly** from your VCR or TV (it's the "Aux" input jack on the back of the card).

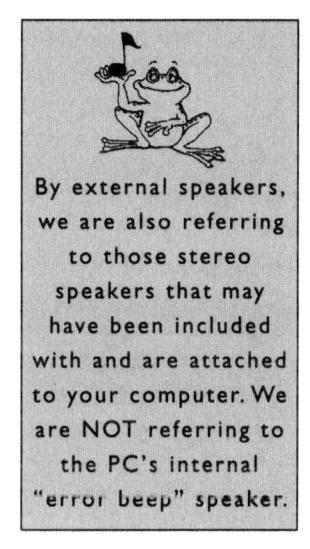

Microphone Input
This is needed to record **indirectly** from external sound sources via microphone (it's the "Mic" input jack).

Name brands
Buy name brands for a guarantee of vendor support, current software and drivers, and upgrade offers

16-Bit, CD-Quality, stereo sound
This is needed for state-of-the-art, quality sound during both playback and recording.

Audio compression
Audio compression reduces the size of sound files. ADPCM and Mu-Law are the two forms most frequently used in gaming and multimedia. Compression reduces audio fidelity somewhat, and is primarily used for speech and game sounds.

Sound Cards

DSP (Digital Signal Processing)
A DSP chip included on a sound card allows capabilities such as voicemail and speech decoding. Business users will find these capacities useful, but they can increase the price! High-end cards also use DSP for reverb, pitch shifting and 3D sound.

Low noise level
The better the card you buy, the better the sound you'll get—obviously! Those who seek great audio quality get the most benefit from cards that have low noise levels. This is especially important for those who are using sound for multimedia business presentations or producing demos of original songs. Higher-end cards provide shielding against electrical noise, thereby delivering better quality wavetable synthesis.

Memory on Wavetable-Capable Cards
Many cards that are wavetable capable allow for the installation of up to 28 megabytes of additional RAM on the card, where samples of real instruments can be stored. The more memory you add, the more MIDI sounds you can add.

Letdowns And How To Avoid Them

Some sound card packages will indicate that they are "wavetable synthesis compatible," "MIDI compatible," "sample compatible" or "wavetable synthesis upgradeable." This should alert you that such hardware (MIDI adapter, extra memory for sampling, or wavetable synthesis) may *not* be included in the package you are purchasing.

You may need to acquire further hardware, such as a daughter card or extra memory, to use these features. Check the documentation to see if these items are included in their full capacity, or if you will need to acquire other hardware.

Sound Cards

Most wavetable cards support the 128-instrument General MIDI (GM) specification. However, make certain you also know that the card meets the General MIDI requirement to play back at least 24 notes (voices) simultaneously; this should be written on the outside of the box, often cited as "GM compatibility."

There are two more refined specifications which we will explain in the software chapters, called GS and XG. Cards that additionally support one or both of those specifications will allow you access to a multitude of additional MIDI instruments.

Other things that are sometimes included in sound card packages are microphones and CD-ROM and MIDI cables. This will save you the aggravation of trying to locate these parts individually. You can replace a low-quality microphone down the line if you want; it's nice to have one to start using right away!

Buy Now Or Later?

If your needs or wants are limited at present, then you have another decision to make. If you are unsure if you want to invest a lot of money in hardware and software you will never use, here's a solution: you can buy a card that is capable of additional features now and upgrade it to use those features later. Unless your budget is extremely tight though, it is wiser to stay as current as possible (using the cautions we mentioned earlier about buying unproved state-of-the art equipment).

Adding on later is not necessarily a bad thing. If you are seeking to economize, and are not certain whether you will use the faculties that wavetable synthesis offers, it is fine to purchase a card which offers that compatibility and make decisions later on upgrading.

If you believe you'll want to go further than listening to sound files, or if there

Sound Cards

is a family member that is already musically adept, then a MIDI connection, wavetable synthesis and sampling are important considerations.

You can have two sound cards in your compute, although currently no applications will use more than one sound card at a time. Some people have a basic, Sound Blaster-type card that they use for simple functions, and a more expensive, MIDI-capable card that they use for composing music. Though you can have both, it creates complications in the internal setup. It's usually best to upgrade by replacing your old card, rather than adding a second new one to your system, since the higher-end card can perform all the actions of the more basic card anyway.

Having two sound cards isn't the same as adding a "daughter card" (wavetable upgrade card) that was designed to enhance an already-installed sound card.

Will you make a recommendation?

Okay, sure! To be certain the sound card you buy will perform most of the functions available today, here is our suggestion:

- 16-bit, CD-quality stereo recording and playback, with sampling rates up to 44.1 kHz (for high-quality sound)

- Sound Blaster compatibility (for games and fun sounds)

- Wavetable Synthesis capability (for real-instrument quality)

- MIDI and WAV capability

- On-board memory capability (for sampling)

- MIDI Adapter Interface (for game joysticks and music keyboards)

- CD-ROM Interface (To connect your CD-ROM player)

Music Keyboards And MIDI Adapters

Inside Chapter 8

Keyboard Basics	105
More Is Not Necessarily Better	108
Built-in sounds	108
Modulation wheel	109
Modulation pedal	109
Pitch wheel	110
Key range transposition	110
Channel pressure	110
Acoustic action	111
Multitimbral capability	111
Standalone capability	112
Try Before You Buy	113
Touch	114
Key response	114
Sounds	114
Construction	115
MIDI Adapters	115

Music Keyboards And MIDI Adapters

Music keyboards, also called synthesizers, come in a variety of types. A music keyboard that attaches to your sound card is referred to as a *controller keyboard*, because it controls the sounds on your sound card via music software. Some controllers can also produce music independent of the computer.

As with most hardware components, the cost of a controller keyboard is primarily dictated by the features. Prices range from as little as $200 to beyond $2,000; you can get a more-than-adequate controller keyboard for as little as $300.

> In order to use a music keyboard with your computer, you must have a MIDI-capable sound card.

Keyboard Basics

Here are some practical, basic features to look for when buying a controller:

Music Keyboards And MIDI Adapters

Full-sized keys

Mini-keys, found on a lot of toy keyboards, make it too easy to strike keys next to the one which you intend to play. If you also play an acoustic piano or organ, the tiny keys on a synthesizer may never feel right.

Five or more octave range (61 keys)

Anything less will limit your music software's range and not allow you to play two-handed parts.

Sustain pedal

If you are new to piano, you may not use this at first. However, without it, you may not be able to play realistic piano sounds. A sustain foot pedal will let notes continue to "ring" after you lift your finger off the key.

Touch sensitivity or touch response

With this feature, the keyboard's MIDI connection is sensitive to the speed or pressure with which you press a key. This allows you to vary the *dynamics* of each note (fast, slow, loud or soft) to more closely resemble the tonal properties of many different instruments, percussion and other sounds, even bumblebees! Some keyboards allow this feature to be turned off and on.

AC power

It is important that your keyboard is not solely battery-powered. Batteries wear out! Imagine being in the middle of your most elegant composition, only to have the keyboard quit working, and maybe lose its memory. Make sure that your keyboard has either a built-in plug or a connector for an AC power supply adapter. The AC power adapter should be supplied with the keyboard.

Music Keyboards And MIDI Adapters

Polyphony

Poly = "many"; *phonic* = "sound." In our context, "polyphony" means that an instrument can play more than one note at a time. Acoustic pianos are polyphonic; horns and other single-note instruments are, in contrast, *mono*phonic. Some inexpensive synthesizer keyboards will also only allow one note to be played at a time. A polyphonic synthesizer keyboard can sound between 8 and 32 simultaneous notes (more is better).

MIDI capability

In order to connect the keyboard to your PC, your keyboard must have a MIDI Out connector. This is a round, 5-pin DIN connector which may (helpfully!) be labeled "MIDI OUT." It is usually located on the back of the keyboard.

Some controller keyboards also have a second 5-pin DIN connector labeled "MIDI IN." If the controller keyboard only has a "MIDI OUT" connector, the controller is not capable of sending any internal sounds it may have stored to the PC; rather, it depends on the internal sounds stored on your sound card or hard drive.

MIDI controllers allow you to compose, record, edit and play back as many as 16 separate instruments, chosen from as many as 128 instruments, percussion and sound effects.

MIDI cables, discussed at the end of this chapter, are necessary to utilize this feature.

General MIDI compatibility

Don't confuse this with MIDI capability—a controller can have a MIDI connector (or two) without being General MIDI compatible, but not the reverse.

General MIDI, often abbreviated as "GM," is the industry-wide standard of compatibility for playing and creating MIDI files. It is a set of musical specifications that dictates which instruments are assigned to which areas of the keyboard, and more. A MIDI instrument labeled "GM compatible" must follow these standards, regardless of make or model.

The packaging or specification sheet may also indicate that a keyboard supports either "GS" or "XG" format. Those are further enhancements of the GM specifications. GS is a proprietary MIDI format developed by Roland, while XG format is Yamaha's enhancement to General MIDI.

If the controller is GM compatible, chances are it says so on the box or has a "General Midi Compatible" logo on it somewhere.

While all of this MIDI talk may sound pretty complicated right now, we'll clear it up for you in the software section of this book. For the moment, the point is to make sure that your keyboard is GM compatible so that you will have the ability to use the features it offers.

More Is Not Necessarily Better

Some additional features you may wish to consider are:

Built-in sounds

When a controller does not have built-in sounds, it needs your computer software and sound card to produce any sound at all.

You don't *need* built-in sounds to use MIDI software with your computer. Having them is not necessarily an advantage. With inexpensive controller keyboards, installed sounds may be so poorly produced that you're better off using quality sounds from computer software instead.

Modulation wheel

This is built into the chassis of the keyboard, and is operated with one hand on the wheel and the other playing the keys. It allows you to add tremolo or vibrato, which are helpful in simulating string and brass instruments.

Modulation pedal

In addition to (or instead of) the modulation wheel, some controllers have connections for a modulation pedal (which should not be confused with the sustain pedal described in the basic features, above).

The modulation pedal performs the same function as the modulation wheel. And since it is a foot pedal, it leaves both hands free to work the keyboard.

Just as the modulation wheel is a good feature to have, so is the pedal. But if the pedal costs a great deal extra, you can consider saving this feature for later on, when you're satisfied that it's necessary. Having it right now is not as important, if it adds a lot to the cost. Here's why: One of the really delightful things about MIDI recording is that you can compose your music note by note, instrument by instrument. For example, you could write part or all of your song using only the guitar voice, then go back and add the horns, one by one. Most beginning keyboardists who are recording their own compositions will only be playing those parts one instrument at a time—a note or two at a time, and will have a hand free for the modulation wheel.

Both the modulation wheel and pedal require some coordination to learn to use. One is not necessarily easier than the other, until you are at a point where you will be playing several string parts at once, and need that other hand to stay on the keys. If you're a beginner, that's not likely to happen for some time. Though if the pedal doesn't cost extra, go for it!

Pitch wheel

A pitch wheel allows you to alter the precise pitch of a note, which is good for enhancing the sounds of instruments that can "bend" notes. Pitch bending would probably not be wise to use on a piano "voice," because notes on a real acoustic piano cannot be bent. Stringed instruments and monophonic instruments, such as those in the brass and reed families, can and often do use this effect.

Key range transposition

This allows you to alter the range of your keyboard.

As you learn to compose for each instrument you'll find that a French horn player, for instance, reads notes differently than a keyboard player does. What looks like Middle C to a keyboard player is actually a G on the French horn. Key range transposition helps players adapt to these differences.

This feature is important on any keyboard that has a limited number of keys. If the keyboard does not allow for very high or very low notes, it is difficult to imitate instruments that play in those ranges. A keyboard that does not have a low range will not allow for bass guitar parts. Likewise, one that does not have a good upper register will not allow flute or high string parts. Key transposition allows you to play these extremes on these limited keyboards.

Channel pressure

Channel pressure allows you to produce vibrato or a brighter sound by varying the pressure you apply to the keys. Professional keyboardists like this feature, but it requires a good deal of finger technique. Since you can produce the same vibrato or tremolo more easily with a modulation wheel, channel pressure is not as important for novices.

Acoustic action

The "feel" of piano keys is called the *action,* because the feeling reflects the movement of parts inside a piano that are connected to the keys. "Acoustic action" or "piano feel" indicate that the controller imitates the response of an acoustic piano. Without this feature the controller keyboard has a softer, spring-loaded action that plays more like an organ.

Keyboards that boast "piano feel" are usually more expensive. If you are a keyboardist already, or if price is no object, you should seriously consider this feature. It never hurts to have a controller that feels something like an acoustic piano. Someone who also plays an acoustic piano might be dissatisfied with anything less. For a beginner, it's more a matter of what feels comfortable. Having this feature won't automatically make you more (or less) of a keyboardist.

Multitimbral capability

"Multitimbrality" means the keyboard is capable of playing back several parts synchronously, with each part assigned to a different melodic or percussion instrument, or even other sound effects such as a bell or a train whistle.

A controller that comes equipped with its own internal sounds can play these separate instruments simultaneously, with each under independent control on its own MIDI channel. 16 is the maximum number of instruments (also known as "patches" or "voices"), because there are only 16 channels in MIDI specifications.

Standalone capability

You may prefer to have a keyboard that can also be used independent of your PC. Consumer-type and beginner keyboards usually include some method which allows you to listen to the keyboard as a standalone product. This may be headphones or speakers that are built into the chassis with an amplifier. Professional models rarely come equipped with these features and thereby require other MIDI connections or external amplification.

Standalone keyboards sometimes include a number of added thrills and frills. Some keyboards allow you to use separately purchased music cartridges. You can use blank cartridges to record your own music and buy pre-recorded ones in either complete orchestra or "music minus one" format. With a music minus one (commonly called "MMO") composition, you can listen to the whole band or orchestra or mute any instrument in the orchestral arrangement and play along, either on the keyboard or on another instrument.

However, you can do this same thing with the MIDI software on your computer! You can even do this with complete orchestrations—all you have to do is mute (turn off) the part which you want to play. Additions such as cartridges and extra floppies offer little extra beside added cost. In order to keep the price within reasonable consumer limits, this may also mean a sacrifice in the quality of sounds the keyboard itself contains.

Some consumer-type synthesizers also come equipped with a drum pad, which includes several preset rhythms.

Even with all these available features, you'll still want to use the keyboard with your PC. The PC allows you to save your files in one location, as well as providing you with sophisticated music software The extra sounds and drum rhythms available in cartridges don't translate in to a MIDI format that will allow you to use them with your computer music software. You may be using music compositions in other documents or programs on your computer. And it's very likely that you won't be able to share externally created files with

Music Keyboards And MIDI Adapters

anyone who does not have the exact same keyboard. Without the ability to save compositions to computer disks, whether fixed or floppy, you won't be able to send them across the internet, or integrate the music into another program. It is the PC that bridges these gaps.

In summary, if you want to use a consumer-type controller keyboard and all the added features with your PC, that's fine. The frills are great fun, and quite wonderful for beginners or advanced amateur musicians. In actuality, though, they can sometimes add to the price, and are superfluous for the purposes of the PC musician. What is most important is that the keyboard connects properly to your PC and offers the basic features described above.

The preset drum rhythms, karaoke capabilities and accompaniments on these type of beginner or consumer keyboards do not usually translate to the PC, because they are not part of the MIDI implementation. In addition, there may be some sacrifice in terms of MIDI sound quality in order to keep costs low for hobbyists and amateur musicians. Keep in mind that the fancy "extra" features usually translate to "extraneous" when considering a keyboard for PC use.

Try Before You Buy

As with other musical equipment, it's important to price and to test before you buy. Sometimes, the quality keyboard offers these exciting features in addition to the necessary ones for PC use, at a more fair price than some no-name keyboards.

If possible, try the keyboard you are thinking of buying. Take a good pair of headphones with you! It's also good to try the demo models that are on display, rather than just listen to someone else play for you. Many other people may have played those demos; it's not a bad idea to see how durable is a keyboard you are considering. Here are some important things to consider, some of which are a matter of personal preference:

Touch

If your keyboard's touch does not feel right to you, it may end up back in its box! Check the response time and pressure of touch sensitivity, described above. In either instance, some keyboards may respond too quickly; others may require a jackhammer to produce sound or to effect any changes in tonality.

Key response

In the case of both a demonstration keyboard that has probably been played by many shoppers and a fresh-out-of-the-box keyboard, watch out for:

- ♪ "sticky keys," which don't spring back after you press them,
- ♪ "stubborn keys," which are too hard to press down,
- ♪ "floppy keys," which respond far too easily.

Each of these things may indicate that the quality or key response is not what it should be. They will affect your playing.

Sounds

Listen to the keyboard's internal sounds, if it comes equipped with them, to see whether they are appealing to you. Use your headphones to evaluate the direct "internal sound to headphone" quality, too. Are the sounds clean and sparkling? Do the instruments resemble the ones they claim to represent? Do you hear any extra noise, pops or buzzing in the headphones?

Music Keyboards And MIDI Adapters

Construction

Does the case feel sound, or is it made of flimsy plastic? How about the keys—have any become detached? Are the connectors wobbly or poorly designed? Any musical connector, such as headphone jacks or MIDI cords, can only take so much abuse, no matter how well designed they are. Check to see that the connections on both new and demo keyboards are snug and do not appear flimsy. Since many people may have tried out a demo model, you have a chance to see connectors that may have become loosened by being jostled about.

If you are purchasing a keyboard that can also be used as a standalone keyboard, be extra sure it can withstand all the connecting and disconnecting inherent in that use. It might cost you more to have a keyboard connector repaired than to replace the whole keyboard!

MIDI Adapters

Finding the right MIDI cable is fairly easy today—it is often supplied with sound cards or MIDI instruments, like the controller keyboard. If it is not, several companies supply them, some of whom we've listed the internet section of this book.

- A keyboard that doesn't make any sound by itself doesn't need a MIDI IN jack. Any keyboard that has internal sounds and needs to control a sound card or record musical parts does need a MIDI OUT jack. Almost all music keyboards made recently have both.

- If you've bought a sound card that has no MIDI capabilities, you won't need the MIDI adapter. Sound cards that are not MIDI capable will not have the MIDI ports (DIN jacks) you need to connect a keyboard or joystick.

Music Keyboards And MIDI Adapters

♪ Sound cards that include MIDI features, MIDI add-cards or MIDI daughterboards will need the MIDI adapter.

To connect a keyboard with a "MIDI Out" connection, you will need 2 MIDI cords, in addition to the external MIDI adapter already mentioned. Some keyboards come equipped with both a MIDI adapter and MIDI Cords. If your sound card and your keyboard both come with these cords, either set will do fine; you won't need both complete sets!

On both the sound card and the controller, you will likely see a "MIDI Out" and "MIDI In" jack. Plug the "MIDI In" connection on the sound card to the keyboard's "MIDI Out," then use the remaining cord to connect the "MIDI Out" on the sound card to the "MIDI In" on the controller keyboard.

The cable should also have a connector that attaches to your PC sound card's 15-pin joystick port, but with some cards and cables you have to alternate your joystick with your controller keyboard, which can be inconvenient. You can usually get a cable that will provide both a MIDI instrument connector and joystick connector. With your PC, a sound card, and a MIDI keyboard, this cable and some software is all that is needed to be up and running!

Most sound cards can use a basic Sound Blaster-compatible cable. Some sound card manufacturers require their own special cable for MIDI applications. Some sound cards need a MIDI adapter with a circuit board in it, because the straight connection on a non-circuit board MIDI adapter will not work. You need to be sure which one your sound card requires.

A final reminder—inform yourself, then trust yourself rather than an inexperienced salesperson! If that person cannot answer many or all of the questions covered above, then you have already become more of an expert than they. Remember, too, that your best pal who just won't tolerate anything but that one particular brand of keyboards will not be playing your keyboard very often—*you* will!

9

Speakers, Headphones And Microphones

Inside Chapter 9

Making Sound Decisions On Sound Equipment 119

    Built-In speakers 119
    Choosing external speakers 120
    Your home stereo speakers may be an option 120
    Adapters 121
    Listening to speakers before you buy 123

Tips On Getting The Best Sound From Your Speakers . 125

    Room acoustics 125
    Positioning speakers for balance 126
    Check your connections! 126
    Consider headphones 127

Microphones 129

Speakers, Headphones And Microphones

Making Sound Decisions On Sound Equipment

In order to hear the sounds produced by your sound card, you will need either headphones or a pair of speakers connected to the sound card. Normally there are jacks or mini-plug connectors for this.

Built-In speakers

Some computers come with two speakers (for stereo) already incorporated into the computer or monitor. Most are not awful and some are quite good. If you already have built-in speakers, they will be fine for at least beginning to work with music and sound.

Speakers, Headphones And Microphones

Choosing external speakers

If you're going to purchase speakers separately you have several considerations. Choosing quality speakers for your computer sound and music studio is as important as the other components we have discussed. The basic science of how speakers work has not altered considerably in decades. To put it very simply, as with any other sound we hear, speakers work by moving air to create sound waves.

Differences between a $29 and $149 pair of speakers will include the material used to form the speaker cone (cardboard or more upscale materials), the size of the magnet that moves the speaker coil (bigger is better), whether the case includes one or multiple speakers (separate woofers and tweeters are better), and so on. The power and quality of the built-in amplifier can also vary widely between different models. While it's easy to pay too much for poor speakers, you can't expect to enjoy great sound from the matchbook-sized $7.95 special at the local grocery shop.

It is important that the speakers are a magnetically shielded, amplified type that is designed for use with computers. If they don't specifically say so, they probably aren't. Improperly shielded speakers can damage your computer.

Your home stereo speakers may be an option

If your budget's too pinched for buying computer speakers right now, you *may* be able to use either home-stereo or Walkman-type speakers with your computer.

There are some significant pitfalls to watch out for, but this move could potentially save you money and—in certain configurations—produce even better results than computer speakers. Normally, however, the best choice is shopping for good computer speakers. They're optimized for the type of signal and sounds produced by a computer, and designed to co-exist safely with your other computer equipment.

Speakers, Headphones And Microphones

Before you do anything at all, read the documentation that came with your sound card to see if it offers any precautionary information.

For example, the compact speakers often sold for portable cassette players (such as the Sony Walkman) may not look or sound much different than computer speakers, but they may not have the same electrical shielding. To test this, play music through the speakers as you normally do, while carefully moving them closer to your computer monitor. Does the picture begin to get wavy or discolored? If so, BACK OFF and forever keep them away from your computer! They are radiating electrical energy that could mess up your monitor and perhaps even your data.

Using "normal" speakers might be tricky

However attractive this sounds, please note this next point! *Serious damage can be done to your hardware* if proper precautions aren't taken. More often than not, the damage will be to your home-stereo system rather than to the sound card, and it could be an expensive mistake.

There are several ways you might use home-stereo speakers with your sound card—each with its own "safe" and "risky" configurations. All will involve using jack "adapters" that won't prevent you from hooking things up incorrectly and causing damage to electronic components. Read what's below and your product manuals carefully, and proceed with caution!

If you haven't got the documentation, or it doesn't refer to using speakers other than those designed for computers, you should contact the vendor to ask which output on the back of your sound card (if any) is the one to use with a home stereo system.

Adapters

Due to the need to keep components small in computers, most sound cards have 1/8-inch mini-plug jacks. You will need to visit an electronics store to obtain adapters that switch from "mini-plug-to-RCA-jacks," or whatever is needed for the connection.

Speakers, Headphones And Microphones

Take your sound card and the stereo plug with you when you shop for adapters so you can get the right adapter the first time.

Typical connections

1. **"Line Out" or "Aux."**—If your sound card has a jack labeled "Line Out" or "Aux.," it is likely what's known as a "line level" signal. This is a relatively weak 1-volt current just like the output cables from your home stereo's tuner unit, audio CD player, cassette deck, and so on.

   If so, you would connect this jack from the sound card to the same input jacks that your home-stereo amplifier provides for a CD player and similar add-on components. Look for an "Aux." (Auxiliary) input on the back of your amplifier, or use any other inputs except "Phono," which is designed for even weaker signals. You'll need to turn on your stereo and switch it to the corresponding source to hear computer sounds through your speakers.

   A line-level signal must first go into an amplifier in order to produce sound through speakers. If you hook it up directly to speakers, you won't hear anything unless the speakers have a built-in amplifier. (Computer speakers usually do.) This is not a dangerous connection to try, since line-level signals are relatively weak.

   Because this "Line Out" to "Aux. Input" option uses all of the components the way they were designed to be used, you are likely to obtain sound as good as anything else produced by your home stereo.

   If the "Line Out" or "Aux." jack has a volume control, play it safe and try it on the lowest setting at first.

2. **"Speaker Out"**—If you have an older, 8-bit card, or even a new one, be extra careful using an output labeled "Speaker Out." This output channel is probably intended for use only with speakers especially designed for a computer system. The signal on this jack may electrically overload your amplifier—it's too "hot" for a stereo amplifier to handle.

Speakers, Headphones And Microphones

It may have enough power to drive speakers without using an amplifier, so that's how it should be used. If it's connected to an amplifier, or to speakers with their own built-in amplifier, you are almost certain to get screeches and distortion. You also run the risk of "blowing out" internal components of the amplifier.

However, if you have small speakers that normally plug into the "Earphone" jack of a portable cassette player, it's probably safe to connect a sound card's "Speaker Out" line to them.

3. **On-Board Volume Control**—Some older, 8-bit sound cards have a built-in volume control on the back of the card. This usually means that it should be hooked up directly to speakers, with no intervening amplifier.

As with the "Speaker Out" jack, you should be careful about hooking this up to an amplifier, or amplified speakers. If you do, make sure the volume is lowered to its minimum setting. You may also check the sound-card documentation for advice on disabling the internal volume control. If you know who made your sound card, a quick phone call or e-mail to the manufacturer may uncover this information.

Listening to speakers before you buy

Speaker quality is not only a matter of taste, it's also affected by the environment. Speakers that sound great in a store's carefully constructed listening booth may not seem so wonderful in your computer workspace.

Bringing along your favorite music CD-ROM is one good way to discern the difference between speakers. When music passages are familiar to you, you'll more readily notice which speakers sound tinny, boomy, and so on. Some stores have a "no returns" policy on hardware items that have been unwrapped, so you may just end up with the first pair of speakers you buy.

Speakers, Headphones And Microphones

Trust your ears instead of simply heeding what a salesperson recommends, but as we've said, don't count on identical results in different settings. It won't hurt to ask the store whether you can "try before you buy." That is, take home the pair of speakers you *think* you want, with the possibility of returning them for little or no financial penalty if they suddenly sound awful in your computer room. (But before giving up, read the advice below on adjusting room acoustics and speaker placement!)

Don't be too surprised if your "try before you buy" pitch is not welcomed by your local computer store, especially if you're a complete stranger and you have done no advance research on the model you want to take home. It may waste your time and money to buy and return several sets of speakers until you are satisfied, so try to get it right the first time around!

Another source of speaker advice is computer magazine reviews. Amidst the technical specs, you should be able to judge whether the reviewer likes them. Perhaps the most trustworthy advice will come from friends—perhaps in torrents when you ask what computer speakers they use and like. (Some people are passionate about their sound equipment.)

As with most other components, most computer stores carry a limited range of the most popular brands. By visiting additional stores, you might gain exposure to more speaker models or find the same speakers at a better price.

Although it is not the most important consideration, one thing to look for is the construction of the speakers' enclosure. If the pieces don't fit together well or the material is obviously cheap, parts may break off or be reduced to shards if the speaker is dropped.

Aside from sound quality, you may wish to consider other design issues. These speakers may be in your face for hours on end. Do you like the design? Is the color pleasant or unobtrusive? Do you have sufficient room on your work surface for speaker boxes? Do you have a shelf above your monitor? Do you know how to safely fasten heavy things to the wall?

Speakers, Headphones And Microphones

Finally, consider features such as multiple audio input jacks, and conveniently situated volume, bass, treble and balance controls.

Tips On Getting The Best Sound From Your Speakers

Room acoustics

Depending on the setup of your computer area, the room can be "live" (overly resonant, with echoes), "dead" (absorbing too much sound) or "flat" (seeming to have no ill effect either way).

A simple handclap can help you determine! If you hear a sharp, brief echo, your room might be too "live." Carpeted rooms are likely to sound just about right, but there is much fine-tuning you can do to affect the sound.

Watch for loose components near the computer speakers, such as picture frames that wobble. Notice whether hard surfaces behind you are creating a sharp "bounce-back" effect. Adjustments may include hanging tapestry or drapes on the bare walls or relocating a mirror or other reflective surface.

These adjustments may not be critical if your goal is to simply listen to game sounds. But others prefer to have the best possible situation for listening to music or hearing the sounds they create or trade.

Different room acoustics also come into play when you're recording with a microphone. Most likely you'll prefer a "dead" room for recording, so the mike will pick up your voice or instrument with minimal extra sounds that may be hard to control.

On the other hand, recording studios sometimes go to great lengths to achieve the same "reverb" you enjoy while singing in the shower. Enjoy experimenting!

Speakers, Headphones And Microphones

Positioning speakers for balance

Normally you'll want your speakers positioned to the left and right of your computer monitor—each about the same distance from you. This helps balance their sound levels.

If they go on a shelf or wall above your monitor, try to separate them by at least 18 inches. If they're too close to each other, you'll miss out on stereo effects that enhance the overall sound quality. For the best sound, you may need to angle them slightly inward, toward your head.

Some computers speakers are highly "directional." That is, the sound travels out at a limited angle, so it matters a great deal exactly where they are aimed. If speakers on your desktop are pointed at your chest and they sound too muddy, see if it improves by propping up the front edges so they're aimed up at your ears.

Computer speakers are designed to be located only a few feet away from your ears. This gives your ears more direct contact with the actual sound being produced, with less interference from room noise. Also, because computer speakers are usually smaller than typical audio speakers, they are less capable at filling up a big room with great sound.

There's no need to set the volume at full-blast. Usually, the higher the speaker volume is, the more distorted the sound becomes. There are several means both externally and within Windows 95 for adjusting your speaker volume, both for playback of files you are editing and for those you have downloaded. Finding the "happy medium" between all of these is not the easiest of tasks, but we will simplify it as best we can.

Check your connections!

I've often heard people who have new computers (and even those who have been using theirs, musically, for a long time) complain that their speakers don't seem to balance properly.

Speakers, Headphones And Microphones

One reason for this may be that the speakers themselves are not plugged into the sound card completely. This can result in one speaker being softer than the other, or no sound at all coming from one of them.

Check to see that wires to the speakers are properly connected according to the diagram provided with your speakers. If the amount of wire exposed on the ends is not adequate, this can interfere with sound transmission. In addition, if those wires are reversed, they may been connected to the wrong inputs and create a hollow, "out of phase" effect. Turn off your computer, unplug the connector and re-plug it, gently, but make sure it "snaps" in to the connecting plug entirely before trying again.

If the connectors on the back of the speakers is a "snap-in" type connector, be sure that the metal contact points on the speaker itself are touching the exposed wire rather than insulation on the wire.

One test to see whether the wires are the problem is playing a CD-ROM, with the volume turned very low, but enough for you to hear the music. Gently wiggle the wire connector at the back of the speaker. If you hear a sputter, or interruption of sound coming from the speakers, this could be the problem. Turn off your computer, re-seat the wires, and try again.

You may also need to replace wires that have become broken, pierced or damaged in any way. The signal could be stopping along any point of the wiring. This is the least probable situation, unless the wire has been visibly severed, but is a consideration.

Consider headphones

Headphones, or earphones, can be a valuable addition for sound playback from your computer. Quality headphones may sound far superior to computer speakers, despite usually costing quite a bit less. They're virtually a "must-have" for careful sound recording and editing.

Speakers, Headphones And Microphones

Headphones are also a good option if you're in an apartment, or live with people who don't appreciate your music, hate your game sounds, or complain about the hours you're playing on the computer while they're trying to sleep!

Compared to speakers, it's a lot easier to discern the quality of headphones before you buy them and bring them home. Take along your favorite music CD and listen! You won't have to worry about room acoustics, exact placement of the speakers or sacrificing desk space.

Choosing between the two basic types is largely a matter of personal preference. Headphones that make a point of enclosing the entire ear, thus reducing or sealing out external noises, are usually best for your recording and editing efforts. You'll hear every little pop and click, and know where it came from. They're also a good choice if you want to enjoy quiet music despite a noisy environment.

Although usually less expensive, the kind with a only an oval sponge or flat foam plate over the ear piece are not inherently inferior at putting sound in your ear. The main difference is that outside noises remain more audible. This may or may not be a problem in your setting. You may actually desire "sound leakage" if you need to hear a crying baby or a telephone ringing.

The very best, most expensive headphones are usually of the ear-enclosure style, but don't assume they all sound good. Sometimes most of your purchase price goes toward the extra padding and finishing materials of the ear piece, while the internal workings are sonic junk.

Another consideration is comfort. The non-enclosure type is usually lighter in weight, and less prone to heat buildup on your ears because air can circulate. On the other hand, enclosure headphones rest over a larger area of your head, while the smaller headphones often exert pressure directly on the ears. Remember, you may be wearing these for hours at a time.

Speakers, Headphones And Microphones

Microphones

The microphone is an important consideration in any musical venture. It receives the external sound and turns those signals into electrical impulses that are sent to your sound card.

There are three types of microphones (mics, for short) that can be used with sound cards. Dynamic microphones, which are either desktop or hand-held mics, and two types of condenser mics. Some condenser mics, called "electret mics," need batteries.

The small mics that usually come with computer sound cards are of the condenser variety. They can also be purchased separately, costing as little as $5 to $10. Their construction is usually less than solid, and they are not noted for a fantastic frequency range. What this means to you is that, in order to produce good recordings, your small condenser mic would have to be positioned fairly close to the input source. It sometimes requires a preamp, which allows its volume to be adjusted, though it can also add noise and distort quality.

The electret battery needs replacing every now and then. It cannot, as with other condensers, take such a strong signal as the dynamic, thus again creating noise and distorting quality. The electret condenser mic must usually have its battery installed in order for it to work properly with sound cards.

Dynamic mics will have more power, are usually larger in size, and have a better range. Recordings using this type of microphone will usually be of higher quality than the condenser mics.

If you are considering using your microphone only for voice recognition, the inexpensive condenser mic may be just fine.

Speakers, Headphones And Microphones

The dynamic mic will give you more professional results, especially in terms of recording music vocals or a sound file that will accompany a business presentation. It is a pretty hardy mic, and requires no external power supply. Older dynamic mics are known for their poor response in high frequencies, but newer ones have been vastly improved. Even the newer ones, however, are not noted for good response at either end of the audio spectrum. They distort less than the condenser mics, however, and can handle a heavier load of high volume sounds.

It is best to check with the manufacturer to see which type of mic works best with their sound cards. Those that come supplied with a mic will obviously work with that mic, but may not with some others.

Mono vs stereo mic inputs

It is also important to ascertain whether your sound card will work with a stereo microphone, as some will not. Again, it is best to consult with the manufacturer or the card's documentation.

10

CD-ROM Drives

Inside Chapter 10

Internal vs. external	134
Drive Speed	**134**
Types Of CD-ROM Drives	**135**
CD-ROM playback-only drive	135
Recordable CD-ROM drive	136
Multi-disk CD-ROM drive	136
SCSI	138
Headphone connection and volume	138
Optimizing Your CD-ROM Player	**138**

CD-ROM Drives

CD-ROM drives have won widespread acceptance in the computer world. CDs are the preferred choice for distributing software programs because of their small size, large capacity (600Mb), durability, and relatively small manufacturing cost.

A CD-ROM drive also allows you to use your computer for playing audio CDs, playing interactive games that involve vast sound and graphic resources, and accessing libraries of other informative material ranging from clip art and fonts to medical data and dictionaries.

Some sound cards provide a CD-ROM connector, which allows you to play audio CDs through the sound card. There are other means of connecting CD-ROM players to your PC as well.

Along with internal vs. external configurations, you have a choice of three different types of CD-ROM units: playback-only, recordable, and multi disk (or "jukebox") changer drives.

We'll also address other important specifications that should be part of your purchase evaluation, including drive speed and interface type.

CD-ROM Drives

Internal vs. external

Computer CD-ROM drives are available in two fundamental configurations: 1) as an internal component (similar to the floppy-disk drive inside your computer), or 2) as an external device that connects to the back of your computer.

Most multimedia computers already have an internal CD-ROM player installed. Pros and cons to consider if you're adding a unit later: Internal mechanisms cost considerably less and don't occupy any of your precious desktop space, but they also aren't as easily portable as external CD-ROM units for hookup to other computers, or moving with you to a new computer someday.

Drive Speed

There are two factors involved in assessing CD-ROM drive speed. One is *data access time*, sometimes known as "seek time." The other is *data transfer rate*. Both of these are quite a bit slower for CD drives than a typical hard drive.

Data access time

Data access time refers to how quickly the laser "read" mechanism can be positioned in the correct place to gather certain data. The faster the mechanism can move across the CD, the lower the access time. A drive with an access time of 150 ms (milliseconds) will begin to retrieve data twice as fast as one with an access time of 300 ms. This matters more than you might think, because reading data often requires skipping around to different parts of the CD-ROM.

When scouting CD-ROM players, look for an average access time of less than 200ms for 4x drives and 175ms for 8x drives.

Data transfer rate

You'll see the speed of CD-ROM players described with an "X"—1x, 2x, 4x, 6x, 8x, 10x, 12x and perhaps higher. Think of this as a math formula. It compares the CD-ROM player's disk-spinning speed to that of the original standard for audio CD players. A 4x drive spins the disk four times faster than a standard (1x) CD player. An 8x drive spins it eight times faster than a 1x, twice the speed of a 4x drive, and 80% as fast as a 10x drive.

When the disk spins faster, more data will pass under the read laser in any given millisecond. Theoretically, an 8x drive could access in one second what a 1x drive would require eight seconds to read.

Now, although this "X" math all seems straightforward, actual performance differences aren't as simple to calculate in the real world. Due to the effect of data-access delays, CPU delays and other bottlenecks, an 8x drive will probably give you less than twice the sustained throughput of a 4x drive. Consider both data access time and data transfer rate when buying a CD-ROM drive.

If you already have a 4x drive, it will probably serve you well for years. If you're shopping for a new drive, consider the 8x. Higher speed makes a difference only when software is specially written to take advantage of it. Of course, that is happening, and someday today's speedy CD drives will be obsolete, but that's a ways off yet.

Types Of CD-ROM Drives

CD-ROM playback-only drive

The vast majority of computer CD-ROM units are "playback-only"—good for accessing software resources and playing audio CDs.

CD-ROM Drives

Anything slower than a 4x drive speed is probably less than adequate for software being produced today. Multimedia CD-ROMs (those with video clips, music and elaborate games) are prone to stutters and jerky playback at lower speeds.

The price range for 4x CD-ROM drives begins at about $100, with a typical price of $250-$300. Internal models are usually considerably less expensive than external units.

It is possible to get an 8x CD-ROM player for not much more than the price of a 4x from the same manufacturer. Software that can take advantage of those 8x drives is beginning to appear.

Recordable CD-ROM drive

The recordable CD-ROM is the new kid on the block, and allows you to record to a blank CD-ROM disk, as well as playback. They are more expensive ($500), but fill the role of a backup drive, too. They are generally available in 2x record speed, with 4x reading ability.

Some recordable drives will write only to permanent disks. There are others that will allow you to overwrite information on a disk you've already used, but at present they're only readable by other CD-ROM drives that allow overwrites.

The former is more beneficial for those who are writing software or creating music for distribution; the latter is useful for storage of backup data.

Multi-disk CD-ROM drive

The multi-disk CD-ROM changer allows you the luxury of having two or more CDs readily available, in the same way a jukebox is poised to play one of several music records stored within it. This will mean you'll spend less time manually loading disks and lessen the risk of damage by handling your CD-ROMs less frequently.

CD-ROM Drives

Multi-disk drives, sometimes called "CD towers," typically hold two or four CDs. There are models with yet higher capacities, but they're probably not worth the money for a home user. A 4x (speed) CD-ROM unit holding two disks can cost as little as $250.

ATAPI vs. SCSI Interface

What a mouthful! Simply put, this indicates what hardware the CD-ROM player requires to connect to your system.

Some CD-ROM players come with their own proprietary interface cards. Unfortunately, not all of them work properly without some tweaking. Using that interface card is usually not the best of choices.

ATAPI has replaced these proprietary configurations. If you're buying a new CD-ROM player, avoid proprietary cards.

ATAPI Interface—AT Attachment Packet Interface

You can use this type of CD-ROM drive if you have one of the following:

- An enhanced IDE hard-disk controller card that allows two hard disks to be installed

- A sound card with an IDE CD-ROM connector

It is important to read the documentation with this drive, and understand that the configuration may not always be easy. If you have a second hard-disk connection available, that will probably be the best place for your CD-ROM.

Some sound card connectors are proprietary, and may not work with every CD-ROM drive. As with every piece of hardware you buy, it's best to make a list of what you think you would like, and check with the manufacturer's specifications before purchasing.

CD-ROM Drives

SCSI

Pronounce this acronym "scuzzy." A SCSI connector provides the means to connect a half-dozen peripherals to your computer in one long line, or "daisy chain." In this type of installation, the CD-ROM is "daisy-chained" into an interface card along with other external equipment.

It's not always easy to make every peripheral in the SCSI chain behave properly, but this type of connection doesn't demand as much of the CPU's attention and memory to work. Thus, your system has more resources to use for other tasks.

Headphone connection and volume

If you want to listen to your audio CDs on your headphones, you may wish to make sure that the CD-ROM player you buy has a front headphone jack and volume control. Though you can connect headphones to the auxiliary output on the back of your sound card, the jack on the CD-ROM player will be much more accessible.

Optimizing Your CD-ROM Player

When your computer receives data from the CD-ROM, it stores it in a buffer cache which receives the data in uneven amounts and feeds it to your monitor in a steady stream. A larger cache will provide better performance. To optimize performance of your CD-ROM drive in Windows 95:

- ♪ Double-click "My Computer."
- ♪ Double-click "Control Panel."
- ♪ Double-click "System."

CD-ROM Drives

- Click the "Performance" tab.
- Click "File System..."
- Click "CD-ROM."
- Adjust the slider next to the words "Supplemental cache size" to "Large."
- Select your CD-ROM player's speed in the drop-down box next to "Optimize access pattern for:."
- Click Apply, then "OK"
- Close the System Properties box by clicking "OK" again.

You will definitely want your computer to have a CD-ROM drive. Not only can you use it to play and sample audio CDs, but many software developers use CDs' large capacity to distribute programs. Without a CD-drive, you'll have to contact the manufacturers of these programs and ask them to send you multiple floppy disks (potentially hundreds of disks) to install a program that fits easily onto one CD-ROM.

Use the information provided here (and elsewhere in this book) to select the CD-ROM drive that best fits your needs and budget.

11

Hardware Installation & Maintenance

Inside Chapter 11

Putting It All Together **143**
    Making sense of it all 143
    About your system 145
    Computer installation and your kids 146
    Tools and supplies you'll need 147
    Preparing your workspace 150
    Before disconnecting your computer 150
    Cleaning your computer 150
    Collecting your components 151
    Filling out warranties and registration forms 152
    Manuals 153

Installing Your Music Hardware **153**
    Installing your sound card 154
    Installing your CD-ROM drive 156
    Installing your speakers and microphone 156
    Connecting your keyboard 157

Guitars And MIDI - The Present & The Future **157**

Hardware Installation & Maintenance

Putting It All Together

Making sense of it all

Bringing home a lot of new computer equipment at once is exciting—here comes a major improvement in your computing environment! But installation can also be bewildering and frustrating. Read on for helpful suggestions about installing, maintaining and troubleshooting your hardware and software.

We've all seen those holiday cartoons with a befuddled person squinting and frowning at instructions such as "Insert Tab A unilaterally into Crumpet B while rotating Widget IV toward its front (nonshiny) side. Do not overtighten!"

It's not so funny when *you* are Person A on the verge of angrily throwing Computer B out of Window C, is it? But if you take a deep breath and follow the advice here, it will all go smoothly.

Hardware Installation & Maintenance

Adding new parts and software to your computer is also a great time to clean your computer's area. Because you'll be moving and opening it, you'll have access to areas you normally can't reach.

Gather more tech support with honey

A very important person in your life can turn out to be someone you've never met—your peripheral's technical support specialist. If we get to the end of this section and your new hardware doesn't work—this person may save your day.

To that end: Before anything else is done, back up your computer system software! "Well, er, no, I didn't think I needed to back up my system" is a sad comment too often heard by technical support specialists.

Remember that the technical specialist did not design or build your new music peripheral. He or she is only employed by the company that did, so be fair. Kindness goes a long, long way with tech support people—they often do the most and get the least thanks.

Ask his or her name and use it! It's a simple courtesy. And if you get a grumpy, uncooperative tech support operator, do ask their name and request their supervisor's name. You shouldn't have to be treated badly by them, either.

But remember that these people are usually very well trained to help you with their product. Usually, the nicer you are, the more helpful they will try to be. It's probably better to try and call them when you haven't been tearing your hair out for hours over a problem. Take a few moments and make some notes for yourself so that you get the most out of your conversation. Be sure you have serial numbers and documentation handy, and a notepad for taking down instructions.

Hardware Installation & Maintenance

Of course, you may have plenty time to calm down if it takes days to get through to a tech support operator—that in itself can be frustrating. Be sure to ask whether there is a code you can dial directly if you need to make a second call. Some companies help their users by this method, so that you do not have long wait times each time you need help with the same problem.

About your system

Hopefully, when you obtained your music peripherals, they came with instructions and the necessary and appropriate parts--both hardware and software. We wish that were the end of the story to insure smooth installation and operation. Often, in the world of PCs, it's not.

The sheer number of possible equipment combinations makes it difficult for manufacturers to test every configuration. No matter how easy it is to install hardware, there are bound to be problems at one point or another. It's one very good reason to avoid no-name brands, as we've cautioned all along.

You can minimize headaches and teeth-gnashing when installing hardware with basic considerations. Of course, you could simply dump everything out on the floor and go at it, and skip this chapter altogether! But the small amount of time it takes for proper preparation can save you hours of installation glitches and frustration.

Let's start with installation, and talk about preventive maintenance along the way.

Cautionary information—electricity and you

Your computer and all of the connected components must be unplugged before you begin to move it, open it, or install new components. Unplugging the computer and peripherals will prevent them from accidentally being switched on while you are working. Working with the computer plugged in can cause irreparable damage to the computer, and worse, to humans also. Plugged-in computers can carry enough electricity to easily electrocute someone.

Hardware Installation & Maintenance

Do not ever, for any reason, open your monitor, even when switched off and cold. Leave that to the experts. Even unplugged, your monitor contains voltages high enough to risk serious injury or death.

Computer installation and your kids

Children should never be unsupervised around an open computer unit, nor handle or install computer hardware unsupervised. While this process can be a great learning experience for an interested child, it's important to include a serious talk with your child in that learning process before you begin. Make certain a child of any age knows not to reach into the computer; even to help you catch that slipping part or lost screw. Very young children should not be discouraged from participating and asking questions, but should only be permitted to watch and learn about that open computer. There are many helpful tasks children of any age can help you with that don't involve being near the electrical components. They can hand you the "un-pointy" tools or be put in charge of other harmless activities, like getting the workspace ready.

Remember that children's attention span is often short—especially when they can only watch. Your children may lose interest just as you are warming to your subject. They'll be back when it's time to enjoy!

It's also a wonderful time to share with your child the knowledge you have of how the inside of a computer works. You don't know? You may be in for a nice surprise—your best learning resource may turn out to be that bright child of yours. This can be a good opportunity to have him or her teach *you* what it's all about!

If you feel your child is old enough to help, make sure he or she takes the same precautions as you do and understands the rules before you begin.

This involvement can help a child in many ways—to connect to the jobs the new hardware and software can perform, to have respect for proper care of the equipment and a joy of having participated. Better yet, this look behind the scenes can add to their musical involvement later.

Hardware Installation & Maintenance

WE'RE SAYING IT AGAIN, FOR FURTHER EMPHASIS: Please memorize the following three computer safety rules and follow them faithfully:

1. Make sure all electrical connections and power supply sources on your computer are turned off and unplugged before you begin!

2. Never, ever open your monitor, even out of curiosity. Leave that to a professional.

3. Never, ever let your child near the internal components of the computer, whether it is plugged in or not. Unplugged power supplies can still contain a significant charge.

Tools and supplies you'll need

A budget of about $25 should buy all of the tools you'll ever need for your computer, if you don't already have them:

- #1 (medium) Phillips screwdriver
- 1/8" (medium) flat screwdriver (it's unlikely you'll need this one, but just in case!)
- Set of miniature screwdrivers
- Surgical gloves
- Can of compressed air
- Manual air brush
- Tweezers
- Long-nosed pliers
- Cups or containers for small screws
- Pen and paper (for taking notes!)

Hardware Installation & Maintenance

- A clean cloth as a drape for your workspace
- A hand towel (not the fuzzy kind!) or dry, clean rags
- Bandages!
- An anti-static wristband
- Power strip
- Y splitter cable

Do *not* use wrong-sized tools! An oversized or undersized screwdriver can strip the screw heads and cause other damage. Also make sure that the screwdrivers are not magnetized—this too, can cause damage.

Have a supply of extra jumpers and small screws on hand. Jumpers are small plastic squares that fit over one or more tiny metal pins attached to your sound card (or other peripheral, such as a modem or hard drive controller card). You can find both the screws and jumpers at a computer supply store.

Keep a few small cups (paper cups work well) close at hand to hold the various small screws, jumpers and the like. They seem to have a fondness for disappearing into the rug or between the cracks of a wood floor.

A clean old sheet or cloth that does not attract lint will be useful in your computer installation workspace, to protect the underside of your computer (and the motherboard) and help prevent screws and other small parts from rolling off the table and disappearing.

While not completely necessary, thin, strong surgical gloves are very handy, for many reasons.

The contact points on most peripheral cards (usually gold in color) should not be touched. Skin produces oil which can corrode these contacts. Rubber gloves will prevent this.

Hardware Installation & Maintenance

Since rubber in an insulator, surgical gloves add to your safety and the safety of your components by reducing the chance of electrical shocks. They will also protect you from tiny scrapes and cuts you may get while installing your hardware. They fit pretty snugly, so can help you keep a firm yet gentle grip on those screwdrivers and tiny screws.

You can find these gloves at most drugstores. They usually come packaged sets of three for about a dollar, or you can splurge on a box of a hundred for around US$10. They're handy for other home projects, too!

Compressed air can be obtained at most computer stores. You may prefer a manual brush with a small bulb at one end that blows air more gently; some feel that compressed air can cause damage by blasting bits of dust into places from where it cannot be dislodged. We use both, and you are likely to find both at a computer or photography supply store.

A pair of shielded or plastic tweezers is great for recapturing small screws that have dropped into your computer. Shielded tweezers have plastic coverings over most of the metal. A long pair of regular tweezers is okay, too, in a pinch, but do cover the handles with electrical tape for insulation.

Electrostatic charges are unlikely to damage you, but even one as small as 5 volts can spell ruin to one or more of your computer components. An anti-static wristband is the best choice; an alternative is to frequently touch the PC's chassis or another grounded object. Always do this prior to handling other components.

A power strip is great for easily connecting peripherals and electrical outlets in your installation workspace. You'll need power to do some testing before you move your computer back to its usual place.

A Y-splitter cable can be found at a computer supply store. This will come in handy when you need to install your CD-ROM player, which needs to be connected to the power supply inside your computer, but often there are no additional connectors left at that stage.

Hardware Installation & Maintenance

It's not a bad idea to keep your computer tools in their own container. Label the box with your own creative threat of what will happen to the person who is foolish enough to borrow them, and keep them under lock and key!

Preparing your workspace

Your work area should be well lit, away from drafts and fairly free of dust and debris. A card table or unused workbench will work well. Moving your computer off of your desk to do your installation procedures is a good idea, even though you have to move it back when finished. Moving the computer gives you an opportunity to clean any dust and debris that has collected on your desktop, and gives you more access to components and connecting plugs.

Before disconnecting your computer

Make note of how your current computer peripherals are connected, so that you are confident you can reassemble them once you're done installing your sound card and any other internal parts. Make a diagram or Polaroid snapshot, if you need to, of where any plugs and connections hook together.

Carefully disconnect each part. You'll want to have your monitor, keyboard, mouse and power strip close to your installation workspace for testing.

Move your computer and the necessary components to your workspace.

Cleaning your computer

Computers can collect dust easily, both inside and out. Other things that can damage your computer equipment are residue from cigarette or pipe smoke, cigarette ashes and liquids. If your computer has not been maintained and cleaned on a regular basis, now's the time. The internal fan that carries the heat from inside your computer also allows dust to be pulled through vents on the case—turning hard and floppy drives and CD-ROM units into virtual air filters.

Hardware Installation & Maintenance

Before you open the computer case, clean the exterior with a lint-free cloth. Use a fine brush for vented areas.

Remove the back of the computer and clean any clogged vents in the casing. Then do the same with the interior of your computer with the brush. Use the compressed air for any hard to reach areas. Be sure not to touch or bend transistors and pins!

Do not remove the casing on the computer's power supply. Instead, brush around the vents where the fan is installed, and use compressed air to blow out the dust.

Once this is done, you're ready to start installing.

Collecting your components

No matter how much research you do ahead of time, there may still be a "missing link" that you overlooked. Oops! Did you misread that package? Did it say that such-and-so was available for purchase separately, while you thought it was included in the package? Rats—it's back to the store, again!

Remember that ring binder we suggested earlier? Now's the time to have it at hand. Open your packages one by one. The amount of documentation that comes with some peripherals can be staggering—the most flimsy of which might be the manual! The minorly interesting stuff that you will find falls under the category of "necessary for later on or never" and might include advertisements for free time on the internet, various magazines and the like. These can be put aside for another time.

It's a good idea not to co-mingle the sound card documentation with the keyboard information, and so on. Instead, create a "pocket" in the binder for each of your components. Another level of documentation you'll want to keep is Warranties and Registration forms.

Hardware Installation & Maintenance

Now remove your components and make sure all of the parts that are supposed to be included with your hardware are, in fact, present. If they are not, stop here. Sometimes people buy, open and then return items. Stores are supposed to return those opened packages to the manufacturer. Some do, others don't. If the store personnel has not checked the returned material carefully, there may be parts or documentation missing.

Filling out warranties and registration forms

Once you are sure you have all the parts you need, and you are sure that those parts are in good working order, some further record-keeping is important.

There's only one way to approach the warranties and registration forms—grab that pen, fill out the forms, and send them in! Before you mail away any important hardware serial numbers, make sure you have a copy for your files. Make a record of any serial numbers and versions of any software. Most companies are intelligent enough to leave you with a copy of those numbers, but we've found that some don't. How annoying to not have that serial number when you need to contact the company for one reason or another. Most times, it's the first question they will ask.

We've found instances where we've installed parts and closed the computer back up, only to find that the company has put a serial or part number in only one place—on the part itself. That part is now, of course, carefully installed in such a way that those numbers aren't visible. Taking the time to note those numbers now will save you time and aggravation later on.

If your documentation says there are serial numbers pasted on your hardware, make sure to verify this.

Hardware Installation & Maintenance

You may find that a sound card manufacturer offers to replace a faulty chip later on, but they will need to ascertain the serial number on that chip. Write it down! You may find a diagram of your sound card in your manual. This is a good place to make note of the serial numbers found on the face of the card or other part. If you're consistent about this, you'll always know where to find your serial numbers. Keep your copies in your binder.

You may also want to make a list of any contact addresses and telephone numbers you find. If you need to get in touch with a manufacturer or distributor, you'll know where to look for the contact information.

Manuals

If you take the time to store your manuals in this binder, you will be doing yourself a great favor. Some peripherals only come with a flimsy sheet of instructions which can be easily lost under piles of other documentation. Put the smaller ones in your ring binder now—you'll be glad you did.

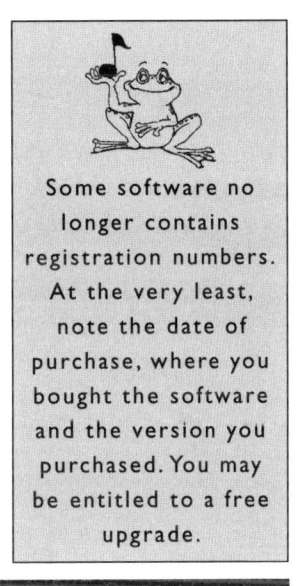

> Some software no longer contains registration numbers. At the very least, note the date of purchase, where you bought the software and the version you purchased. You may be entitled to a free upgrade.

Installing Your Music Hardware

We suggest you read all installation material carefully prior to installing your components. Here are some general installation hints for you, together with some helpful photographs!

Hardware Installation & Maintenance

Installing your sound card

Because different brands of sound cards are configured differently, it is important to read the documentation for your particular card prior to installation. Some have software programs that help you with installation and configuration procedures; others may have hardware that requires adjusting. The hardware adjustments can be either jumpers (which are small plastic coverings) over various pins mounted on the card itself, or on/off switches on one end of the card. Check to see which method your card uses!

If the appropriate jumpers are not already provided on the sound card, someone may have removed them. Contact the place of purchase or the manufacturer immediately to find out why.

If switches (sometimes referred to as "dip switches") are used, they are usually located on the end of the sound card that also has the connectors for your other equipment.

If your card is Plug-and-Play, Windows 95 may or may not recognize it upon installation. The documentation that came with your sound card should tell you what procedure the manufacturer recommends. If Windows 95 finds your card by itself, it will notify you that it has found the card. Sometimes, Windows 95 will recognize that you have a new piece of hardware, but can't determine its function. There may also be software drivers that must be installed via accompanying diskettes.

Before handling the sound card, your hands should be clean and dry. Before removing the card from its packing, be sure the computer is turned off and disconnected entirely from any power source.

As we mentioned earlier, if you don't have an anti-static wristband, be sure to frequently touch the chassis of your computer or another grounded source to prevent static discharge that can damage circuitry.

Hardware Installation & Maintenance

Remove the card carefully from its packaging, being sure not to bend or dislocate the components. Usually cards are packaged with a piece of soft foam—set this beside your computer. You can use this to cushion your sound card if you need to set it down for any reason.

Seat the card carefully in the slot you have chosen inside your computer, and make sure it is snug in the socket. A bit of gentle downward pressure along the top of the card will not hurt the card, and will make sure the fit is snug. With some card slot configurations, you can even hear a card click into place. Do not try to jam the card into the slot; if it won't click in smoothly, check to see that it is seated properly and try again.

A non-Plug-and-Play card may have to be configured manually. The maker of the sound card will usually provide such information in the documentation enclosed with the card. If this information is missing, you should first check with the store where you purchased the card, to see what happened to it.

Most sound card manufacturers also maintain a site for technical support on the World Wide Web. In the internet section of this book, we have included web addresses for many of these manufacturers.

Hardware Installation & Maintenance

Installing your CD-ROM drive

Your CD-ROM drive should be packaged with a flat ribbon cable that connects it to the motherboard or controller card inside your computer. The other thing you may need is a Y power cable splitter from your toolbox, if there are no power supply connectors left.

Your computer should have also come with a small plug that attaches to the CD-ROM on one end and the sound card on the other.

Installing your speakers and microphone

We've included quite a few tips for positioning your speakers in the section of this book that tells you how to shop for your speakers. You'll not need to position them perfectly right now, but you will want to hear how your sound card is behaving!

Once you have installed your CD-ROM and sound card, you can put the casing back on the computer. Replace only one or two of the screws for now, because you may need to remove the cover again for troubleshooting.

Set up your speakers according to the manufacturer's instructions, then refer to your sound card diagram to make sure you connect the speakers to the proper plug on the back of the sound card.

Hardware Installation & Maintenance

Connect your microphone to the sound card as indicated on your documentation.

Connecting your keyboard

You will need the MIDI adapter that came with your sound card or keyboard in order to connect these components. If your keyboard has a MIDI Out connector, plug one end of the cord into the back of the keyboard, and the other end to the MIDI In connector on the sound card.

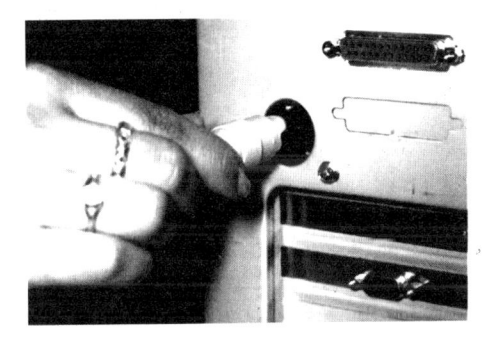

Guitars And MIDI - The Present & The Future

There are many who do not play piano or synthesizer who are curious about recording their acoustic or non-MIDI electric instruments on computer, especially those interested in creating recordings of their own compositions.

Hardware Installation & Maintenance

Though there is quite a selection of MIDI Controller Keyboards available, the components designed for Guitar MIDI are few and equally expensive, ranging from $500 to $3,000 and above. Translating the dynamics of how guitars and pickups work to the world of MIDI has involved years of research and scientific study, as you will soon see.

You can, of course, do what we call a "quick and dirty" setup for your guitar. Position your instrument in front of the computer microphone attached to your sound card, and record from there. This is the quickest "fix" for just getting your guitar or other acoustic sound on computer; however, as we've mentioned, you may be greatly disappointed with the sound. There is ambient room noise between your instrument and the microphone that can cause unwanted echo and hiss, especially that "noise" issuing from your CPU fan and any other sources of electrical output.

> We want to remind you to be very careful with this kind of configuration. The same cautions apply here as for connecting any external audio source, such as your VCR or Stereo system. Be extra careful of volume settings, as you might overload your sound card or speakers.

So, what's the answer? Well, you can input your electric guitar using a direct connection between it and your sound card and record it as a WAV sound. It's not MIDI, but you can at least record your guitar into the computer direct, skipping the disappointment of the sound it would produce through your microphone. You can make sure the software you use compatible - some editing and composition programs such as the Cakewalk Home Studio are very guitar friendly. Acoustic guitars have work-abounds, too.

How is this accomplished? First, let's talk about electric guitars. Simply use your guitar patch cord! You'll also need a small adapter that you can purchase at most electronics stores. You may wish to take your patch cord and your sound card with you to the store to insure you've gotten the correct part. You'll need a 1/4" mono to 1/8" stereo mini-jack.

158

Hardware Installation & Maintenance

Connect your electric guitar to its patch cord as usual, and on the other end of the cord connect the mini-jack adapter. Plug the small jack at that end into your sound card at the input that you use for your microphone, usually labeled "mic input". If you wish, you could also try the one labeled "line input", which may also work.

If you have an effects rack for your guitar, you can also run your electric guitar through that as you usually do and use the patch cord from the effects rack "line out" on many sound cards.

Be aware that on many sound cards, the mic input could either be stereo or mono; the "line in" input is usually stereo. You'll need to be sure of that by reading the documentation on your sound card.

Next, let's discuss your acoustic guitar or saxophone or any other non-electric instrument. As we mentioned above, you can try playing these into the computer microphone; this may be sufficient for your purposes, although you may be disappointed at the results. You can buy an instrument-specific amplification device for most acoustic instruments at many music stores and some of the online mail-order Web sites we've listed in the bookmark included on the companion CD-ROM. Attach your amplification component to your instrument as recommended, and attach the patch cord for it. You may or may not need the mini-jack adapter depending on the size of the cord used on your instrument amplifier. If the patch cord has 1/4 inch mono plugs, you will still need the mini-jack adapter as described above.

All this doesn't address the idea of the MIDI guitar. The state of the art for MIDI enthusiasts who are also guitarists is an important issue. There are as many guitarists out there, we believe, as keyboardists, who want to be using their guitars as MIDI controllers with their computers.

In order to use MIDI with your guitar, you will need a guitar, of course — acoustic nylon or steel string or an electric guitar, a proper pickup such as the one mentioned below made by Richard McClish, a pitch-to-MIDI converter, and your sound card.

Hardware Installation & Maintenance

The components currently available cannot be as widely found as Keyboard controllers. The manufacturers we've found mentioned most often are Roland Corporation, Starr Labs, Godin Guitars, Fender and Axon make a line of MIDI guitar components, along with a few others.

That's only a handful in comparison with all the other MIDI gear out there, but watch for that to change in the near future. We'd like to now let you know what's soon to come!

It's interesting to note that the creators and visionaries in the guitar arena are fine musicians and lovers of music themselves; each in their way in quest of the perfect sound, each of whom has been in touch with the idea of guitars and MIDI. Here are the voices of some of those who shape our industry today. These "behind the scenes" experts each have a great reverence for the historical nature of the guitar and at the same time are paving the path towards the future of the stringed instrument. Here are some of their thoughts on that issue:

We first called on Roger Sadowsky, restorer, repairer and custom builder of fretted string instruments. Roger's artistry has received raves from the likes of Lee Ritenour, Will Lee, Marcus Miller and Keith Richards amongst others. Roger spoke to me briefly about the exciting mixture of computers and acoustic instruments:

"I never had any intention of building a MIDI instrument until I was asked to do so by Earl Klugh, who had two of my electric nylon-stringed guitars and wanted a third built with a MIDI interface. After doing some research, I chose an electronics package made by Richard McClish of RMC Pickup Company and much to my surprise, the instrument tracked and performed better than any MIDI guitar I had previously heard.

Hardware Installation & Maintenance

In spite of my reluctance to get involved with MIDI guitars, I built a second one and sent it to Lee Ritenour, who also had two of my electric nylon guitars. Lee, who had used every guitar synth system ever introduced, reported that the guitar I sent him was the best he'd ever used and purchased the instrument! I now offer it as a model for discriminating MIDI guitarists.

I don't know what the future will bring, technology-wise, but the present has brought an alleviation of the fear that MIDI would replace regular guitars and guitarists, which was a genuine worry 10 or 15 years ago. In the 15 years since, what's interesting is the technology and research of acoustic guitar music, and how disparate paths cross and recross to braid new paths. I think that guitarists need have no fear of the technology rendering them obsolete."

For a look at his master creations, you can visit Sadowsky's Web site at

http://www.sadowsky.com/

Roger suggested we speak with Richard McClish. We did. Allow us to introduce you.

Richard McClish is the owner of RMC Pickup Company in Berkeley, California and one of the original founders of Zeta Music Systems of Oakland CA. Canadian-born, Richard came from Quebec to California in 1983. He and other engineers there founded Zeta in 1985 for the purpose of producing MIDI violins, which seemed like a good niche for their research and development at the time. With the artistic and financial support of many, including Jean Luc Ponti and the fine minds of Richard and friends, the company began to thrive. At the end of the startup phase, Richard left Zeta in 1989 to start RMC Pickup Co.

Here are some of Richard's words on MIDI and the state of the art for guitar:

Hardware Installation & Maintenance

I have to say that all the new MIDI converters on the market work very well, and that's where my concern really lies. The pickups used with these devices must be compatible with both technologies. Fortunately, we have no significant compatibility problems. My pickups, being bridge saddles, are ideally located for providing an excellent wave form for the pitch converters, whereas the older pickup technology device is a hex magnetic pickup close to the bridge.

Because of its location, such a magnetic pickup will produce very little fundamental and a dominant amount of harmonics in the signal. That's not quite ideal to obtain the relevant data for pitch detection. You'd like the pickup to have a fair amount of fundamental and a wide response

There's an order of important things to consider in the quest for good MIDI Guitar performance as well as good sound quality:

1. Strings / the playing surface of the pick, nails, etc.

2. Instrument setup: action, neck relief, etc.

3. Pickup & electronics, cable(s)

4. Pitch detection system and converter that outputs MIDI commands

5. MIDI input device in the computer

6. MIDI software you use

7. Computer type and speed

That's the fingers-to-MIDI chain ! Remember: garbage in >> garbage out.

My expertise is, of course, mostly about pickups and adjacent electronics, but my work spans four engineering categories:

1. Acoustical (sound production, distribution, propagation, and absorption)

2. Mechanical (interactive behavior of strings, diaphragms, beams, trusses, etc.)

Hardware Installation & Maintenance

3. Electromechanical (sensors, actuators, loudspeakers, motors), and

4. Electronic-analog (signal conditioners which drive the amplifiers and the converters)

Ah, prices, prices - what can I say? Again, MIDI Guitar is a niche market. Because it's new, it's a "sports car-type of market." By that, I mean, it's a luxury. Since the music industry is not the defense industry or the computer industry, it has to market the new stuff at relatively higher prices for awhile to make the R&D worthwhile.

What other advice can I give? Well, before I advise anyone who wants to know more about guitar and MIDI, I need to find out their individual needs. Then I can make a valid contribution. With changing times and new markets popping in and out all the time, it's difficult to address a broad audience in the same old way. I want to know why they play, what they play, what their goals are. What do you want to do? That's what I like to hear -- I like to evaluate who I'm talking to.

The best gear sounds the best . . . well, if you know how to use it, of course. Sometimes, when you're creative, you can take some old used stuff and fix or modify it or put it together in a certain way and get surprisingly good results. If I had been rich at the onset, I would have just bought what I needed or commissioned someone to do it rather than building it myself. And I would have probably missed out on a lot of great experiences dictated by my condition.

This is the dawn of the hybrid electric guitar. You can already see that more and more electric guitars come equipped with regular magnetic pickups and piezos in the bridge. I believe this trend will continue for a number of years because:

1. There are very nice sounds that can be generated by piezo pickups; the type of sounds that can be mixed with the sound of magnetic pickups in a synergistic way.

Hardware Installation & Maintenance

2. Current MIDI access calls for a polyphonic pickup system in the instrument and the piezoelectric saddles are the best candidates for the job. You can still have your magnetic (bridge) pickups in their normal place doing their normal job without interfering magnetically with a MIDI pickup that has optimal tracking ability !

Whether hybrid guitars will have MIDI access is an economic consideration. Not everybody wants MIDI right now, but an increasing number of electric guitarists want the sound of the piezo with the magnetics.

As far as acoustic guitars are concerned . . . of course you have two types: nylon string and steel string. The acoustic steel string can have both the magnetic and the piezo, just like the electric guitar. With the nylon string, however, magnetic pickups don't work, since there's no ferrous

(steel) element vibrating. So you have to have some kind of piezo pickup in the bridge for amplification.

About what's coming up for the MIDI/Guitar connection, I think that the bottom line is this: the future will be what the players make it. The marketplace for MIDI electronics has grown significantly in the past five years, and the recent increase in demand for MIDI Guitar products is

beginning to accelerate the research. Currently, I'm busy designing and manufacturing high-end pickup systems and sound processors that are catalysts in the MIDI guitar marketplace. And I'm very happy in that kind of work.

What can you do about that right now? Well, you have to let the people in the industry out there know what you want. Communication is every thing. The internet is a great medium for that! I think that's your real power!

Author's note: You can visit RMC Pickup Company's Web site at

http://www.california.com/~rmc/

Hardware Installation & Maintenance

We wanted to let you hear from one who has preserved the artistry of music in his own manner by making that a part of the retail side of the music industry. We therefore called on a long time friend Rudy Pensa. Rudy is the owner of Rudy's Music Stop in New York City, which is also the home of the superb Pensa Guitar, used by renowned guitarist Mark Knopfler as well as Eddie Martinez and many other professional studio musicians.

I value his knowledge of the world of musical instruments immensely, and asked him to offer his thoughts on the state of MIDI and guitar:

"We feature the new MIDI guitar by Robert Godin, the MultiAc. The possibilities are absolutely limitless. It's incredible how it opens peoples creative minds, because it's not just like playing guitar! Now, you can listen to the sound of a baby grand piano or a violin quartet coming through your fingers. It's fantastic attacking the strings in such a multitude of different ways to get violin or cello sounds. We're busy here at the shop - so I don't have a much time as I would like to experiment with it myself, regretfully! But in the short time I've had to try it, I'm simply amazed that you can now create a whole concert orchestra on one instrument through the computerized setup and MIDI sound, while still retaining the fine output of a quality guitar!

As to pricing, well, most of my customers right now are the real pros. But I see that kids are becoming involved, too, and that's exciting. It's a new era, and I see the prices going down already. Truthfully, even some no-name guitars without the new mechanics are way up in price compared to 10 years ago, some as many as $2,000. I'm not saying that paying $2,000 for a fine MIDI guitar isn't a lot of money to spend, but when you think that a no-name guitar may cost just as much, and not give you what you want, it's a bargain! People are spending as much as $15,000 for vintage guitars these days - and it's hard, with all that in mind, to think that prices for MIDI-capable guitars are going to ever plunge down to the $200 range. The price paid for such an instrument today is not even equal to all the research and development put in to these instruments. I do love that Godin...."

11 Hardware Installation & Maintenance

We cannot speak of Rudy Pensa without saying that Rudy's Music Stop is a "don't miss this" stop on any aspiring or professional musician's visit to New York's Music Row. Argentinian-born, Rudy arrived at Kennedy Airport in 1974 and headed straight for New York's Music Row - West 48th Street. "I bought a Rickenbacker bass and a P-bass; I wanted to shop where the Beatles and the Rolling Stones had shopped! I was so unbelievably happy!!!!" Four years later, Rudy opened the Music Stop at the same spot on which it stands today — but now it's expanded to four floors, including an on-site repair shop. It's an un-splashy, non-glitz place from the outside. I like that. No pretense - and an exact statement of what you'll find inside - a warm, yet entirely professional atmosphere. They know their stuff!

I've seen Rudy and his staff spend as much time and care with a young, seriously interested, unknown musician as with the celebrities that are proud to count him as friend. I cannot think of being in New York without a quick stop at Rudy's! The shop offers an unmatched standard of professional gear, including a magnificent selection of vintage instruments and acoustic and classical guitars, many of which are handmade.

If you're only interested in "checking out the scene" - looking for flash and no substance — just keep moving on down the Row. Rudy's isn't the place you want to be. But if you're looking for the real thing and you're ready to be amazed - just walk on in!

Music Software

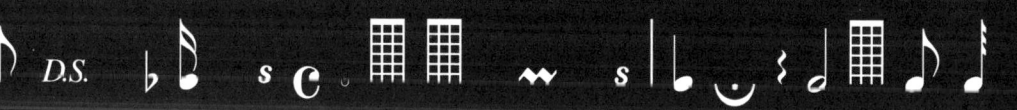

SECTION 3

12

The Windows 95 Sound Utilities

Inside Chapter 12

Exercise One : Playing WAV Sounds 172
    Windows 95 Sound Recorder 172
Exercise Two: Playing MID or RMI Sound Files 175
    The Windows 95 Media Player 175
    What you need 177
    Adjusting sound quality 177
    The Windows 95 CD Player 178

Exercise Three: Creating An Audio Clip In
    WAV Format 181

Exercise Four: Creating A Voice Recording In
    Wav Format 185
    Recording your new vocal WAV sound 186

Exercise Five: Recording WAV Files From
    A VCR Or Stereo 187
    Your VCR or stereo connection 188
    Your sound card connection 188

Exercise Six: Adding Effects To A Sound File 189

Exercise Seven: Cutting & Snipping: Editing A
    Sound File 191

Exercise Eight: Insert A Sound File Into A Second
    Sound File 193

Exercise Nine: Cut And Paste 195

Exercise Ten: Overlaying Sound Files (Mixing) 196

Conclusion 198

The Windows 95 Sound Utilities

Let's look at the features of the Windows 95 utilities we'll be using for the exercises in Chapter Twelve.

There are several methods that you can use to play a WAV sound using the sound recorder, or a MID file using the Media Player. We'll give you instructions on opening the Sound Recorder and Media Player in the first and second exercise groups; after that, it's up to you!

Group One: Playing Sound Files

Exercise One shows you how to play WAV sounds. Exercise Two shows you how to play MIDI (MID and RMI) sounds.

12 The Windows 95 Sound Utilities

Exercise One
Playing WAV Sounds

Here are two methods for opening the Sound Recorder.

Windows 95 Sound Recorder

Here's the Sound Recorder!

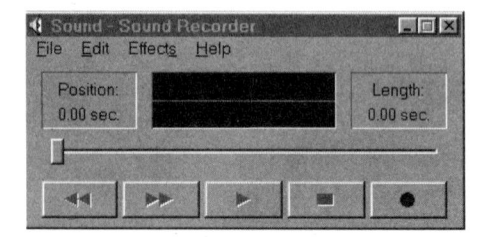

The Windows 95 Sound Recorder

The Sound Recorder is a very basic program that allows you to do a number of things: listen to WAV files you have stored on your computer or CD-ROM, record segments of CD-ROMs, add effects to those sounds and save the altered sounds with either the same or a different filename.

Think of the Sound Recorder as a software tape recorder. Just like any "real" tape recorder, it's got these buttons: Play, Forward, Rewind, Stop and Record.

A visual meter on the screen lets you "see" the sound wave that is playing. There's also a slider that allows you to move from one section of the sound to another.

Playing a WAV Sound

It's not at all difficult to play sound files in Windows 95. First, we'll show you how easy it is to play a .wav sound. We will describe two methods and point out why each might be useful.

The Windows 95 Sound Utilities

Method One is the easiest, and is most useful for "just checking" to see what a sound might be or for listening to a new sound you've created or downloaded.

Method one: Start Sound Recorder from the WAV file

Here's how to locate a file with a .wav extension or icon and double-click it with the mouse.

Use the Windows 95 Find Command to find a WAV file in the C:\Windows\Media folder. Use the Browse... button to locate the Media directory and enter "*.wav" as the name of the file. Then click "Find now."

Select a WAV file from the Media folder (listed by the Find command). If you do not see the extension ".wav" on your file, look to see which files have the little sound icon next to them that indicates a .wav file (see the icon immediately on the right) and double-click it.

Windows 95 will open the Sound Recorder program, play the file and close the program!

Method two: Start Sound Recorder to play a WAV file

Method Two is the procedure we suggest you use for the exercises which follow in this section. Unlike Method One, Sound Recorder will remain active after playing the file.

If you put the Sound Recorder on your Desktop as we suggested in the Introduction to Software, you can simply double-click it to open. If you did not, use this path to open it:

Click Start/Programs/Accessories/Multimedia/Sound Recorder.

From the Sound Recorder File menu, select **File/Open**. The Sound Recorder **File/Open** menu defaults to the C:\Windows folder.

The Windows 95 Sound Utilities

You will see a dialog box requesting a file name. Locate the Media folder within the C:\Windows list and double-click it to open.

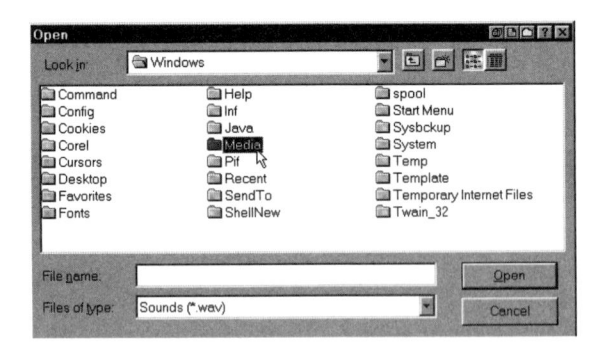

Choose the WAV file that you wish to use and click it. When highlighted, it will automatically be listed in the box to the right of the words "File name." Remember, a WAV file will be indicated by the icon on the right:

Click the "Open" button.

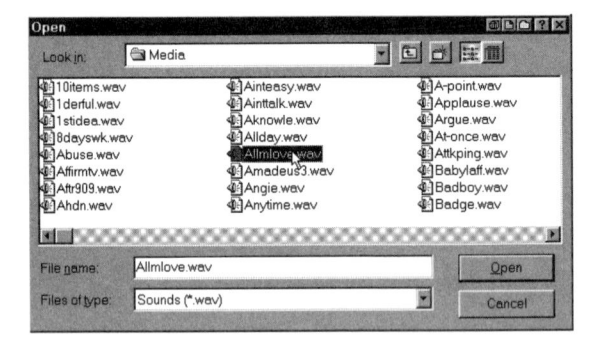

Click on the Play button '>' to play the file.

Click the square Stop button to stop playing the sound.

Click the reverse arrows '<<' to move to the beginning of the sound file.

To move to the end, click the Fast Forward arrows '>>'.

The Windows 95 Sound Utilities

Before clicking Play, grab the slider with your left mouse button to move to any section of the sound. Click Play to begin at that point.

To close the Sound Recorder, click **File/Exit**.

That was easy! Now let's try playing files that are in MIDI format.

Exercise Two
Playing MID or RMI Sound Files

The Windows 95 Media Player

The Media Player plays audio WAV files just as the Sound Recorder does (if you have a sound card installed, of course!). It will also play MIDI files in MID and RMI format, something the Sound Recorder cannot do.

In addition, Media Player can also play video and animation files. Since the Media Player is designed more for audio and video functions, we will not be using it much in this book. When we get to creating MIDI files, we'll be using software from the companion CD-ROM.

So, here's a brief overview of the Media Player; it's a helpful, basic player for listening to MIDI files.

Method one: Start Media Player from the MID or RMI file

Locate a MID or RMI file to play using the Windows 95 Find Command described earlier. Substitute "*.mid" or "*.rmi" for the filename used earlier.

Select a MID file or RMI file from the Media folder and double-click it. Windows 95 will open the Media Player program, play the file and close the program!

175

The Windows 95 Sound Utilities

There's also second way to open the Media Player.

Method two: Start Media Player from the MID or RMI file

If you put the Media Player on your Desktop as we suggested in the Introduction to Software, you can simply double-click it to open. If you did not, use this path to open it:

Click Start/Programs/Accessories/Multimedia/Media Player. From the Media Player menu, select **File/Open**. The Media Player will default to the C:\Windows\Media folder to look for sounds.

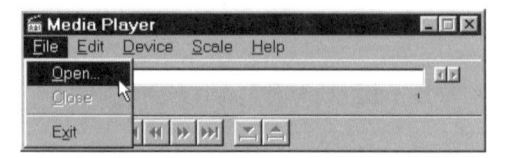

Media Player File Menu

You will see a dialog box requesting a file name. Select the MID or RMI file that you wish to use and click on it. It will automatically be listed in the box to the right of the words "File name." Remember, a MID or RMI file will have this large icon or a smaller icon that only shows two music notes, depending on the viewing choices you've selected.

Click the "Open" button.

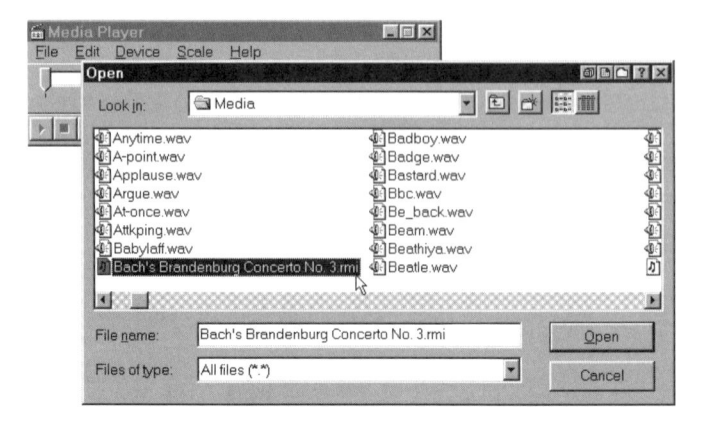

176

The Windows 95 Sound Utilities

Click on the Play button '>' to play the file.

Click the square Stop button to stop playing the sound.

Click the reverse arrows '<<' to move to the beginning of the sound file.

To move to the end, click the Fast Forward arrows '>>'.

Before clicking Play, grab the slider with your left mouse button to move to any section of the sound. Click Play to begin at that point.

To close the Media Player, click **File/Exit**.

Group Two: Recording And Editing Your WAV File

Exercise Three will teach you how to record a sound from your own favorite audio (music) CD. Exercise Four will teach you how to record your voice.

What you need

To do these exercises, you need a CD-ROM drive and a microphone connected to your sound card. We'll be using the Sound Recorder and the CD-Player programs, too.

Don't worry if these sounds aren't quite what you want them to be. Just do the exercise as described, so you can learn the basics. Later, you can use these same files, or create new ones, and apply the techniques we will learn later in this chapter to improve your sound samples.

Adjusting sound quality

Before you begin recording, you should select the default sound quality:

Open the Windows 95 Sound Recorder by using WAV Method Two.

The Windows 95 Sound Utilities

On the Sound Recorder menu, click **Edit/Audio Properties**, then click on one of the format choices listed under "Preferred quality." (From high quality to low, the options are "CD Quality" (44.1kHz, 16-bit, stereo), "Radio Quality" (22kHz, 8-bit, mono) and "Telephone Quality" (11kHz, 8-bit, mono).)

Then click "OK."

Remember that two attributes create larger sound files: one is higher quality, the other is the length of your sound file!

The Windows 95 CD Player

The CD Player is one of the "extras" provided when you buy the Windows 95 CD-ROM installation disk. Here are a few neat features of this utility, which you may choose to try before beginning the next exercise.

As we've mentioned, this player is initially configured to start automatically ("AutoPlay") when you insert a music CD. The program starts and appears as an icon in your Windows 95 taskbar, instead of an open window on the Desktop.

The CD Player allows you to save your CD by a name you choose—usually the CD's title. It will also remember the names of songs that you enter.

Here's how:

Put the audio CD you wish to identify in the CD-ROM drive and close the door. It's a good idea to have the CD sleeve available with the titles of the songs.

The CD Player should begin to play, and the icon appears on the Windows 95 taskbar.

The Windows 95 Sound Utilities

Click on the icon to maximize the CD Player.

Click on **Disc/Edit Play List** to open the Disc Settings dialog box.

Select File/Edit to add the CD artist, title and playlist

The dialog box provides spaces in which to enter the artist's name and the title of the CD. Do that now by clicking in each box and backspacing over any existing words.

CD Player also knows the number of tracks on this CD; you can enter the title for each song in the right-hand panel. To do this, click on Track 1 in the Available Tracks field. Note that the words "Track 01" appear to the left of the box at the bottom of the screen, and "Track 1" is written in that box.

Click in that box and backspace (if necessary) to get rid of the existing words "Track 1." Type in the name of the song and click "Set Name." The song title will be copied to the Available Tracks list to replace the words "Track 01," and you will now see that the notation to the left of the box at the bottom says "Track 02."

The Windows 95 Sound Utilities

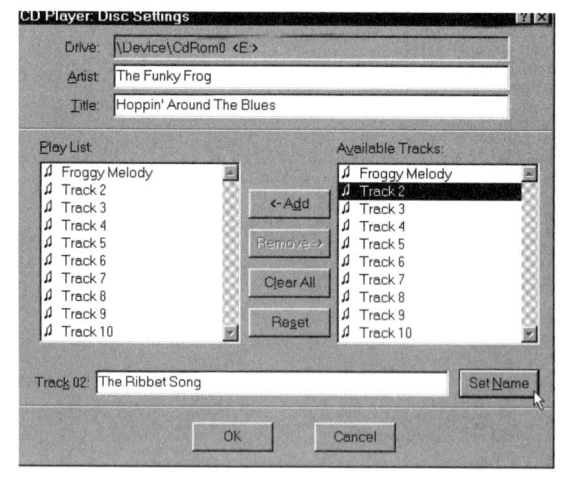

Naming the songs on the CD

Continue until all of your tracks are named. When you are done, click "OK." This will save your information. You may select which tracks to play by removing the songs you don't want to hear from the Play List on the left.

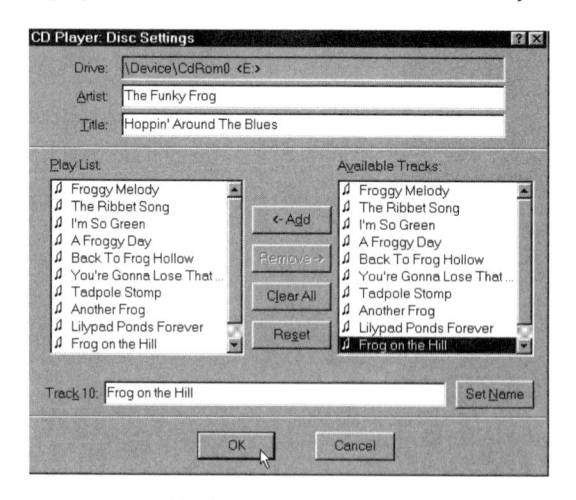

Click OK when finished

You can re-edit this list or the selections you wish to play at any time by clicking on **Disc/Edit**, as long as the proper CD is in the drive.

180

The Windows 95 Sound Utilities

To choose which song you would like to hear from the CD, you can use the drop-down list on the CD Player.

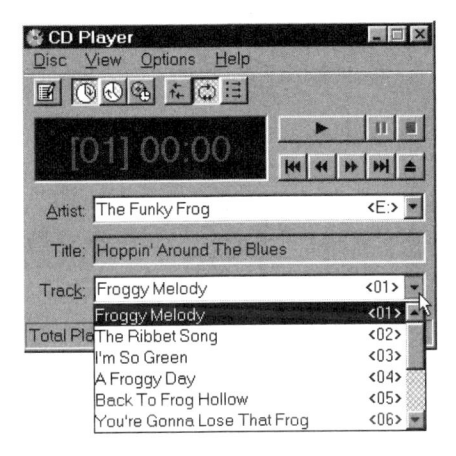

Use the drop menu to select a song

Each time you put a new audio CD in your CD-ROM drive you can use this process to enter information about that CD. The next time you play that particular CD, Windows 95 remembers its title and tracks. That's pretty neat!

On to the exercise...

Exercise Three
Creating An Audio Clip In WAV Format

For this exercise you'll need the Sound Recorder and CD Player, and your favorite audio CD.

Start the Sound Recorder using WAV Method Two.

Remember to specify the default sound quality before you record.

The Windows 95 Sound Utilities

Place your favorite audio CD in the drive; it will start to play automatically. You will only be able to record a small sample from your song—about 5 seconds at first.

Maximize the CD Player by clicking on the icon on your taskbar, if necessary.

Use the forward and back arrows to locate the song on your CD from which you wish to record a sample.

Click the Pause button on the CD Player.

Click **File/New** from the top menu of the Sound Recorder.

Click on the red circle '•' to begin recording.

Begin playing your audio CD.

To stop recording, click on the Sound Recorder's solid rectangle and then stop or pause the CD.

Now name your new file "myfile1.wav" and save it to the C:\Mymusic folder:

Click **File/Save**.

The Save dialog box will appear. Click on the "up arrow" to get to the C:\ drive.

The Windows 95 Sound Utilities

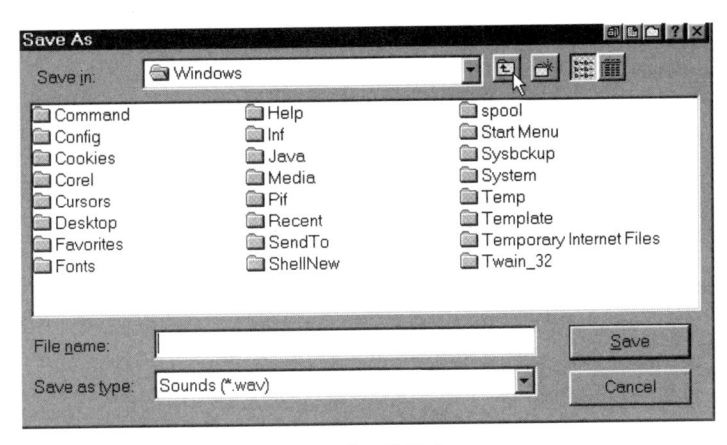

Go to the C Drive

Locate your Mymusic folder.

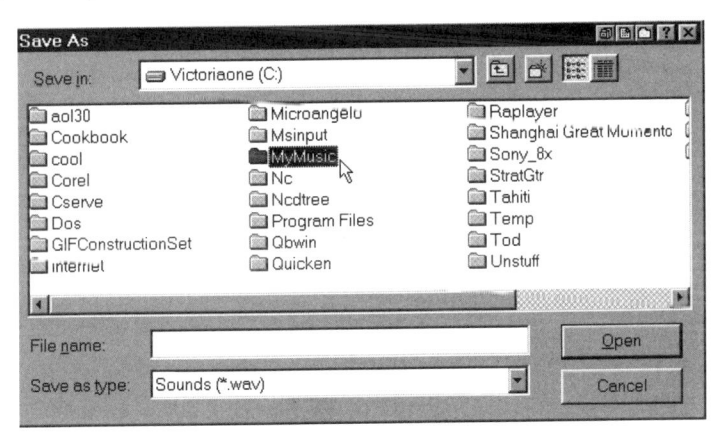

Find your Mymusic Folder

Double-click it to enter the folder. Now click on the box to the right of "File name" and enter "myfile1.wav"—or simply "myfile1." Click on the "Save" button to save it.

The Windows 95 Sound Utilities

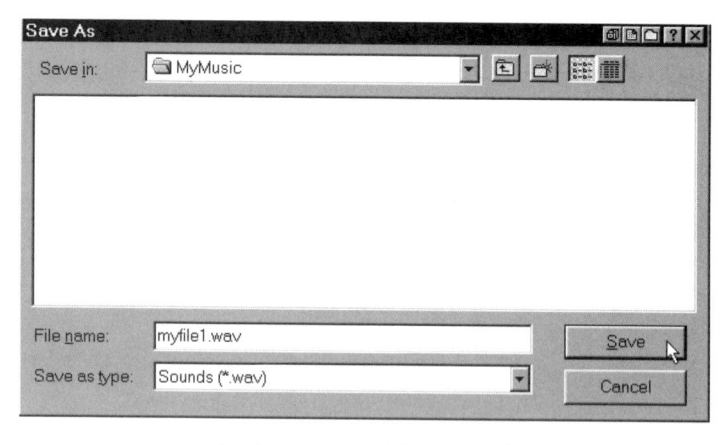

Saving your myfile1.wav file

Windows 95 will save that file for you in the Mymusic folder as a WAV file.

To play back your recording in Sound Recorder:

If the file is already open, click the << arrows to return to the beginning of the file and click on the > arrow to play it. Otherwise:

From within the Sound Recorder, select **File/Open**.

Locate your C:\Mymusic folder and double-click to open it.

From there, locate your myfile1.wav in the dialog box and click it so that myfile1.wav is entered on the line to the right of "File name."

Click "Open" in the dialog box.

Click > to start playing the sound.

Click the Stop button to cease playing the sound.

Now try a second one by selecting **File/New**. Remember to save it with a new name!

The Windows 95 Sound Utilities

The Sound Recorder's maximum default recording time is 60 seconds. If you want to make the playing time of your clip longer, you can use one of two ways.

Method one—plan on not using the first "take." Instead, when the file stops playing, move the slider to the beginning of the file and click the record button again. This will increase the size of your file. Choose a section of your CD to record and start the recording process again. Don't forget to re-save your file!

Method two—open Sound Recorder and click on the record button. Let the slider reach the end of the file, at which point the recording will stop automatically. Look at the notation next to the view meter to see how many seconds of empty sound you've recorded. If you wish, you can extend the length of that by clicking Record again. Let it play to the end of the file. Click on **File/Save** and save the "empty" sound as "nosound.wav."

Use this file any time you wish to extend your recording time! To begin a new long recording, click on **File/New**, then **Edit/Insert file** and select your nosound.wav. Sound Recorder will insert the empty file. Rewind, then start your recording!

When you have increased the file size two or three times, you may wish to do a test recording to see how large your finished effort is before you save the file. Long WAV files take up a lot of space!

Exercise Four
Creating A Voice Recording In Wav Format

For this exercise you'll need the Sound Recorder microphone. Make sure your microphone is ready to use and attached to your sound card. We can really have some fun with this one!

The Windows 95 Sound Utilities

Recording your new vocal WAV sound

Have your microphone ready.

Open the Sound Recorder using WAV Method Two.

(Optional: specify the default sound quality by clicking **Edit/Audio Properties**, and then click the quality that you want from the "Preferred quality" list.)

Click **File / New** from the menu of the Sound Recorder.

Click on the red circle '•' to begin recording.

Start talking or singing. Shorter is better!

To stop recording, click on the solid rectangle.

Click **File/Save**.

The Save dialog box will appear. Click on the "up arrow" to get to the C:\ drive.

Locate your Mymusic folder.

Double-click it to enter the folder. Now click on the box to the right of "File name" and enter "myfile2.wav"—or simply "myfile2." Click on the "Save" button to save this file.

Windows 95 will save it in the Mymusic folder as a WAV file.

The Windows 95 Sound Utilities

Exercise Five
Recording WAV Files From A VCR Or Stereo

A lot of people enjoy making their own WAV files with excerpts from their favorite movies or television shows. This exercise will teach you how to set up your system to do just that.

This exercise is also useful if you don't have a CD-ROM player installed in your computer, because you can connect your sound card to your stereo system to record CDs instead!

While you could just place the computer's microphone close to the TV speakers and record in that manner, the results will be of much poorer sound quality.

Before proceeding, we want to give some cautionary advice. If volume levels from your VCR or stereo are too high, you risk damaging your sound card or computer system. We are including this information because it is a popular and fun activity, but ask that you use your own judgment in deciding to record from your VCR or stereo.

For this exercise, you need some inexpensive additional equipment. Most electronics stores will have the two inexpensive items you need: an audio patch cord and a mini-jack adapter. Make sure the cord is long enough to reach from your sound card socket to your VCR or Stereo!

If you are unsure of the size of the plugs or how to connect them, you may wish to take both your VCR player and your sound card with you to the electronics store. If you let the salesperson know what you are trying to do, he or she can usually help you make the right choices.

It's also helpful to have your VCR or stereo documentation handy, as well as your sound card's manual.

The Windows 95 Sound Utilities

Your VCR or stereo connection

You will find on the back of most VCRs or stereo amplifiers an output socket labeled "Audio Out." This, or the equivalent according to your documentation, is the socket you will use to send your signals out from your VCR to your sound card. Plug one end of the audio patch cord in to the "Audio Out" socket on your stereo or VCR.

Your sound card connection

Look at the exposed end of your sound card on the back of your computer. You will probably see three mini-plug sockets, "Audio Out," "Line In" and "Mic." "Audio Out" is probably being used by your computer speakers; "Mic" may be connected to your computer microphone. Attach the mini-jack adapter to the other end of the audio patch cord and plug it into the "Line In" socket on your computer's sound card.

This completes the connection. Plug in your VCR and put in a tape. If your connection was made correctly, you'll hear the same sounds through your TV and your computer speakers from the VCR.

We'll use the Windows Sound Recorder for this exercise.

Start the Sound Recorder using WAV Method Two.

The Windows 95 Sound Utilities

Play the VCR tape to slightly before the sound you wish to record and press the VCR's Pause button.

Start the Sound Recorder and select **File/New**.

Click the Sound Recorder's Record button and then release the pause button on your VCR.

Leave some space at the end of your recording for editing—cutting away bits of sound you do not want—then stop the tape and recorder.

Wind back the recorder and play the sound to be sure it's what you wanted!

Remember to save the file! It's a good idea to save this to your C:\Mymusic folder until you've edited it to your liking, then you can drag it to the C:\Windows\Media folder.

Group Three: Editing Sound Files

Exercise Six
Adding Effects To A Sound File

Now that you know how to create a sound of your own, let's do an exercise with another file we've provided for you. Put the companion CD-ROM in your CD-ROM drive. We can get really silly with this one.

You can add some basic sound effects to any WAV sound file you choose. You can use the limited effects in the Windows Sound Recorder to alter speed and add echo, or even play the sound backwards! Though the selection of effects in the Sound Recorder is limited in comparison to software we'll look at later, we think it's a good place to start learning these techniques.

12 The Windows 95 Sound Utilities

Before we begin, you can teach yourself a good habit. When editing files, if you save what you've done, then you have overwritten the original file. That's okay in this case, because you can always load the original from the companion CD-ROM. But what if it's one you've carefully worked on?

In order not to lose your original file, when you open a file, save it immediately with a different name. Let's try that with this one, then go on to adding effects.

> If your sound card does not support 44,100kHz sound files, you will not be able to play the files that end in 44. Instead, use the ones ending in 11. Example: Rather than choosing file exer644.wav, chose exer611.wav from the same folder on the CD-ROM.

Open your Sound Recorder.

Click on **File/Open** and select the exer644.wav (or exer611.wav) file in your C:\mymusic folder. Once it's open, you'll see "exer644.wav - Sound Recorder" on the Sound Recorder title bar.

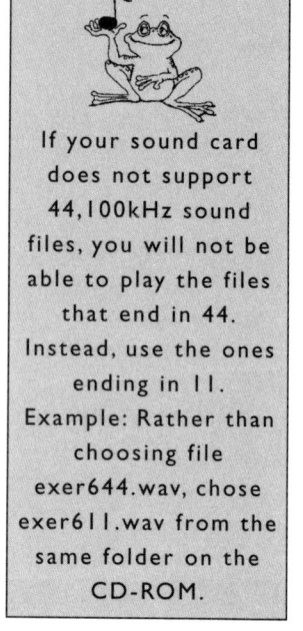

Click on **File/Save As...** and rename the file to "myfile6.wav." You will now see it appear at the top of the Sound Recorder as "myfile6.wav" and the original exer644.wav (or exer611.wav) will still be intact.

Play myfile6.wav by clicking on the > button.

Rewind it by pressing <<. It's the word "music," right? If not, you've got the wrong file! Remember to rewind it every time you add effects, too.

Now just have fun! Click on the Effects menu. While increasing the volume is a handy tool, the others are more fun. First, speed up the sound so that instead of a female speaking voice, it will sound like a chipmunk. Each time you speed up the sound, it increases in speed by 100%, just as it tells you.

The Windows 95 Sound Utilities

Now rewind and try some other effects. To add echo, click on **Edit/Echo**. Then click on the play button to hear it. You can do this as many times as you like, but remember to rewind it if you play it back. After awhile, though, the sound will get pretty muddy!

To play the sound backwards, click on **Edit/Reverse**, then click on the play button. (It didn't work? Did you remember to rewind it, first?)

When you're satisfied with the effects added to this file, you can save it with the same name by clicking on **File/Save** or you can rename it to something else by clicking on **File/Save As...** and renaming it. Make sure you save it into your Mymusic folder. This is a good habit to have, otherwise you'll have sound files all over your hard drive, but you won't be able to find them!

> If you don't like the changes in the steps that follow, you can always go back to the sound's original form by clicking on File/Revert, until you re-save myfile6.wav. After you've saved changes to myfile6.wav, you cannot revert. If you make further changes, you can only revert to the sound as you last saved it.

Now, if you like, you can try this exercise by making a CD sample of your own or by recording your voice with your microphone. Remember to save the file!

Exercise Seven
Cutting & Snipping: Editing A Sound File

For this exercise, we'll need the Sound Recorder and the file called "exer744.wav" (or exer711.wav if your sound card doesn't support the larger file) from the companion CD-ROM.

Open the Sound Recorder. Click **File/Open**.

The Windows 95 Sound Utilities

Locate the exer744.wav file (or exer711.wav) in your Mymusic folder.

Now, before we do any editing, we'll save this as a new file to work on, leaving your exer744.wav file (or exer711.wav) intact.

Click **File/Save As...**, and when Windows 95 prompts you, name the new file "myfile7.wav."

Play the file. You hear the word "speak," then Ellie the dog barking, with space in between, we hope!

We're going to cut out everything before Ellie's bark.

If you've rewound the file, play it again! This time, note where the slider is right after the word "speak" is played.

When the file has finished playing, grab the slider by placing the mouse arrow directly over it and slowly slide it backward. Try to put it right where you noticed the word "speak" stopped.

Note the position of the slider, then click Play. Did you get it right? It takes a little work, because the Sound Recorder's slider isn't precisely accurate.

If it's not exactly what you want, go back and try it a few times, until you've gotten the slider to a point where all you hear when you click the play button is Ellie the dog. Leave some space at the end of a spoken word or phrase. You'll need that space in your sound files for more sophisticated editing in the next chapter, where we'll be using Ellie's voice again.

The other reason it's good to leave some empty space at the beginning and end of sound files is that sometimes the actual sound begins before the human ear perceives it. You can accidentally cut off a sibilant "s" sound at the beginning of the word "speak," for example. Leaving that space helps you avoid this. Leaving room at the end does the same. It also allows you to smoothly "fade in" and "fade out" the sound, so it doesn't seem to begin and end abruptly.

The Windows 95 Sound Utilities

Unlike the "fade" at the end of a song, this fade might go undetected by the human ear, but you will be able to detect the difference between one that has been smoothed out at the beginning and end and one that has not. This will be exemplified in a later exercise.

Once you feel you've found the right cut-off point (if you're not sure, about 0.70 seconds is a good place), put your slider at that position and click **Edit/Delete Before Current Position**. When prompted, confirm the deletion by clicking "Yes." This will "cut away" all but the bark.

Click the Reverse and Play buttons to play the file from the beginning again, to make sure you got it right. If you didn't or are unhappy with the results, you can try again without exiting. Be sure to click on **File / Revert** before re-trying.

Once you are happy with what you've done, save the file.

Now try one yourself! Open the original exer744.wav (or exer711.wav) again, and this time save it as "myfile7a.wav."

This time, try positioning the slider so that you will only have the spoken word "speak," leave a bit of empty space after it, and click **Edit/Delete After Current Position** to slice away the last part of the file, including Ellie's bark.

Feel free to use other techniques you've learned in this section, including adding echo and volume, and even reversing the sound!

Exercise Eight
Insert A Sound File Into A Second Sound File

Now, let's try putting those two sounds, myfile7.wav and myfile7a.wav, back together! This will teach you how to combine two WAV sounds into one file. We're going to put them together in the reverse order, though.

The Windows 95 Sound Utilities

Open the Sound Recorder.

Click **File/Open** and select "myfile7.wav."

Click **File/Save As...** and rename the file to "myfile8.wav."

Move the slider to the end of the myfile8.wav file (or play the file!).

Click on Edit/Insert File.

Go to your Mymusic folder and select the myfile7a.wav file you created.

This will insert myfile7a.wav into the myfile8.wav.

Play the file.

If you like what you've done, save the file again. Otherwise, you can always click on **File/Revert** to get back to the clean myfile8.wav (without the word "speak" in it), as long as you did not save the file.

Independent study: Choose a sound effect that you like. We've included some on the companion CD-ROM for you. Think of something spoken you'd like to add to that file, and create a new file as in exercise four, above and name it myfile8a. Open the sound effect file you've chosen and re-save it as "myfile8b.wav," then append your myfile8a.wav to it. We know you'll use your own imagination, but just to get you started, you might choose the sound of glass breaking and say "Oh, no!" at the end. Technically, you could just have appended those words to myfile8b.wav by starting to record at the end of it, but this teaches you more about combining sound files.

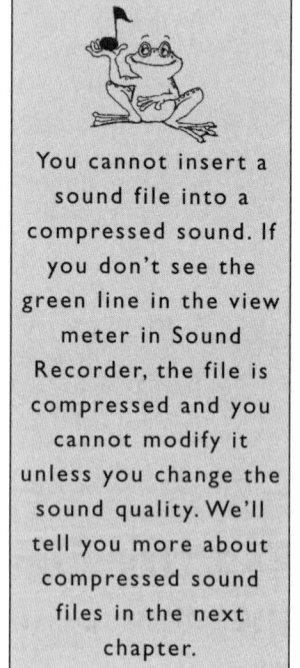

> You cannot insert a sound file into a compressed sound. If you don't see the green line in the view meter in Sound Recorder, the file is compressed and you cannot modify it unless you change the sound quality. We'll tell you more about compressed sound files in the next chapter.

The Windows 95 Sound Utilities

Exercise Nine: Cut And Paste

Again, we're going to use the exer944.wav or exer911.wav to try copying the barking sounds in this WAV file and pasting it into itself. This will make the file twice as long. Although this is a simple example, with the software in the next chapter you can do more sophisticated cutting and editing.

Open the Sound Recorder.

Open the exer944.wav (or exer911.wav).

Save the file in your C:\mymusic folder as "myfile9.wav."

Play the file. You should be able to count seven barks!

Rewind the file, and select **Edit/Copy**. We're copying the whole file here to add to a new file. It will be saved to the Windows 95 clipboard so you can use it soon.

Move the slider to the middle of the file somewhere—make sure you see a flat green line! If the line is not flat, you will be cutting out part of a bark.

Click **Edit/Delete** before current position. NOTE: If you select **Edit/Cut** by mistake, this will erase what you have on the Windows 95 clipboard, and copy the cut section instead. So be careful with this, what you want to do is copy the original seven barks and add them on to the new two or three barks you've just edited.

Play the new file and count how many barks there are. Remember this number—for our purposes, let's say you reduced the number of barks to two.

Now click **Edit/Paste Insert** to add back in the original seven barks.

Add the number of barks you counted in your own file to the number 7.

This is the number of barks you should hear!

The Windows 95 Sound Utilities

Save the file and exit Sound Recorder.

Independent study: Create your own WAV using your microphone. Try finding one word and cutting it out. It will be easier with Sound Recorder to pause between each word. If you try some of the exercises in the next chapter, you'll see that visually, some of the software we've included for you on the companion CD-ROM is easier to manipulate for cutting and pasting.

Exercise Ten
Overlaying Sound Files (Mixing)

The object of this exercise is to show you that you can combine two WAV files and have them both play back at the same time.

Copy the sound called exer1044.wav (or exer1011.wav) from the companion CD-ROM to your C:\mymusic folder. That's Ellie, barking several times in succession!

We'll use two techniques here. First, we will use an older file that you've created, and cause it to repeat itself several times. You can choose one of two files from above, myfile6.wav (the word "music") or myfile7a.wav (the word "speak").

If you use myfile6.wav (the word "music"), this exercise could get pretty silly and fun. Using myfile7a.wav makes more sense—having the word "speak!" and the dog barking at the same time is a reasonable WAV file. Having the dog bark at the word "music" doesn't make too much sense, unless, of course, you happen to have a dog that barks when someone says "music!".

But, we're here to have fun, right?

The Windows 95 Sound Utilities

Open either one of those files, and save it as myfile10.wav in your C:\mymusic folder. Select **Edit/Copy**, then move the slider to the end of the sound file and click **Edit/Paste Insert** several times. Play the file. You should hear either the word "music" or "speak" repeated over and over. Save the file again, and leave the Sound Recorder open with your file loaded.

Now we're ready to try the last new technique—overlaying this file with a number of dog barks that will occur at the same time the voice is saying "speak" (or "music").

If your Sound Recorder is still open, as we suggested, you should have myfile10.wav loaded.

(If you closed the Sound Recorder, open it again, click **File/Open** and open the myfile10.wav from your C:\mymusic folder.)

With myfile10.wav open, rename the file by clicking on **File/Save As**, and call it "my10a.wav." (Otherwise, the file name may be too long for some sound programs that are not conversant with Windows 95's long file names. We want to go easy on you, here!)

Move the slider to pick a place where you want to overlay the exer1044.wav (or exer1011.wav) file.

Click **Edit/Mix With File**.

Double-click the exer1044.wav (or exer1011.wav) file (The one you want to mix in).

Play back the file. You should hear the word "speak" (or "music") several times, and at the same time, hear Ellie barking!

If you wish, click on **File/Revert** and try placing the barking sounds in a different place in the my10a.wav.

When you're satisfied with your results, click on **File/Save** to save my10a.wav

12 The Windows 95 Sound Utilities

Conclusion

This ends the basic WAV exercise section. We've now learned most of the basic techniques of manipulating sound files. We'll get to some more fun activities in the next chapter. It's fancy stuff, but you can do that, too, having learned these basic techniques!

13

The Fun Continues

Inside Chapter 13

Advanced Exercise One : Inserting One Sound File Into Another 205

Advanced Exercise Two::How to Overlay Sound Files ... 208

Advanced Exercise Three: Stereo Recording 210

Advanced Exercise Four: How To Change Sound File Format (Audio Codecs) 213

Advanced Exercise Five: How To Convert Sound File Types 217

Advanced Exercise Six: How to Both Overlay and Combine Sound 220

    Polishing and refining your sound files 221

Advanced Exercise Seven: Removing "Dead Air" 221

Advanced Exercise Eight: Get Rid Of Unwanted Noises 223

Advanced Exercise Nine: Fade In, Fade Outs 224

Some Final Tips 226

    Throw out the trash 228

The Fun Continues

We'd like to introduce you to some of the wonderful software we've provided for you on the companion CD-ROM. The following advanced exercises help you try out some of those programs. We'll start with that, then at the end of the chapter we'll introduce you to some of the other delightful programs we have provided.

We have three very fine and popular programs—Cool Edit 96 from Syntrillium, AWave and Gold Wave. Each is far more sophisticated in nature than the Windows Sound Recorder.

The Sound Recorder is capable of some of the activities described below, and we've included instructions on how to use that program for these exercises also. Unlike Windows 95, the Sound Recorder application in Windows 3.x cannot record sounds in stereo. It is capable of playing stereo WAV files, but the 3.x Sound Recorder records sounds in mono.

13 The Fun Continues

We think you'll be thrilled at the more graphic interface of each of the new programs we're introducing. Don't be intimidated by all the new functions—the ones you've learned in the last chapter are easy to use in these new programs—in fact, we suggest you try just that! After we've completed this chapter, you can go back to earlier exercises and experiment with the fine additional capabilities of these programs. You may find that one pleases you more than the other, or that you enjoy using each of them.

For those who are new to Windows 3.x or Windows 95, be aware that many software writers keep their commands fairly similar from program to program. For example, to exit the Windows 95 Sound Recorder, the command is **File/Exit**. That's the same for the Windows 3.x Sound Recorder, and in fact, for most if not all software designed for use in Windows, including word processors, spreadsheets and almost anything else you can think of.

So, you're going to find that you recognize many commands you've already used in other programs, such as **File/Save**, **File/Save As**, **Edit/Copy** and so forth. Better than that, they're likely to mean the same thing in every program!

Let's begin learning about the software from the companion CD-ROM. We hope you will install each of them and try the exercises in the previous chapter using these programs. You're in for a real surprise!

Each of these programs comes in two flavors, one for Windows 3.x and one for Windows 95. We've provided both. We'll illustrate the exercises with the Windows 95 version, but the activities are pretty much the same in the Windows 3.x versions.

Each of these programs performs beautifully, and though they all do many of the same functions, we thought showing you each one with an example or two would give you a feel for each.

Cool Edit 96

First, allow us to introduce you to Syntrillium's fine program, Cool Edit 96.

The Fun Continues 13

Cool Edit 96 is a digital audio editor for Windows 95 and Windows NT. With it, you are able to record and play WAV files. But that's not all! You can also record and play files in a very wide variety of audio formats, including Mac sounds! You can also edit, add effects and combine files together. Perhaps most useful, you can convert them from one format to another.

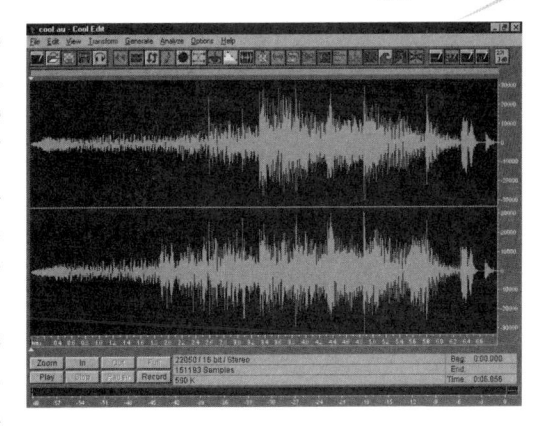

You can open more than one copy of Cool Edit 96 at a time. That means you can be working simultaneously with several files, chopping them up, reversing them, adding echo, slowing them down and speeding them up. In addition, you'll see that the View Meter on the front of Cool Edit 96 is very fancy! Instead of a straight green line, you'll actually be able to see the shapes of the sounds interpreted in sound wave form. You'll be able to zoom in close and snip out a tiny piece of unwanted noise in the exact spot where it occurs, rather than "best guessing" as you might with the Windows Sound Recorder.

Especially fun are the features used to enhance sounds. More than just Echo, Reverse and a change of speed, you'll find a wide choice of Echo Chambers, Delay and Distortion. You can keep the pitch of your sound the same, but speed up the tempo. Or you can do the reverse.

One really fantastic feature of Cool Edit 96 is that it has a multiple Undo feature. That means that you can keep undoing effects you have added to back out of changes you've made, or pieces that you've cut from your file. Though you could exit the file without saving changes, this makes it much easier than the "Oh, darn!" experience of having to start over from scratch.

The Fun Continues

Compliments go to Syntrillium for the wonderful toolbar they've created for you. When you position your mouse over any of them, it displays a very understandable explanation of what each icon means. How great!

Formats supported by Cool Edit 96 are WAV formats: ACM, Windows PCM, Microsoft ADPCM, IMA/DVI ADPCM, CCITT mu-Law and A-Law; Sound Blaster voice file format (.VOC), Apple AIFF format (.AIF, .SND), ASCII Text format (.TXT), 8-bit signed raw format (.SAM), Next/Sun CCITT mu-Law, A-Law and PCM format (.AU, .SND), SampleVision format (.SMP), Dialogic ADPCM (.VOX), Raw PCM Data (.PCM), Amiga 8SVX (.IFF, .SVX), DiamondWare DWD (.DWD), RealAudio 3.0 (.RA), and MPEG Layer I & II (.MP2).

Best of all, if you can't find an answer in their very complete Help file or the Troubleshooting menu, you can email them for support at support@syntrillium.com. Syntrillium Software's Web site is at http://www.syntrillium.com

Please refer to the chapter on installing your CD-ROM programs for installation instructions.

We have included dozens of WAV files for you. To copy them to your drive we suggest you create a directory called MYMUSIC. You need to run the MENU program and select Copy Wave Files. Follow the directions and select the WAVs you want to copy. If you have any difficulties, simply run your Windows 95 Explorer and copy individual files to your MYMUSIC directory.

Advanced Exercise One
Inserting One Sound File Into Another

In the upcoming exercise we're going to combine five different sound files to create a whole sequence. For this exercise, you need Cool Edit 96 and the files we've provided for you: cardoor.wav, carstart.wav, hornhonk.wav, tirestop.wav and shatter.wav. Can you guess what we're up to, here?

We chose these four files to show you how to use multiple WAV files to create a sequence of events. If you play each file separately, you'll quickly see what we're going to do—start the engine of a car, have it honk its horn then put on the brakes (you'll hear the tires squeal) and, oh, dear, too late—crash through that piece of plate glass (don't worry—no one gets hurt!).

If you insert one sound file into the middle of another, the new file will replace the old one from that insertion point on. In the Sound Recorder, if you do that, you'll lose the last of your other file. Not so with Cool Edit 96. You can place a sound anywhere you like.

We'll just tag each of these files in order at the end of the previous file, then we'll do some refining later on. If you like, you can further edit this on your own to insert your own voice saying "Watch out!!!" or whatever else you'd like to say.

TIP: In Cool Edit 96, to scroll your file back and forth, locate the green and/or black bar above the waveform. This indicates which portion of the entire wave is being viewed at that moment. When Zoom In is chosen, the bar gets smaller, because the portion being viewed with respect to the entire wave is smaller.

To move back and forth through your file, you can click and drag the green bar at any time. That will scroll the portion being viewed left or right. Clicking in the black region outside the green bar will scroll the bar exactly one screen to the left or right.

The Fun Continues

To select a portion of a WAV file to listen to, click on the center bar in the view meter. You'll notice a dotted line running vertically across the wave form. Place your mouse on that line, hold down the left mouse button and drag the mouse in the direction of the area you wish to select.

To play that selection, click on "Play."

Double-clicking in the slider bar region above the waveform display brings up the Viewing Samples text-entry box. You can enter exact starting and ending points in this box.

Now here's how to combine those sound files:

- Open Cool Edit 96.
- Click **File/Open** and choose cardoor.wav from your C:\mymusic folder.
- Click **File/Save As** and save the file in your C:\mymusic folder as "carcrash.wav."
- Click **File/Open Append** and select carstart.wav.
- If you click "play" right now, it's possible that all you will hear is the new portion of the file. Don't panic! To get to the beginning of the file, grab the slider and move it all the way to the left. Click on the middle line in the View Screen. Now click "play." You should hear both your car door slamming and the engine starting up.
- If you're happy so far, save the file!
- Now repeat the **File/Open Append** procedure and select hornhonk.wav.
- Repeat the **File/Open Append** procedure and select tirestop.wav.
- And last, repeat the **File/Open Append** procedure and select shatter.wav.

The Fun Continues

♪ Play your file! You should now have a sequence of a car door opening, the engine revving up, a tire squeal, horn honk and the crash of plate glass.

♪ Save your file and exit.

Instructions for Advanced Exercise One using Windows Sound Recorder

♪ Open Sound Recorder.

♪ Open cardoor.wav.

♪ Click **File/Save As** and save the file as "carcrash.wav."

♪ Move the slider to the very end of the file or play the file, but do not rewind.

♪ Click **Edit/Insert File** and select carstart.wav.

♪ Click **Edit/Insert File** and select hornhonk.wav.

♪ Again, move the slider to the end of the file.

♪ Click **Edit/Insert File** and select tirestop.wav.

♪ Move the slider to the end of the file.

♪ Click **Edit/Insert File** and select shatter.wav.

♪ Play the file to see if you've accomplished what you wished. If you forgot to move the slider to the end you can click on **File/Revert** to start again with the carstart.wav file as it was before you inserted the other files.

♪ Once you're satisfied with the result, click **File/Save**. That's it!

Advanced Exercise Two
How to Overlay Sound Files

This technique is also called *mixing*. What we'll do here is have one sound file running and put another file "on top." Both will be running at the same time once we're done, having been combined into one sound file. It will be as if both you and a friend were talking at the same time—but we've tried to make it more sensible fun, so you won't end up with a bunch of noise.

Ready? We're going to create our own dog and cat fight using two separate files, elliedog.wav and catnoise.wav.

♪ Open Cool Edit 96.

♪ Select **File/Open** and locate the elliedog.wav file in your C:\mymusic folder.

♪ Save the file as "dogcat.wav."

♪ To overlay a file in a particular place, you would move the slider to the place in the file where you want to overlay the sound file. This one can really be overlaid anywhere you like, and you can experiment with that.

♪ Click **File/New Instance**.

♪ From that screen, click **File/Open** and locate the catnoise.wav file in your C:\mymusic folder.

♪ From the catnoise.wav screen, click **Edit/Select Entire Wave**. Select **Edit/Copy** to copy the catnoise.wav file information to the Windows clipboard.

The Fun Continues

♪ Now go back to your dogcat.wav file, position the cursor where you want to place the start of the cat sounds and select **Edit/Paste Mix**. Make sure the Overlap box is checked. Choose the mixing volume, and click on "OK."

♪ Play it back. If you don't like the change, try it again by clicking **File/Revert** and starting again by moving the insertion point and clicking **Edit/Mix Paste** again.

♪ Once you have a sound you like, click **File/Save** and exit all instances of Cool Edit96.

Instructions for Advanced Exercise Two using Windows Sound Recorder

♪ Open the Windows 95 Sound Recorder.

♪ Click **File/Open** and select elliedog.wav.

♪ Save it as "dogcat.wav."

♪ To overlay a file in a particular place, you would move the slider to the place in the file where you want to overlay the sound file. This one can really be overlaid anywhere you like, and you can experiment with that.

♪ Click **Edit/Mix With File**.

♪ Double-click on the catnoise.wav file to mix it with dogcat.wav.

♪ Play it back. If you don't like the result, try it again by clicking **File/Revert** and starting over by moving the insertion point, clicking **Edit/Mix With File** and selecting catnoise.wav.

♪ Once you have a sound you like, click **File/Save** and exit Sound Recorder.

The Fun Continues

Now that you've learned how to insert and overlay files, we hope you'll use your good imagination to really learn how Cool Edit 96 can work for you. There are so many wonderful effects you can use—stretching the sound, compressing it, and using a variety of echoes and reverb sounds from the echo of a small garage to a huge arena—you can create an entire collage of sound with one file and overlay it on another.

Let's suppose you just thought up a new song. You want to play guitar on it, but when you play and sing into that tiny computer mike, you just can't hear both voice and guitar. No problem! You can record your guitar or piano through your sound card, then put a voice track over that, and if you'd like, add distortion, echo and other effects to both or to each one separately.

Yes! You can. Here's how:

Advanced Exercise Three
Stereo Recording

- Open Cool Edit.

- Select **File/New** and make sure you select 22,050 Hz Mono 16 as your selection if your sound card allows it. (16 will be cleaner, but if you cannot make a 16-bit recording, choose 8 bit.)

- Click Record and begin to record your instrumental part either through the microphone or direct connection to your sound card. Make sure you have an instrumental introduction that will let you know when to begin singing, or tap near the microphone in tempo to give yourself a "click track" before you begin. You can cut that part off later.

The Fun Continues 13

- Save your file as "comp1.wav."

- Click **File/New Instance** and you'll see a brand new window open while your comp1.wav file still exists on your desktop. Have your microphone ready to record your vocal track. In that window click on **File/New** and make sure the settings are the same as for comp1.wav.

- Click "record" and then go back to comp1.wav and click on "play." While comp1.wav is playing, you can record your vocal track to another WAV file.

- Once you are done recording, save your new WAV file as "comp2.wav."

> You will need to have a line-in connection to your sound card in order to record your instrument. If you wish to write out a musical line, you can read Cool Edit's Help file on how to use the Transform/Special Music feature.

- Now you can combine those two files! To do so, first let's create a new, blank stereo file. Click **File/New Instance** while both comp1.wav and comp2.wav are still on your desktop. Select 22,050 Hz Stereo 16 bit as your choice. (Note: this is stereo, your other files were mono.)

- Go to comp1.wav and select **Edit/Select Entire Wave**, then click **Edit/Copy** to copy the WAV file to the Windows clipboard.

- Go to your new stereo file. Select **View** and you'll note that both Right and Left Channel have a check mark next to them. Click on "Right" to uncheck it. That means we're going to be "viewing" only the Left Channel. You'll still see both Left and Right channel in the View screen, but we'll only be working with the Left one.

- We're going to copy your comp1.wav information from the clipboard to the Left Channel, simply by clicking **Edit/Paste**! Save your file as "compmix.wav."

The Fun Continues

♪ Do not close the file! Now go to your comp2.wav file and click **Edit/Select Entire Wave**, then click **Edit/Copy** to copy it to the Windows clipboard.

♪ Return to compmix.wav and select **View/Left Channel** again to de-select it. Now click **View/Right Channel** to select it. Paste the file in and you're done.

♪ Now click **View/Left Channel** and make sure both Left and Right Channel are selected. Play back your file.

You may have to do some adjusting on your original mono files to cause your two tracks to match up, but you get the idea by just trying this exercise.

♪ Save your file!

Sound compression

When trying to insert files, you may sometimes come across a file that has been compressed. You can tell if a sound file is compressed when using the Windows Sound Recorder in this easy way: if you don't see the green line in Sound Recorder's view meter when you open the sound, the file is compressed and you cannot modify it unless you change the sound quality.

So, why don't we learn how to do that now?

The Fun Continues 13

Advanced Exercise Four
How To Change Sound File Format (Audio Codecs)

Before we begin this exercise, it's time to talk about compressed audio files. An Audio Codec is a mathematical algorithm. Sounds like a mouthful, right? Well, what it does is compress and decompress sound files for you in the background—you don't even know it's going on!

What on earth would you want this feature for? Well, as we've said all along, WAV files are big, bigger and biggest. The higher the recording rate, the larger the file, remember? Codecs help you with that. It's useful because a compressed WAV file takes up less space on your hard drive and also takes less time to download or upload from or to the internet.

Changing the sound quality of your recording may be a genuine improvement in the sound quality. A file recorded at 11,025 Hz in 8-bit mono format will invariably sound less glamorous than one recorded at 44,100 Hz in 16-bit stereo format.

But while changing the compression ratio of a WAV file may cause the file to increase or decrease in size, it doesn't normally improve the sound of the file.

You can see for yourself whether you like this. We will change a file that is at CD Quality of 44,100 Hz to 11,025 Hz to hear what it sounds like. If it's bearable to you in a smaller format, you'll see that it takes approximately half the space on your hard drive in the first exercise, and one-fourth the space of the original file in the second exercise.

Before we do this exercise, let's make sure we have all the default codecs (compression tools) installed.

♪ Make sure you have your Windows 95 CD-ROM handy.

The Fun Continues

♪ Click Start/Settings/Control Panel/Add-Remove Programs.

♪ Click the Windows Setup tab, scroll down to Multimedia and click to highlight it.

♪ Click "Details."

♪ If the Audio and Video Compression check boxes are empty, click each to select them and then click "OK." Windows 95 may ask for your installation CD-ROM. Insert it in the drive and allow it to install the Codecs.

♪ Click "OK" to close the dialog box.

Now, on with the show.

To do this exercise, let's use the file called "advx4.wav" from your companion CD-ROM. It's a 44,100 Hz 16-bit stereo file. We're going to compress it now to a 22,050 Hz, 8-bit mono file. Conveniently, you don't have to remember all that! Windows 95 has codified that, as you will see, into what it calls "Radio Quality."

♪ Click **File/Open** and select advx4.wav from your C:\mymusic directory.

♪ Click **File/Save As** and rename it "compres1.wav," so you don't overwrite the advx4.wav file, but don't click Save yet!

♪ In that same dialog box, look to the bottom right. Find a button called "Change." This is where you change the Codec.

♪ You'll likely see that the choice appearing in the top drop-list box is "CD Quality," which is described as a 44,100 Hz 16-bit stereo file. Click the drop-list button and select "Radio Quality" and note how the description below changes.

♪ Click "OK" to accept that, and now save your file.

The Fun Continues

Play it back. Does it sound better, worse or just the same? Try opening advx4.wav and comparing it to what you just heard.

Now, let's save advx4.wav to a "Telephone Quality" file by repeating the same steps above, only this time, when you get to the Save As dialog, save the file as compres2.wav and click on "Change" to change the Codec to 11,025 Hz, 8 bit mono by selecting "Telephone Quality" from the drop-down list.

Compare the quality of all three files. The decision is yours!

Instructions for Advanced Exercise Four using Windows Sound Recorder

♪ Open the Windows 95 Sound Recorder.

♪ Click **File/Open** and select advx2.wav from your C:\mymusic directory.

♪ Click **File/Save As** and rename it "compres1.wav," so you don't overwrite the advx2.wav file, but don't click Save yet!

♪ In that same dialog box, look to the bottom right. Find a button called "Change." This is where you change the Codec.

♪ You'll likely see that the choice appearing in the top drop-list box is "CD Quality," which is described as a 44,100 Hz 16-bit stereo file. Click the drop-list button and select "Radio Quality" and note how the description below changes.

♪ Click "OK" to accept that, and now save your file.

AWave for Windows 95

Allow us to introduce you to AWave, and show you what it can do

13 The Fun Continues

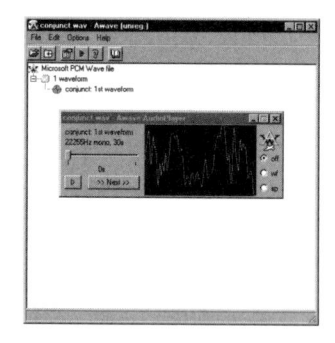

AWave for Windows 95

http://hem.passagen.se/fmj/fmjsoft.html

AWave (from FMJ Software Productions) is an extraordinary audio and wavetable instrument file format converter, editor and player.

This amazing program is capable of reading more than a hundred audio file formats from different platforms, synthesizers and trackers. When you open the program you'll see the instruments available contained as a graphical tree. Saving an item to any of the supported export formats is done with the click of a mouse.

There is also the "AudioPlayer" feature, a nice audio playback control. It is available from inside the main program as well as integrated into the Windows95 shell so that you may easily play any of the supported file formats either in your Windows programs or on the internet. You'll find it an ideal addition to your web browser for that reason. It also has the capability to do some audio processing and editing.

If you have one of the supported wavetable synthesis sound cards you can just click on an item, and directly "audition" it using a MIDI keyboard or the computer keyboard. If you just have a basic sound card capable of audio playback, you can use it as a crude, but realtime, software synthesizer to get an idea of what it should sound like.

AWave recognizes the following import file formats:

The Fun Continues

669, AIFC, AIFF, AIS, AMS, AMS, ASE, AVI, AVR, C01, CDR, DCM, DEWF, DIG, DMF, DSF, DSM, DTM, EMD, EDA, EDE, EDK, EDQ, EDS, EDT, EDV, EFA, EFE, EFK, EFQ, EFS, EFT, EFV, ESPS, EUI, F2R, F3R, FAR, FNK, FSM, G721, GKH, GSM, HCOM, IFF, INI (MWave DSP synths) and INI (Gravis Ultrasound bank set).

AWave can export to the following formats:

AU, AIF, ALAW, DES, EFE, G721, IFF, INI, MAT, MWS, PAT, PRG, RAW, SBK, SF2, SB, SDS, SW, TXT, UB, ULAW, UW, VOC, W01, WAV and WFP.

The clipboard copies audio data to the Windows clipboard and the AudioPlayer plays back on any digital audio device.

We think you'll most likely find this program a great addition to your sound studio.

Advanced Exercise Five
How To Convert Sound File Types

First, let's check to see if AWave is configured!

♪ Open AWave.

♪ Select **Options/Program setup**.

♪ Select the AudioPlayer tab.

♪ Under "Primary" check to see that your primary audio playback device is selected. If not, enter it now (this should be your sound card!).

The Fun Continues

- Next, let's select the method that should be used for audio playback. If you are using Windows 95 and have Microsoft DirectX (v2 or later) installed on your computer, we recommend you select that. NOTE: Windows 3.1 does not support DirectX. For those who use Windows 3.x or do not have DirectX, select "Use Windows multimedia services, buffered output." If (and only if) you have problems with no sound in the AudioPlayer, try "Use Windows multimedia services, unbuffered output."

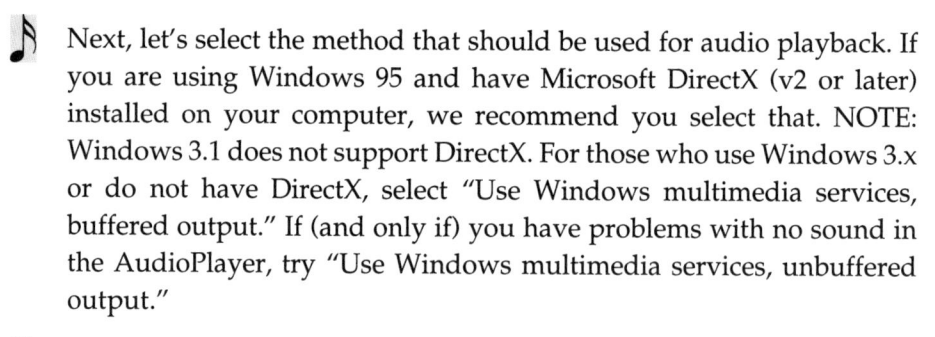

- Select the Auditioning tab and check the "Enable auditioning" box.

- In the MIDI-Input list, choose what device you want to use for playing. If you don't have, or don't want to use, a proper MIDI-in device, then select "None" from this list. If you check the "Enable virtual keyboard" box, you can use the computer keyboard as a MIDI keyboard.

- In the Wave-synth list, choose any you might have, or simply select the AWave software synthesizer.

- There is a button on the program toolbar to toggle the auditioning feature on and off.

- Click "OK" to finish.

We'll use the file yakety.voc from the companion CD-ROM. A VOC file is a Sound Blaster file format, as we've mentioned. We're going to convert it to a WAV file.

- Select **File/Open new** from the program menu and select yakety.voc.

- Click "OK" to load the file.

You should now see an expanded folder containing the yakety waveforms that you just loaded.

- To convert it to a WAV, select it and click on **File/Save waveform as**.

The Fun Continues 13

♪ In the dialog box that appears, name the file "yakety.wav" and click "OK."

♪ To play the file, click on **Edit/Play Audio**.

You now have a WAV file in your C:\mymusic folder called "yakety.wav!"

GoldWave

For the final exercises, we will be using GoldWave. Allow us to introduce you!

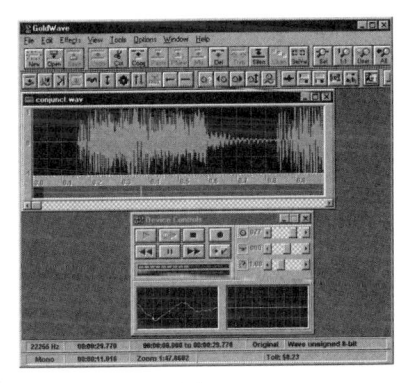

GoldWave

GoldWave is another fine sound editor, player, recorder and converter for Windows 95/NT.

It is speedy and slick, opening huge files in the blink of an eye, and includes all standard editing functions as well as file conversion capabilities and a huge variety of effects! It also allows for realtime playback when you are rewinding and fast forwarding, and has a lot of user configurable options. It has a comprehensive help system and none of the features on the shareware demo version are disabled. You can also have multiple instances of Gold Wave running simultaneously.

Gold Wave supports WAV, VOC, IFF, AIF, AFC, AU, SND, MAT, DWD, SMP, VOX,

13 The Fun Continues

SDS, as well as the ability to open RAW files as 8-bit, 12-bit, 16-bit, mu-Law, A-Law or IEEE floating point Transparent Audio Compression Manager support for WAV files.

Advanced Exercise Six
How to Both Overlay and Combine Sound

For this exercise we're going to combine the splash of an ocean wave with the sound of a ship's horn. We'll use the files ocean.wav and shiphorn.wav from the companion CD-ROM.

- Open Gold Wave.

- Click **File/Open**.

- Select the file ocean.wav from your C:\mymusic folder.

- Click **File/Save As** and save it in your C:\mymusic folder as "overlay.wav."

- Select **File/Open** and open shiphorn.wav.

- Click **Edit/Copy**.

- Move to the overlay.wav screen by clicking on its title bar.

- Click **Edit/Mix**, then click "OK."

- Play the file by clicking the forward arrow in the "Device Controls" box.

You'll hear that the splash of the ocean is very short, and the ship's horn is very long! Let's now add another splash at the end of the ship's horn.

- Click **File/Open** and select the file ocean.wav.

The Fun Continues 13

- ♪ Click **Edit/Copy**.
- ♪ Move to the overlay.wav screen by clicking on its title bar.
- ♪ Click **Edit/Paste At** and select "end."
- ♪ Play your file and save it! You should hear the overlaid sound of the ship's horn and the ocean, then another ocean splash at the end.

Polishing and refining your sound files

Although we are currently using Gold Wave, Cool Edit 96 or AWave will also perform these functions nicely. However, these tasks will be all but impossible using the Windows Sound Recorder, because you cannot see the tiny clicks, pops and dead spaces as well in the Sound Recorder's view meter. For that reason, we'll not be giving you the cleanup equivalents for the Sound Recorder in the exercises that follow.

Advanced Exercise Seven
Removing "Dead Air"

Polishing tip one is that you cut out "Dead Air" space on your sound files. This keeps the file size down to a minimum. Here's a tip on how.

We've included a file for you that has a lot of "Dead Air." Using Gold Wave, let's snip out those sections quickly. It's not difficult!

- ♪ Open Gold Wave.
- ♪ Click on **File/Open** and select deadair.wav from your C:\mymusic folder.

The Fun Continues

♪ Click on **File/Save As** and save it in your C:\mymusic folder as "deadair1.wav."

♪ Play the file by clicking on the forward arrow in the Device Controls screen. You'll note that there's a lot of silence in this file—we've exaggerated it for you so you can try this exercise!

Now, let's trim the beginning of the file.

♪ You'll need to set your editing markers first. To do that, move the start marker to the position where you want to begin by placing your mouse in the deadair1.wav screen near the middle line, and position it at marker 0, the beginning of the file. Click your left mouse button to select the start point.

♪ Point your mouse to the area at position 1.5, and right-click.

That portion of the file should now be lighter than the rest of the file.

♪ Select **Edit/Delete** from the menu. Bingo! It has cut out that portion of the file.

♪ Now try eliminating dead air from other parts of the file.

♪ Click on **File/Save** when you are satisfied, and close the file.

NOTE: As another option, you could have selected just the two areas of sound with the same clicking procedure and selected **Edit/Trim**. Try that now, if you like, by beginning the exercise over, opening deadair.wav and saving it as "deadair2.wav." Use your markers to select just the middle of the file where the two sounds occur. Then use **Edit/Delete** to eliminate the dead air in the middle.

The Fun Continues **13**

Advanced Exercise Eight
Get Rid Of Unwanted Noises

Look for those annoying "clicks" at the beginning and end of your sound file created by the stopping and starting of your input (such as your CD Player). They're often there. Be sure you leave enough space at the beginning and end of your recording to allow for this kind of editing.

Here's a "sound file housekeeping" exercise that will be an easy task. We've put a very unwanted sound at the beginning of the file—a click. See if you can hear it. If not, try turning up the volume on your computer speakers.

♪ Open Gold Wave.

♪ Select **File/Open** and choose clicky.wav from your C:\mymusic folder.

♪ Click **File/Save As** and save it to your C:\mymusic folder as "clicknot.wav."

♪ Play the file by pressing the forward arrow in the Device Controls panel.

♪ Do you hear that exaggerated click at the beginning of the file?

♪ Select that click using the method described in Exercise Seven, above.

♪ Click **Edit/Delete** to get rid of the unwanted noise.

♪ Play the file to see if it's gone!

♪ Click **File/Save** once more, then close the file.

13 The Fun Continues

Advanced Exercise Nine
Fade In, Fade Outs

It's nice to have a sound file begin and end smoothly. For that reason, we suggest you learn how to cause the file to "fade in" at the beginning and "fade out" at the end. These are not the ordinary "fade" sounds you hear at the end of a musical recording where the song fades away on a repeated ending phrase or instrumental solo, although you can certainly do that, if you wish, once you've learned this technique.

These refinements are almost undetectable, but do round out the beginning and end of a sound file very nicely so that the sound does not appear to start and stop abruptly.

Of course, if, in your original recording, you do not allow the speaker, instrumentalist or singer to finish their phrase, or leave some space at the beginning and end of your file, you'll get a very "clipped" sound. Be sure to include that in planning your sound recording. If you are cutting and snipping prior to doing what you learn in this next exercise, be careful not to cut too close to what you think is the beginning or end of the sound file, be it music or spoken word. There are still minute sounds happening after a word is spoken or a note is played. Cutting those away will alter the sound and cause it to sound "chopped off" at the end.

Let's try this. It's easy, but it's a sign of professional sound editing. You're learning, see?

- ♪ Open Gold Wave.
- ♪ Select **File/Open** and pick the file smooth.wav from your C:\mymusic folder.
- ♪ Save the file to your C:\mymusic folder as "smooth1.wav."

The Fun Continues

- Play the file. You'll first hear silence, then the actual sound begins. We're going to trim the "dead air" at the beginning and end of the file and smooth out the start and stop points.

- Using the method in Exercise Seven, above, trim the beginning of the file, but leave enough room to "fade in." Do the same with the end of the file, leaving enough space to "fade out."

- Save your file once more.

- Now, move the start and finish markers to the part of the sound you want to fade in—including the blank space at the beginning of the file and a bit of the beginning of the sound.

- Choose **Effects/Volume/Fade In**.

- Enter the initial volume percentage. We suggest you try 50% first. Choose "OK."

- Use your markers to select the entire file and play it back. If you're not happy with the result, you can click on **Edit/Undo Fade In** and try again to see just how much fade in effect you want!

- Once you're satisfied with it, save the file.

- Now, go to the end of the file and select the portion you wish to fade out.

- Click **Effects/Volume/Fade Out** and select the percentage, then choose "OK."

- Play back your file and save it when you're satisfied with the overall picture!

13 The Fun Continues

Some Final Tips

When you're doing hobby recording and using the spoken word, the inexpensive unamplified microphone that came with your sound card is probably quite adequate. If you're creating a presentation or musical composition that you will record at 44,100 Hz or more, you may want to consider investing in a more expensive microphone.

As we've said all along, the higher the number, the better the sound will be. If you're uncertain as to what will be a quality recording, try doing a sample recording at 11,025 and the same one at 22,050 and 44,100 and compare.

You can also use codecs such as ADPCM to reduce file size, although ADPCM will degrade the quality of the recording somewhat. It's best used in speech, though you might not want to use this when planning on addressing a large crowd.

While both Windows 3.x's and Windows 95's Sound Recorder handle a good number of compression methods, Windows 95's version adds the ability to set sample rate and resolution from within its menus, as we've shown you.

Be sure your choice of speakers is adequate. Small speakers in your home office area may not sound the same in a classroom or board room, or with larger groups of listeners. You may want to consider regular stereo speakers and an amplifier. But try it out at home with that hookup, before you do your presentation. The small errors that you could live with at home may be more pronounced over a larger sound system.

Also, consider what you are planning to do with your recordings. In our opinion, a Sound Blaster is quite acceptable as a game board and plays your system sounds nicely. It is not a card for the discerning musician. Sometimes scouring the Microsoft Knowledge base at their Web site and/or the Sound

The Fun Continues 13

Blaster site are required for solving problems that are less likely to occur with high-end sound cards. Those problems are in the areas of MIDI resources, IRQ settings and the like, which is okay if you plan to become a PC tech expert, or if you already are one.

If you're really going to get serious about the quality of your sound recordings we'd suggest looking into something more glamorous and delightful. An excellent card can be acquired without a significant difference in pricing. Voyetra's Turtle Beach Sound Systems offer a fine line of sound cards that will amaze your ears, so much so that we've taken the huge step away from impartiality to recommend them to you. It's part of why we gave their site our Author's Award. The Turtle Beach line has long been a favorite—they are easy to install and use, are well shielded against noise and have great MIDI sounds via wavetable synthesis! Over the years, we've found both the friendly but intelligent tone of written documents and the voice tech support to be of the highest caliber. Interestingly, you may note there are not an overabundance of Tech FAQs on their site. How nice to be able to tell you that we feel it's because when you're dealing with Turtle Beach sound cards, there are usually very few problems.

There are other very fine-to-excellent sound cards on the market that you're less likely to see in a computer superstore, including Advanced Gravis, Digital Audio Labs, Roland and Star Multimedia Corp's Kurzweil Sound Cards—these are some of the others we suggest you research by checking out the Web sites! We've included a list for you of such sites you can visit in the bookmark on your companion CD-ROM.

You may need to add additional memory to any sound card you acquire to allow it to sample sounds, but all in all, with a little research, you can have top-notch MIDI sound for around the same price as those cards found in most computer outlets. Do check out Voyetra's Turtle Beach line first.

The Fun Continues

You may find it difficult to locate any one of these stunning cards in some local computer stores. Sadly, it seems that most are not dedicated to those of us who enjoy quality sound, and assume people don't want to do much more with a sound card than have some capacity for speech or hearing the sounds that come in our gaming or software packages. It's an unfortunate thing, and yet you should have absolutely no trouble locating and purchasing one of these fine cards and even doing price and feature comparison right on the Web.

Throw out the trash

Finally, consider what you'll be doing most. If you are planning on using your sound recording and editing program mainly for home dictation and transcription, or just for silly fun, then you may not want to have large WAV files cluttering up your drive.

If you make a habit of using C:\mymusic, or a folder of your own choosing, to do your sound editing and creation, you can move the final result to C:\Windows\Media and get rid of the rest of the intermediate files. If you just don't have the heart to throw out all of your work copies, you can put them on a floppy disk or back them up. But do get them off your hard drive! You'll find that "CD-Quality" WAV files can pile up quickly, and if we haven't said it often enough, WAV files can be huge!

You can set the recording quality of your files permanently in Windows 95. If you plan to spend an afternoon recording clips off of your favorite CD, you may prefer to have those files be of very high quality. Tomorrow, you may wish to record some short spoken phrases to store in a document. Those don't need to be of such a high caliber, do they?

You could, if you wish, select the quality of your recording in Windows Sound Recorder every time, by selecting **File/Properties** and selecting, for example "CD Quality," or "Radio Quality" for your recording. But why do this time after time?

The Fun Continues 13

Windows 95 has a better idea. Click Start/Settings/Control Panel/Multimedia. A dialog box appears, asking you to select your preferred devices and the quality of sound. In the "Playback" section you can change the volume of your playbacks, and click in the "Show volume control on the taskbar" to place a small icon on your Windows 95 taskbar. By clicking that icon, you can instantly control the volume. Therefore, you can set a reasonable volume within this dialog box, then tweak it further by using the taskbar icon.

The lower portion is where you set the default quality of your recordings. You know about CD Quality, Radio Quality and Telephone Quality now. If you want an average overall sound, select "Radio Quality." Size-wise and quality-wise, CD Quality is highest. Radio Quality will put you at 22,050 Hz 8 bit mono recordings, which is the average selection for newer WAV files you'll find on the Internet.

That's it! There's lots more to learn, but we think you're already well on your way! With the lessons we've shown you, you've learned an awful lot about sound, recording and editing. Each of the programs we used here have very fine documentation with the help files right in their program. So if you're as eager as we think you might be to learn more about each or any of them, open the program and click "Help."

14

Here's MIDI For You

Inside Chapter 14

Defining MIDI For The Newcomer 233
EarlyProblems-And The GM Solution 234
System Exclusive — What Is It? 237
What MIDI Means For You 239
Computer Music Education 241
    Let's Take A Cakewalk 244
    Digital Orchestrator Plus for Windows© 3.1 and 95 by Voyetra 247
    DrumTrax for MIDI 247
    Harmony Assistant 248
    MOZART the Music Processor 248

Here's MIDI For You

Defining MIDI For The Newcomer

Let's first learn a bit about just what MIDI is. Not a big, long explanation. There's a wealth of information online and elsewhere about MIDI. Our purpose here is to get you started, and the opportunity to decide if you want to go further.

MIDI stands for "Musical Instrument Digital Interface," and it started being used by the general public in about 1983. It's a way for any instrument that is MIDI-capable to "speak" to another MIDI-capable instrument. It was standardized further to incorporate the General MIDI Standard, which you'll often see described on instruments and software you buy as "GM compatible." That means that the 128 instruments that are provided with your MIDI equipment or software all conform to the table we'll show you later.

14 Here's MIDI For You

EarlyProblems-And The GM Solution

Since MIDI songs are computerized data, there quickly became a need for standardization. That's where GM (General MIDI) saved the day, as it were, for MIDI users.

Early on, MIDI programmers began to realize there was a file incompatibility between different MIDI programs. You might have written a great MIDI song, but if the friend with whom you shared it didn't have the same MIDI components and software, the file could end up sounding very odd! What a disappointment after all that hard work. Instead of hearing that lovely flute solo or jazz guitar you'd written a part for you'd hear a bass guitar playing that line of instrumentation. Not a fun thing to have to put up with.

There was an urgent need to standardize the instrument setup for MIDI files, so that creation and playback guaranteed that when you wrote a part for a saxophone, the listener was going to hear a saxophone part no matter what MIDI equipment he or she owned. That's where the General MIDI standard came in. The whole music industry was quick to accept this standardization, which was due in large part to Roland and Passport Designs.

What the General MIDI standard entails is a simple enough concept. GM created a standardized listing of 128 instruments, and associated them with particular program numbers. (Don't worry, you'll see, when you install the Cakewalk demo from the companion CD-ROM!) For now, General MIDI sets up a default list of 128 instruments and associated program numbers. It's not an actual law that you risk being jailed for breaking—you're not locked in to using these parameters. It's nonetheless a good idea to keep in mind, especially for those just beginning to work with MIDI. (We'll show you some fun "tampering" with the GM setup in Cakewalk, too.)

Here's MIDI For You

With General MIDI, the actual composition is "pre-triggered" behind the scenes, sending musical information to the computer which is hidden from you. Those messages reveal which instruments have been chosen for a particular composition, and much more.

We've provided a table for you.

	General MIDI Patches
	Piano		Chromatic percussion		Organ
Nr	Instrument	Nr	Instrument	Nr	Instrument
1	Acoustic Grand	9	Celesta	17	Drawbar Organ
2	Bright Acoustic	10	Glockenspiel	18	Percussive Organ
3	Electric Grand	11	Music Box	19	Rock Organ
4	Honky-Tonk	12	Vibraphone	20	Church Organ
5	Electric Piano 1	13	Marimba	21	Reed Organ
6	Electric Piano 2	14	Xylophone	22	Accordion
7	Harpsichord	15	Tubular Bells	23	Harmonica
8	Clavinet	16	Dulcimer	24	Tango Accordion
	Guitar		Bass		Solo strings
Nr	Instrument	Nr	Instrument	Nr	Instrument
25	Nylon String Guitar	33	Acoustic Bass	41	Violin
26	Steel String Guitar	34	Electric Bass(finger)	42	Viola
27	Electric Jazz Guitar	35	Electric Bass(pick)	43	Cello
28	Electric Clean Guitar	36	Fretless Bass	44	Contrabass
29	Electric Muted Guitar	37	Slap Bass 1	45	Tremolo Strings
30	Overdriven Guitar	38	Slap Bass 2	46	Pizzicato Strings
31	Distortion Guitar	39	Synth Bass 1	47	Orchestral Strings
32	Guitar Harmonics	40	Synth Bass 2	48	Timpani

Here's MIDI For You

General MIDI Patches (continued)

Nr	Ensemble Instrument	Nr	Brass Instrument	Nr	Reed Instrument
49	String Ensemble 1	57	Trumpet	65	Soprano Sax
50	String Ensemble 2	58	Trombone	66	Alto Sax
51	SynthStrings 1	59	Tuba	67	Tenor Sax
52	SynthStrings 2	60	Muted Trumpet	68	Baritone Sax
53	Choir Aahs	61	French Horn	69	Oboe
54	Voice Oohs	62	Brass Section	70	English Horn
55	Synth Voice	63	SynthBrass 1	71	Bassoon
56	Orchestra Hit	64	SynthBrass 2	72	Clarinet

Nr	Pipe Instrument	Nr	Synth lead Instrument	Nr	Synth pad Instrument
73	Piccolo	81	Lead 1 (square)	89	Pad 1 (new age)
74	Flute	82	Lead 2 (sawtooth)	90	Pad 2 (warm)
75	Recorder	83	Lead 3 (calliope)	91	Pad 3 (polysynth)
76	Pan Flute	84	Lead 4 (chiff)	92	Pad 4 (choir)
77	Blown Bottle	85	Lead 5 (charang)	93	Pad 5 (bowed)
78	Skakuhachi	86	Lead 6 (voice)	94	Pad 6 (metallic)
79	Whistle	87	Lead 7 (fifths)	95	Pad 7 (halo)
80	Ocarina	88	Lead 8 (bass+lead)	96	Pad 8 (sweep)

Nr	Synth effects Instrument	Nr	Ethnic Instrument	Nr	Percussive Instrument
97	FX 1 (rain)	105	Sitar	113	Tinkle Bell
98	FX 2 (soundtrack)	106	Banjo	114	Agogo
99	FX 3 (crystal)	107	Shamisen	115	Steel Drums
100	FX 4 (atmosphere)	108	Koto	116	Woodblock
101	FX 5 (brightness)	109	Kalimba	117	Taiko Drum
102	FX 6 (goblins)	110	Bagpipe	118	Melodic Tom
103	FX 7 (echoes)	111	Fiddle	119	Synth Drum
104	FX 8 (sci-fi)	112	Shanai	120	Reverse Cymbal

General MIDI Patches (continued)								
Sound effects							
Nr	Instrument		Nr	Instrument		Nr	Instrument
121	Guitar Fret Noise		124	Bird Tweet		127	Applause
122	Breath Noise		125	Telephone Ring		128	Gunshot
123	Seashore		126	Helicopter		

System Exclusive — What Is It?

SysEx MIDI information is data that is specific to a particular brand of MIDI instrument. If you have a Funky Frog brand keyboard, it will probably contain a code that dictates certain SysEx messages, like the data that is part of the MIDI sound design of our particular keyboards. You can only share that information with other Funky Frog Keyboards.

Though hardware is not part of SysEx, let's use it as a more understandable example. Suppose you had bought our imaginary Funky Frog Keyboard. It needs a new hardware pedal that a lot of manufacturers make, but only Funky Frog manufactures the one that fits on our keyboard. If you don't get the Funky Frog Keyboard pedal, it won't match up with the design of the keyboard.

Maybe someone out there has an identical pedal, but you'd have to know that it's an exact match in order to be sure it would work. So it is with SysEx data. You can exchange certain SysEx data between instruments, but you have to know the designs of the instruments to make sure it works.

Here's MIDI For You

If you and your neighbor both have MIDI instruments that are GM compatible, each of you will find your Acoustic Piano on "Patch 1". What that means to you is that, when you compose a MIDI song, and play it at your neighbor's house, the acoustic piano you chose will play back as an acoustic piano, not a saxophone! And so on... That's pretty important, if you want your compositions to sound right.

Sometimes, though, people choose other instrument patches for their writing. It's a matter of sensibility and choice. Those choices are called "System Exclusive," simply meaning that where you would expect to find an acoustic piano sound, instead the composer has assigned a clarinet.

No matter. System Exclusive is something you're going to see in the Cakewalk Demo when you load some of the sample songs included. You're given an opportunity to load the System Exclusive patch assignments with a simple question, and a request that you answer Yes or No. Hint: Choose Yes.

You can go back later and try to tell it No. You'll hear some interesting differences between the two versions of the song!

By choosing Yes, you can listen to it as it is supposed to sound; choosing No at a later time will allow you to hear what it would sound like with the GM assigned patches are in the places they are supposed to be. A vocal line may become a piano; a trumpet is now a drum. Interesting!

This demonstrates better than how we can think GM has helped to make things easier for MIDI musicians. All you have to do is "expect" everything to be in the right place, if not, the composer should advise you of that so you can hear the sound properly.

Cakewalk does that all for you automatically.

Here's MIDI For You

You can simply listen to MIDI sounds, as we've told you already, with your Sound Recorder or Media Player. You don't need MIDI software to listen to MIDI, as long as you have MIDI capability on your sound card. What you do need the software for is to compose, edit and record your own MIDI compositions.

What MIDI Means For You

With MIDI you can turn your home computer into a music workstation! MIDI-equipped computers communicate with other MIDI-compatible instruments like synthesizers and drum machines. You do need to have a sound card that is MIDI capable? And has a MIDI in and MIDI out connector in order to carry the MIDI data back and forth from your MIDI instrument to the computer? Your computer can send information (data) to the MIDI instrument you have connected to your sound card. You can also play your MIDI instrument and send information to the computer.

Just what is MIDI out and MIDI in, then? Well, think of the words "Out" and "In" as comparable to "send" and "receive". The computer *sends* information from its MIDI Out connector to the instrument's MIDI In. The Instrument sends information to the computer from its own "MIDI Out" to the computer's MIDI in. Simple enough!

So what does all this mean for you? Well, it means that you can do any number of things musical—like using your computer for musical notation. It works like any word processor—you can create sheet music just by using a mouse click to park notes on a staff, for example.

You don't read music? No matter. There are many music programs that do that for you! How nice to be able to play a music keyboard (a software, or "soft", keyboard that allows you to use your mouse or computer keyboard as a piano) and create MIDI files. The bonus is, with the right software you can

239

Here's MIDI For You

also be creating a piece of sheet music at the same time. Suppose you want to send a demo of some music you've created to a music publisher, or you wish to copyright what you've written. Think of the hours you save, and the headaches, when the software will do that notation for you! And, you don't have to know a thing about writing music.

Software programs will also "normalize" your playing for you. How does that work? Well, first, let's explain the term *click track*. Studio musicians who have not put down a drum or rhythm track on their recording use the click track. It's a track of rhythm that doesn't end up being on the recording. The same principle applies to computer music. You'll hear a click track in many of the software programs once you click the "record" button to start playing your song and recording it to a computerized file. There are a wide variety of click tracks to select from in this kind of software.

Suppose you're not the world's greatest keyboardist, and yet you have managed to create approximately the rhythm you want. Well, imagine software that helps you out with that, and "moves" a slight off-beat to the logical point where it should be. Not only does it detect the moment you strike the musical "key" (note) and when you release it, but it guesses what you might be thinking as you are playing along with a click track. That's not a futuristic expectation—it's already in many of the software programs you might buy today.

The subtlety of the MIDI interface is even more amazing. When you have a music keyboard connected to the computer, there are more things that are detected. For instance, the volume at which you strike the key, and the effects you add to that note, like a "bending" sound when you're imitating a guitar note, or a vibrating (vibrato) sound to imitate a long note played on a violin. The instrument you have chosen to use via your "soft" keyboard or your actual music keyboard MIDIed into your computer is another parameter that is recognized. With one keyboard, you could be playing strings, acoustic baby grand piano or glockenspiel. The choice is up to you!

Here's MIDI For You

To sum it up, the computer interface detects all kinds of information about the musical data you are sending, and recognizes each piece of information (called an "event") separately, then recombines them to play them back to you.

If that's not enough, imagine software that will allow you to combine your own digital recordings from direct input sources—like your voice singing into a microphone, or your favorite guitar sent direct into the sound card. What if you could combine that with synthesizer music such as keyboard and drums and a string background to record your own compositions? And store all of that in files on your computer? What if you could take all the music you just wrote, and put it in a different key before you sing along to it, add and remove notes, and change the volume (dynamics) of various notes or sections to loud or soft? What if you could learn to play piano or another instrument right at your PC?

With the right composing software, you can!

Computer Music Education

Computers and music software work wonderfully together as an instructional program! There's software that will teach you piano, guitar, notation, music theory from beginner to pro, and improve your skills right at your computer station.

Ready to get started?

YES, YOU CAN DO MIDI!

Here's MIDI For You

We've chosen the great Cakewalk Home Studio program demo to show you just how easy it can be to do simple MIDI exercise on your computer. You don't even need a piano! The Cakewalk home studio is the program we chose, because it's simply fantastic. It's geared towards the newcomer to computer music. If you are a professional musician, you may wish to consider looking at Cakewalk's more professional packages, are included on the Companion CD-ROM, courtesy of Cakewalk.

The more professional packages contain all the features of the Cakewalk Home Studio and more. The exciting thing about the Home studio is that it allows you to create and play back up to 4 tracks of music at a time. That means you can write for a small classical string quartet or a rock band, right from your computer!

The concept of MIDI is still somewhat haunted by the notion that it's for "professionals only." Many of us have at the very least seen a TV show about the professional artist at work at his or her computer station—creating wonderful compositions through the courtesy of MIDI.

While it's true that there is a learning curve required, MIDI is not something to be daunted by. The software engineers of today have spent years refining their product—from the early days of a simple notation program with complicated commands to what has appeared on the software scene today. Just in the last year, MIDI software seems to be claiming its own place on the computer software shelves.

For those who don't want to learn to compose, there is the listening aspect. True, there is a wide range of MIDI files available on the internet and elsewhere, and this ranges from a professional rating of "poor to superb."

Here's MIDI For You

The internet and MIDI have also proven to be fast friends. Not only can you now listen to MIDI in the background as you work on or off the internet, but you are quite frequently greeted at any given Web site with a fine MIDI introduction. MIDI files are small; it makes them an ideal sound file for use on a Web site. Visitors to a Web site that includes a MIDI tune don't have to sit and drum their fingers impatiently while waiting for a huge sound file to load.

In the upcoming year, we expect to see more and more people incorporating MIDI sounds into their business applications, multimedia videos and Web sites, and using MIDI as a vehicle for teaching both musical and non-music related subjects.

Well, what about those "poor" MIDI files? We want to elucidate on that. If you're new to the MIDI community, and you've done the very best you can do, then "poor" is not necessarily the result. Perhaps a better choice of words is "novice." If you are shy the quality of your files, and about sharing with others, then try to see this as a wonderful opportunity to learn from the masters. Remember, they were all beginners once, too!

With the internet connection, you can converse with other MIDI enthusiasts, read what they have to say, get answers to your questions and learn new techniques from basic to complex. You can even upload your own files attached to a letter in a newsgroup, asking those who are interested to please listen to what you've written and offer advice or give you opinions and pointers. We'll remind you to be courteous, and not overload a newsgroup with every one of your new files. Pick one or two that you are the proudest, and use those to learn from.

Cakewalk is one such program. On their Web site at http://www.cakewalk.com, you will have the privilege of getting the latest news and information; technical support and answers to frequently asked questions (FAQs, as they are called) and even joining a Web discussion group. At this time, Cakewalk has four such newsgroups available to you, including a

Here's MIDI For You

Beginners newsgroup, where questions are answered accurately and quickly by the fine Cakewalk technical advisors. Once you've tried the software we've included on the companion CD-ROM, we encourage you to visit their very fine site to see all the goodies they have in store for you!

Cakewalk and other fine software program manufacturers have dedicated themselves to making music more accessible, fun and amazingly easy. Sure, there's always that first step to learning. Cakewalk knows this, and has included some wonderful tutorials to get you up and running in no time. We've provided those for you on the companion CD-ROM.

Let's Take A Cakewalk

On the companion CD-ROM, we've included three demo programs, in both Windows 95 and Windows 3.x format, from Cakewalk. Those are, from basic to advanced

Cakewalk Home Studio

Cakewalk Professional

Cakewalk Pro Audio

We suggest you try the Cakewalk Home Studio Demo first, as your introduction to this aspect of music computing, for a number of reasons. One, it's a sensational program. Two, Cakewalk has included some wonderful basic tutorials to get you up and running, right along with their demo versions. Three, Home Studio contains some stunning features for the newcomer to MIDI music as well as more advanced features for the professional, all at a very manageable price. They've also been generous enough to include both the Windows 95 and Windows 3.x program on the same CD-ROM; if you're a Windows 3.x user now, you'll have the Windows 95 version ready and waiting for you when you migrate to Windows 95!

Here are some of the other features of the Cakewalk Home Studio:

Here's MIDI For You

Integrated multi-track MIDI and digital audio sequencing, which means you can combine your MIDI and digital recording. This means you can record, edit and play back up to four tracks of audio (digital) along with your MIDI music. "The Virtual Jukebox" which allows you to interactively select your favorite tunes and play them back. You can also print out your own high quality sheet music, including lyrics and guitar chord grids! You can even play along with the included music files and record new parts with Virtual Piano.

The first step in trying this program is to install it from the companion CD-ROM. You cannot save or print any of the music from within the demo version, but it will allow you to edit and play back your own parts to see how Cakewalk Home Studio Works. To install the Cakewalk demonstrations, load the Menu program on the companion CD-ROM and click the Cakewalk Demonstrations button. You will be presented with several demos to choose from. You can make your selection by clicking on one of the buttons.

Once you've installed the Home Studio, make sure you reboot your computer so that Windows recognizes the new installation. Now that you've rebooted, let's make sure the Virtual Piano is up and running. Home Studio's Virtual Piano allows you to use your computer keyboard as a piano. It's fun, and easy to learn.

Click on Start/Programs/Cakewalk Home Studio Demo/Cakewalk Home Studio Demo. The first time you run Home Studio, it will check your sound card and find the settings it needs. Once that's done, let's get Virtual Piano set up.

In Windows 95, click on Settings/MIDI Devices from the top menu. In the left panel, you should see several settings under the heading "Input Devices". Click with your mouse on "TTSVirtual Piano" to make sure it is highlighted. Note: there may be other settings there for your own sound card. You can choose those, too; Cakewalk knows about how to use them all.

Here's MIDI For You

In Cakewalk, go to **Settings/MIDI Devices**, and make sure "TTS Virtual Piano" is highlighted on the input side. The Virtual Piano is only an input device, and doesn't produce any sounds of its own, so you need to make sure a driver is selected for it on the "Output" side. Make sure the correct driver is highlighted on the Output side (SB16 MIDI Out, FM Synth, OPL, Voyetra, etc.).

Load one of the demo songs included with Cakewalk, for example BALLAD.WRK. Select track 1, then go to **Tools/Virtual Piano**. In the Virtual Piano, go to the **Settings/Always On Top**. Make sure "Use PC Speaker" is not selected. You should now be able to play the Virtual Piano.

In the right hand panel, if MIDI mapper is the only parameter visible, you can choose that. Otherwise, look for "Header In" or another descriptive phrase that lists your sound card, too.

Click on "Move Selected Devices to Top"

Now, click on "OK" to close the Dialog Box.

The Cakewalk Help files include a wonderful tutorial for you to use. You can print those files out, and follow along! This program might look at first as though there's a high learning curve. Don't be daunted by the opening screen—Cakewalk helps you through every step.

Enjoy!

Digital Orchestrator Plus by Voyetra is our other choice for fine combined Digital and MIDI composition. It's an excellent program, and we think you'll find it impressive!

Digital Orchestrator Plus for Windows© 3.1 and 95 by Voyetra

Digital Orchestrator Plus by Voyetra brings you the ability to combine digital audio recording and the power of MIDI. Turn your PC into a multi-track hard disk recording system. Combine MIDI and digital audio into dynamic original compositions.

You can combine your vocal tracks and acoustical instruments right along side your MIDI sounds. There are many drag-and-drop features in the user interface, so you can, with familiar Windows commands, record, edit, mix, move or copy both MIDI and digital audio tracks.

Home musicians and professionals alike will find this an amazing sound studio to work with. Imagine being able to assign up to 1,000 tracks to both digital and audio, record, loop, even do "punch-in" recording right on your desktop!

Digital Orchestrator's import techniques are a dream. You can import WAV files and paste them into your composition "right on the beat," without a lot of frustration in trying to line them up with your composition. We think this an excellent feature of this great program.

Here are some other fantastic programs for you to try.

DrumTrax for MIDI

DrumTrax for MIDI Demo is a great addition to any MIDI composer's toolbox. It offers a sampling of drum patterns in Standard MIDI format that give you rock drums, blues, hip-hop and Latin, with a good number of patterns included for each. You can use them as they appear, or make you own modifications!

Here's MIDI For You

Harmony Assistant

This is a score editor, digital sound editor, guitar chords diagram editor and much more. Working with 44KHz, 16-bit sounds, this program offers a digital sound database (GM compatible), guitar tabulator display and much more.

One of the fun parts of this program is its Karaoke features. You'll enjoy using this to create your favorite Karaoke sing-alongs.

MOZART the Music Processor

http://www.mozart.co.uk.

Mozart by David Webber is a neat music processor for Windows 95 and Windows 3.x. You can type in music notation as easily as typing in a word processor. You may view, hear, edit and print full scores and individual parts suitable for professional musicians.

Mozart instinctively knows which operating system you are using, whether it is Windows 3.x or Windows 95, and chooses the proper installation for you.

You only need your computer keyboard to use Mozart, which allows you to create and edit printable sheet music. In addition to being a great way to print out parts for the members of your musical group, you can also import MIDI files you've created or downloaded to hear or print.

We find this program easy to use, and a life-saver for those times you're in a rush to get those parts written out! A very fine program.

15

How To Use Your Newly Made Sounds

Inside Chapter 15

**Practical Exercise One: Assigning Sounds To
     System Events** 252

**Practical Exercise Two: Creating Your Windows 95
     System Sound Scheme** 254

**Practical Exercise Three: Insert Sound Into
     A Document** 255

**Practical Exercise Four: Linking Your Sound File To
     Your Document** 257

What Else Can I Do With My Songs? 259
      Looking to promote your songs? 260

More Treats For You 260
    Educational software 260
    CD Player utilities 262
    WAV Managers 263
    Extra treats from Syntrillium 264

How To Use Your Newly Made Sounds

I've heard this very question many times from newcomers to the world of computer sound. Sure, these sounds, quips and clips of music are fun to trade back and forth with friends, but what else are they useful for?

Sound enhances your workspace in many ways, especially the applications suggested in the four "practical" exercises below. The first one shows you how to make your own choice of sounds for a particular event on your computer. The second shows you how to change all of your sounds in Windows 95, and create a favored "Sound Scheme" of your own. You can even create several of them and change them at will.

Practical Exercises Three and Four will show you how to enhance your business, school or hobby documents with WAV or MIDI sound files. You can create musical clips from your CD-ROMs, voice recordings or even great sound effects to include in your documents. The uses are only limited by your imagination. We've suggested a few below—we're sure you can think of more!

To use the full capability of the sound feature you must have a sound device (usually a card) installed in your computer. If you want to create your own sound files, you will also need a microphone or some other input device.

15 How To Use Your Newly Made Sounds

Depending on your hardware configuration, you can use at least two types of sound files with most word processing programs, such as Corel WordPerfect or Microsoft Word. You can even embed sounds in the Windows 95 Word Pad. MIDI and WAV are the two file types you can use.

Practical Exercise One
Assigning Sounds to System Events

"What are System Sounds?" you may ask. In both Windows 3.x and Windows 95, sounds can be set to play when various events take place. For instance, you might hear a sound when you open or exit Windows. Or you may hear sounds when a file is opened, when a program opens or closes or when the computer tells you that an error has occurred.

Since you'll have to wait while these sounds play, we suggest you pick very short files. You may enjoy making a huge WAV file of your favorite recording artist, but you'll quickly grow tired of that if you have to wait for it to play every time you make an error on the computer! A simple file that you can make by recording your own voice saying "You Goofed!" or even "Wrong!" is a much better choice.

You can create sounds of your own or pick others that you like to define your own System Sounds. Here's how:

To assign system sounds in Windows 3.x:

- ♪ Double-click "Main"/Control Panel/Sounds.
- ♪ Make sure that the Enable System Sounds box is checked in the lower left-hand area.
- ♪ Highlight an Event in the list box on the right.

How To Use Your Newly Made Sounds

♪ Highlight a sound of your choice—you may have to go to another directory to find your sounds, although if you've done as we suggested and put your sounds in C:\Windows\Media, you should find most of them there.

♪ Click on the "Test" to hear the sound.

♪ Now, if you like, you can set up other events and associate them with sounds by highlighting another event and choosing another sound.

♪ Click on "OK" when you've finished picking the sounds you like.

To assign system sounds in Windows 95:

♪ First, copy any sounds you will wish to use to your C:\Windows\Media folder.

♪ Double-click on My Computer/Control Panel/Sounds.

♪ In the Events list, click on the event to which you wish to assign a sound.

♪ In the Name List, select the sound you want Windows to play. You can use the "browse" button to find your C:\Windows\Media folder if it is not selected.

♪ Test the sound by clicking on the name and then clicking on the right arrow button.

♪ If you like that sound, click "Apply" to select it and assign it to that event.

♪ To continue adding other event sounds, click on another event, associate it with a sound, then click "Apply."

♪ Click on "OK" when finished, or continue on to the next exercise to learn how to save your Sound Scheme and create others.

How To Use Your Newly Made Sounds

Practical Exercise Two
Creating Your Windows 95 System Sound Scheme

One great way to take advantage of that wonderful new sound card is to put it to work on a daily basis! You start and stop Windows and all of the programs therein so often that you may get tired of the sounds you've chosen for your system events. Windows 95 has solved that for you.

Suppose you have two favorite recording artists. You've selected sounds from one of them to use for your System Sounds, but after three days, you don't want to hear those sounds for awhile. Now what? Do you have to change them all, every third day?

No!

You can save the sounds you've assigned to events in Exercise Four, above, by giving them a name. Then, you can create a whole new bunch of Systems Sounds and save that, too. In this way, you can change all your Systems Sounds at once with just a few clicks of the mouse.

It's very easy! Shall we begin?

If you are still in the dialog box from the exercise above, let's just continue from here. Otherwise, repeat Exercise Four to make sure you've set up the sounds you want. Once you've finished doing that, save your sound scheme.

To do so, click on "Save As" and create a name for that entire group of sounds, such as "Pop Star Sounds." Windows 95 will now remember that entire scheme for you, and the name will appear in the list of Schemes so that you can change or restore these settings any time you want.

How To Use Your Newly Made Sounds 15

The first time you do this, the Scheme box may be blank. It still "thinks" it's a scheme—and will tell you that if you save this new Scheme, it will overwrite the old one. Go ahead, because there really wasn't a scheme there!

> The Windows 95 CD-ROM contains four schemes for you to try that have been pre-assigned for many events. You can even edit those and re-save them. They're called Utopia, Jungle, Robotz and Musica, and you can install them if you haven't already by clicking on Start/Settings/Control Panel/Add-Remove Programs and clicking on the Windows Setup Tab. Have your Windows 95 CD-ROM ready. Find the Multimedia listing in the list box and highlight it. Click on "Details" and if the Sound Schemes mentioned above have not been checkmarked, do so now.

Then click on "OK" and follow the instructions to insert your Windows 95 diskette. Now, when you click on My Computer/Control Panel/Sounds, you will see those schemes in the drop-down list underneath the word "Scheme" by clicking on the downward arrow in that box.

Practical Exercise Three
Insert Sound Into A Document

Here's a wonderful exercise for use in your business applications, in school presentations and home hobbies. We're going to have some fun with this one. For this exercise you will also need to have a Windows word processing program installed, such as Corel Word Perfect or Microsoft Word.

Your Windows 3.x or Windows 95 Sound Recorder will work just fine with this, but you may want to get fancier with your WAV files later on. For the exercise here, you can use the sound file we've provided or make one of your own. Either way, it's an impressive presentation that doesn't require a lot of difficult work.

How To Use Your Newly Made Sounds

Charts and graphs may make your document look wonderful, but music and spoken words are fantastic. They help your audience stay interested. You can use professional, prepackaged MIDI files for business presentations, too. Best, these documents can be "zipped" into a neat package with your sound files and sent to others across the world with the click of a mouse via your e-mail.

A word of caution. Remember, it's not a great idea to use professional CD music from an audio disk. That music is copyrighted and you need a license to use it in a business presentation. It's a good thing for kids to learn right away—even using their favorite rock artist in a school presentation violates the copyright laws. That's why it's better to compose your own music, or at the very least purchase CD-ROMs that are designed to be used without license from local or internet suppliers.

Here's how to paste that sound file into your document:

- Use the Windows 95 Sound Recorder to create the sound you wish to use or pick one from your favorite sounds. For this example, we would like you to make a new sound file and call it "myvoice.wav," using your own voice repeating the words "This is a sound file that you click on in a business document." (If you don't have a microphone, you can use a pre-made file, but it's more interesting if you can hear your own voice right next to your typed words in the document!)

- Next, create a document in your word processing program or in Word Pad, and type the words "This is a sound file that you click on in a business document." In Word Pad, you'll be offered the opportunity to save the file in MS Word 6.0 format. Save the file as "C:\mymusic\mysound.doc."

- On the Sound Recorder menu, with the myvoice.wav file open, click on **Edit/Copy**.

- Now, go back to your mysound.doc and position the mouse so the cursor is right before the word "This" at the beginning of the sentence.

How To Use Your Newly Made Sounds

♪ On the Word Pad menu, click **Edit/Paste**.

♪ You should see a WAV icon appear in your document, surrounded by corner markers. If you click on the sound right now, it should play for you! Click anywhere outside the icon to "exit" the sound; that is, to remove the corner markers.

♪ Save your document again.

Now that you've tried this, think of all the other things you can do. Create a family page for yourself at home; later, you might even want to put some of these things on your Web page. Record each person's speaking voice, saying his or her own name and something about themselves.

You can learn to embed a photograph of each person, and next to it put a sound icon that someone can click on to hear that person's voice. What a neat "Family Page" to save for your grandchildren!

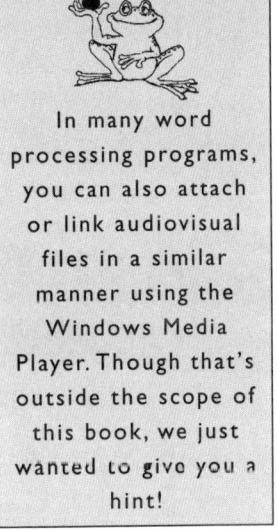

> In many word processing programs, you can also attach or link audiovisual files in a similar manner using the Windows Media Player. Though that's outside the scope of this book, we just wanted to give you a hint!

Practical Exercise Four
Linking Your Sound File To Your Document

Suppose you decide, however, to go back and edit the sound file in some way? What will happen then? Well, the changes will not be reflected in your document. In order for that to happen, you have to link the sound to the document. Here's how to do that:

♪ Make sure you have your mysound.doc open. Go to the end of the sentence and hit [enter] a couple of times to create a new line. On that

15 How To Use Your Newly Made Sounds

line, type "Here's the linked sound file." On the Word Pad (or word processor) menu, click **File/Save**. Leave the document open.

♪ Now, open Sound Recorder and the file you just created, called "myvoice.wav." Using your editing skills, increase the speed of the file by clicking on **Effects/Increase Speed (by 100%)**. Play it now. It should sound quite different. Save the file as "myvoice2.wav."

♪ Now, on the Sound Recorder menu click **Edit/Copy**, as you did before.

♪ Go back to mysound.doc and position the cursor to the left of the word "Here's" in the new sentence.

♪ On the Word Pad menu, click **Edit/Paste Special**.

♪ A dialog box will appear, asking what format you wish to use. Make sure "Wave Sound" is highlighted, then click the radio button to the left of "Paste Link."

♪ Now with the sound linked, you can make changes to that file as you wish and they will be reflected in the document, too. Try changing the speed of the file or adding other effects, or even recording over the file. Be sure and save it again as "myvoice2.wav."

♪ Now open the Word Pad document and the file should sound brand new, with all the updates you've just made. Any time you wish to make additional changes to your sound file, you can do it right within your business document. Maybe you'd like to add some music or add a spoken conclusion at the end. You can, just by double-clicking the icon, which will show the toolbars and menus from your word processing program that allow you to edit the sound file.

Alternately, you can save the document, and go to Sound Recorder to re-edit your sound file.

If you are using a word processing program that does not offer the "Paste Special" command, then that program does not support linking.

How To Use Your Newly Made Sounds 15

> If you need to transport this document to another computer, you need to include the sound file as well, in order for a linked connection to work.
>
> Also, you can use any WAV editor, such as the three we've provided in this book, rather than the Windows Sound Recorder to perform these same tasks.

What Else Can I Do With My Songs?

When you've created a musical composition beyond a small WAV file to use as a system sound, you're understandably going to be emotionally invested in that creation. Whether you're planning to distribute your creations to family and friends, share them with others online or use them as demos to promote your current band, it's wise to consider copyright protection. Copyright laws protect "original works of authorship" including works of music, and is applicable even if your music wasn't professionally published.

You can order copyright forms and brochures from the Library of Congress by telephoning (202) 707-9100, or by mail at:

Register of Copyrights, Copyright Office
Library of Congress
Washington, D.C. 20559-6000

You can also visit their Web site to read or get their Circular 1, entitled *Copyright Basics*, which explains in detail what may be copyrighted, and has the copyright forms you'll need.

However, unless this is a song that you intend to market in some way, and believe it may become a popular song, you don't need to copyright it. Making that choice is yours and yours alone.

How To Use Your Newly Made Sounds

The Library of Congress has a Web site at http://lcweb.loc.gov/copyright/

Looking to promote your songs?

If your songwriting is more than a hobby and you wish to make your music available to publishers and other music business professionals, a good way to start is to visit some of the sites on the Web designed just for that purpose! Try locating songwriting groups on the Web, or promotion sites. We've included a few of those sites for you in the bookmark file on the companion CD-ROM.

Another thing you can do is create your own Web page, and use a site host that allows you some space to upload your songs for others to download. We'll discuss that further in the section on the Internet and the World Wide Web.

More Treats For You

In addition to the above, here are some other treasures you will find on the companion CD-ROM. Where applicable, we've included the Web site for you.

Educational software

Here is a fine sample of the educational software for PC that is available from any number of sources. We've included what we feel to be samples of the best.

Pat's Music Theory

This program provides wonderful information to any newcomer to the world of music, and augments the learning of a professional by testing the user in recognizing musical notes on the staff and much more.

How To Use Your Newly Made Sounds

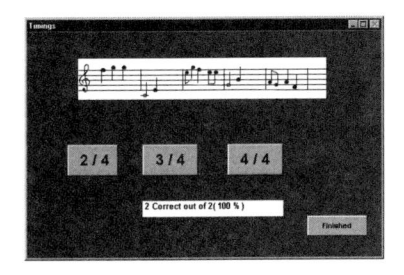

Pat's Music Theory has four categories of testing with as many as eight selections in each category and runs on Windows 3.1 or Windows 95.

DR. Worm's Master Chord Music Theory

This program comes in both Windows 3.x and Windows 95 versions. It teaches guitar chords, chord inversions and music theory, covering major, minor, dominant, suspended, augmented, diminished, power and even more chords. It also features a built-in CD, AVI, MIDI and WAV player.

Ear Power

This program comes in Windows 3.x and Windows 95 versions. It's a great routine for improving your natural ear for music; you will note the improvement day by day. It features voice pitch recognition, rhythm drills, chord recognition, variable difficulty levels and MIDI compatibility.

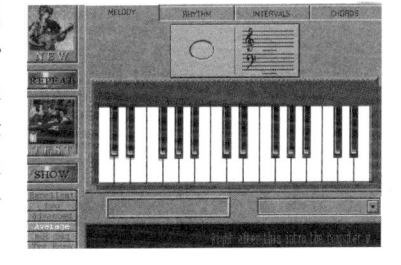

We feel it's a great help for professionals and newcomers alike, and appreciated the polite request to "Please Come Again!" when we exited the program. It's fascinating and well prepared with an attractive interface.

Tune It!

http://www.zeta.org.au/ftp/home/dvolkmer

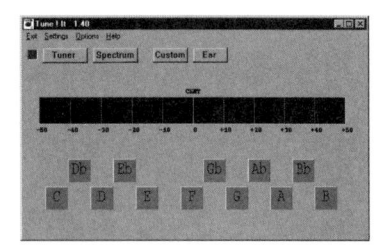

15 How To Use Your Newly Made Sounds

Helps tune your instruments through a microphone or direct connection. It also has exercises to help improve your ear for music. Versions for Windows 95 and Windows 3.x are provided.

Guitar Workshop

http://www.donet.com/~oberwerk/gws.htm

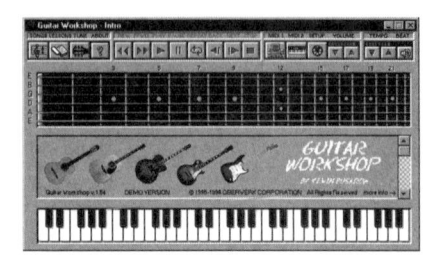

Oberwerk Corporation's Guitar Workshop, by Kevin Busarow, is a fantastic guitar tutorial for Windows 3.x and Windows 95. It is a set of interactive lessons for beginner through intermediate guitarists, and includes about 18 licks appropriate for country, rock, jazz and blues. This program was developed by professional guitarists, and has a good range of skill levels and styles. Included in the program are lessons about chromatic scales, arpeggios, open string runs, ending runs and chordal licks.

Also a composer's tool, Guitar Workshop creates score and tablature on the fly with a simple click of the interactive fretboard. Guitar Tutor also allows you to enter your own compositions or lessons and songs from guitar journals and magazines. You can play them slowly in order to hear them note for note or play them at tempo to learn how they are supposed to sound.

CD Player utilities

Here are some CD Player utilities that you may enjoy!

Autoeject

Automatically ejects your CD from the drive when you shut down Windows! What a nice little utility to have. Now you don't have to remember to remove a CD from your drive; Autoeject will do that for you.

How To Use Your Newly Made Sounds

CDWizzard CD Audio Player

This is a fun replacement by BFM Software for the Windows 95 CD Player. It allows you to save the disc name and the track names in its database, and comes with a full help file enclosed. All this, together with eye-pleasing 3D appearance makes it a good addition to your PC sound system.

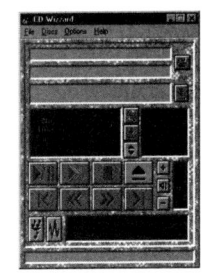

The interface is highly customizable and includes eight large buttons for track selection, eject, scan and other common functions. The volume control allows muting. This great program allows you to perform drag-and-drop programming and includes a searchable, exportable 1,000-disc database with a dialog box. Auto-sample tracks and store them in the database to create a play selection. This program's toolbar displays the current CD status and a track number in the Time window.

3DLEDCD

This is a 3D CD audio player for Windows 95 with an LED that displays track and track times. A treat to use, you can change the colors of the LEDs. You will also need the VB40032.DLL, THREED32.OCX and MCI32.OCX files (also on the companion CD-ROM).

CD32Bit

This is another Windows 95 CD-player for you to try. It provides unique transport controls, colors and lots of user-defined options, including the ability to change the background colors. CD32Bit will run on Windows 95 or Windows NT.

WAV Managers

Sound Play

ebicom.net/~hart/sndplay.html

How To Use Your Newly Made Sounds

Sound Play's main purpose is to sort very large collections of WAV files, and it performs that function magnificently! It remembers a vast number of your favorite WAVs and can play a sample of each WAV file in your directory. A clean, fresh, easy-to-understand interface makes this program really worth trying (versions for Windows 95 and Windows 3.x)!

WavAudit For Windows 95

http://www.stgenesis.org/~leapis/leapware.html

What a wonderful tool! Thanks to LeapWare, Inc., for this fine freeware program. WavAudit is a sound sampling program that allows you to select a group of WAV files in a directory, play them one at a time and then have the option to continue or delete the file. Now you don't have to put up with the tedium of opening one WAV file at a time, playing it and then moving on to the next when organizing your WAVs. A once time consuming activity is now a thing of the past.

Extra treats from Syntrillium

Kaleidoscope

http://www.syntrillium.com/kaleid.htm

Kaleidoscope is a screen saver for Windows (we've provided you with the Windows 3.x and Windows 95 versions). A stunning display is waiting for you—a kaleidoscope with never ending color changes and movement. There are 35 preset styles of kaleidoscope and you can create your own.

Kaleidoscope loves PC music! It will dance to the rhythm of your favorite audio CD. Kaleidoscope for Windows 95 will also dance to the fantastic sounds of Wind Chimes, a fine sound creation by Syntrillium.

How To Use Your Newly Made Sounds 15

You can use Kaleidoscope fully with the shareware version we've included for you. When you register your copy, Syntrillium will issue a registration number that personalizes your copy and removes the registration reminder.

Wind Chimes

http://www.syntrillium.com/chimes.htm

Wind Chimes provides an ambient music background for you while you are hard at work on your PC. It includes sounds that simulate real Wind Chimes, and several other choices such as the sound of a guitar playing, or you can design your own set of sounds and save them in presets to use later.

To hear Wind Chimes you will need a sound card. When Wind Chimes and Kaleidoscope 95 are running simultaneously, Kaleidoscope's screen designs respond directly to the sound coming from Wind Chimes.

Music And The Internet

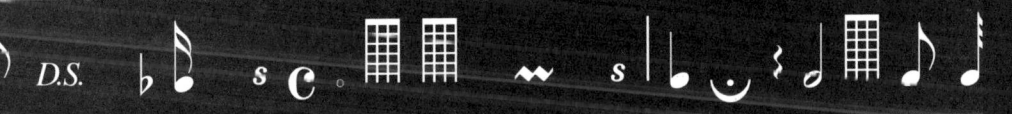

SECTION 4

16

An Introduction To The Internet

Inside Chapter 16

Internet-wise parenting 272
The Internet And Its Components 272
The Internet 272
Newsgroups 274
Mailing lists 274
Netiquette 274
File Transfer Protocol - FTP 277
Connecting To The Internet 277
Online services 278
The World Wide Web 278
Web addresses 279

An Introduction To The Internet

Whether a netizen, a newbie or a luddite, the Internet affects all of our lives. We are inundated with discussions of this growing environment in all forms of media. We hear regularly about the changes in communication trends that the Internet has wrought; it is even accessible through conventional televisions. Some people only vaguely understand what the Internet allows us to do; others avail themselves of its services on a daily basis.

Music is one of the universal topics that has found a niche in cyberspace.

As when moving into a new neighborhood, at first the pathways and stops along the Internet are confusing. But there are good maps out there, and in these pages we hope to provide some interesting information to get you on your way. Before long, you will find your own favorite musical stops, and perhaps create one of your own.

An Introduction To The Internet

Internet-wise parenting

Many of us, including this author, have worked hard as a team to keep online services and the Internet safe and fun for adults and children. Even so, it is best if a parent supervises when children go online, just as he or she would if they were in a shopping mall. (The Internet is like a huge shopping mall, and as you will see, some of the best things in the Internet Mall are free!)

While a teenager may not be as delighted to have company at the computer, he or she may very much enjoy showing you the creations they've made, from "noise" to "music" to "Hiya, Dad!" Helping a child of any age learn new and exciting computer skills can create a wonderful and fondly remembered time for both parent and child.

Last, but not least: if you are a novice to computers, perhaps you'll have the pleasure of learning from the best expert in town—your child!

Details, Details

As an introduction to the workings of the Internet, we've focused mainly on the area of the Internet known as the World Wide Web, or simply "the Web." Most of us have heard these terms, and many of us use the Web on a regular basis. Here are some basics.

The Internet And Its Components

The Internet

Even experts can find explaining the concepts and workings of the Internet to be a challenging task. We'll try to keep it as simple as possible, focussing on the areas of the Internet that suit our musical purposes.

An Introduction To The Internet

The Internet can be described as a collection of computer-generated files stored in computers in many locations—from right next door to your home to a site thousands of miles across the globe, and all points in between. You can visit these other computers from your own PC through telephone lines.

There are some restrictions. A particular area may be locked because you have not "joined" the site. Some sites simply require that you "sign in" before you are permitted to join, others require a paid subscription. They might simply wish to count you as a visitor to their site or add you to their Internet mailing list, or may offer "members only" privileges and/or services. They might also offer the opportunity to notify you about upgrades to your current software, future products or upcoming events.

Once you join these areas, you are issued a password which you will use to gain entry to that site, and which allows you to visit again and again. Fortunately, most musical sites on the Internet are not restricted!

No one owns the Internet. Although it began as a government research project in the late 1970's, it soon expanded from federal scientific research to universities and beyond. Many have predicted what the future will bring; no one knows for sure where the Internet will take us. But the prospects are exciting, even now—just being able to find information about almost any topic that interests you and communicate around the world with others who share those interests!

No one really knows how big the Internet is. Estimates range wildly, from as few as 2 million to as many as 50 or 60 million sites, and the numbers grow daily.

There are many branches of the Internet, and many ways to travel those routes. For our purposes here, we'll mention some of them, and focus on one: The World Wide Web.

An Introduction To The Internet

Newsgroups

Internet newsgroups are areas where people around the globe compose messages from their home or office computers and "post" them with the click of a mouse. Anyone can access a newsgroup to read and reply to these messages, or to create new discussions of their own. One can access newsgroups through a private online service, such as America Online or CompuServe, or via a direct connection through an Internet Service Provider.

Newsgroups number in the tens of thousands, and are organized by topic.

Unlike private online service message areas, newsgroups are usually not well supervised, which increases the likelihood of finding offensive language or topics, or the annoyance of advertising and other posts that do not coincide with the group's purpose. Regardless, newsgroups are an excellent source of information on almost every subject.

Mailing lists

Mailing lists are identical to newsgroups, with one important exception. In order to participate in a mailing list, one must specifically request a subscription, as they are not "public." Some lists are strictly limited; most of them, however, can be joined by anyone.

Mailing lists are one of the oldest part of the Internet, and some estimates place their number at 50,000 or more.

Netiquette

Since the Internet allows us to meet and greet others from across the world, some standards of courtesy have been set, known as "netiquette."

An Introduction To The Internet

Netiquette is suggestions for conduct on the 'net. Internet social behavior is not altogether enforceable, but courtesy and decorum are just as important in the virtual society as in the tangible world. As in any neighborhood, conscientious members of the virtual community abide by these regulations and remind others of them, though there are others who seem to enjoy being offensive. Here are a few of those conventions you should learn about.

When sending e-mail, chatting in a chat area, or posting a message, it's important to be considerate of others by observing these rules:

- **DON'T SHOUT**
  TYPING ALL CAPITAL LETTERS IS EASIER FOR SOME, BUT ON THE INTERNET IT IS THE EQUIVALENT OF SHOUTING AND ANGER. It's also hard to read, so remember to keep your Caps Lock off.

- **Look before you leap**
  Before you post a message or question, read some of the other posts and questions in the area. This will give you a sense of the content and degree of casualness or formality. You may also find the answer to your question without having to ask! Beware of misusing the area. Some areas do not appreciate advertising and others encourage trading and/or sales of goods.

- **Short is sweet**
  Keep your messages short, friendly and to the point. Use several paragraphs rather than one long one to organize your message.

- **Show your best side**
  Take time to check facts and spelling errors, and don't say anything that might embarrass you later. Also, do not give out any personal information, such as your phone number or address.

- **Choose a descriptive subject**
  A post entitled "Please Help" is not as descriptive a title as "Sound Card Problem," or something even more specific, like "Help - XBrand

An Introduction To The Internet

SndCard." This specific title will attract readers who may know the answer to your question or are having a similar difficulty.

Quoting

When you respond to a message from another, do not copy the entire message into your own letter. However, quoting a bit of that person's message can make your response more clear. To differentiate between their comments and your own, use the character ">" at the beginning and "<" at the end to surround the comments you are quoting.

Using Smileys

Internet or online smileys help create expression in your messages. Tone is much harder to convey in writing than in conversation, where we often rely on non-verbal cues to express mood. A friendly smile can deliver the humor you intended, or convey your concern. Internet cues also clarify statements that might be ambiguous in written form. Sometimes, people might not understand that you are kidding by your words, where a smiley will help convey that.

Smileys can be read by tilting your head slightly to the left. Here are a few:

Comments	Chapter comments
:) or :-)	A smile. One has a nose, the other doesn't. Do you see it?
;) or ;-)	A wink and a smile
:D or :-D	A big grin
:(or :-(	A sad face, disappointment or upset
:~(	A frown with a teardrop - crying or sadness
}:>	A little devil
0:>	A little angel
{{{Misty!!}}} {{{Ron!!}}}	Greeting an online friend with curly brackets around his or her name sends a hug

An Introduction To The Internet

♪ Using Shorthand

Internet or online abbreviations are used to shorten common expressions. Here are a few:

Abbr	Definition	Abbr	Definition
BTW	By The Way	ROFL	Rolling On The Floor Laughing
WRT	With Regard To	TTYL	Talk To You Later
IMHO	In My Humble Opinion	WTG	Way To Go!
LOL	Laughing Out Loud		

File Transfer Protocol - FTP

File Transfer Protocol is a basic part of the Internet. It is a repository of software, text and other files you can download from FTP sites on the Internet. You can also upload files to computers to which you are allowed access.

You will find that many Web providers on the Internet have, in addition to their Web sites, an FTP site where files they provide for you to download are stored.

When you download files from an FTP site, or any other location, that process does not remove the file from its original location. You are only making a copy of that file which gets transferred to your own computer's hard drive.

Connecting To The Internet

In order to connect to the Internet, an *access provider* is necessary. This can be a private organization or a telephone company subsidiary that owns a *server*—a system of computers that can connect its subscribers to the Internet.

An Introduction To The Internet

There are a vast number of Internet service providers (ISPs), local and nationwide. In order to get online, a user places a computer phone call to connect to the provider. The provider then connects the user to the Internet.

The speed of the connection and the efficiency of accessing data depends both on the user's modem and the speed of the connection that the access provider offers.

Online services

Besides an ISP, you can go online through online services, such as America Online or CompuServe, which provide access to the Internet with the use of an internal browser. You can connect to these services via your own Internet service provider, or you can dial into these services directly using their own networks. In either case, these systems require an additional subscription.

While you can access the Internet from these services, the reverse is not completely possible. You can go to AOL's or CompuServe's Web sites, but you cannot access their internal areas from the Internet.

The World Wide Web

Technically, the Internet is composed primarily of computers in the US and Europe, and allows users to access text information and computer data files. The Web allows users around the globe to share text, graphics, sounds and even movies and animation. Though some of these Web files are very amateur in design, they are mainly professional, colorful and exciting. These files are accessible to anyone on the Internet (again with some restrictions). There is a wide variety of files available to download, as well—text files, audio and video files, graphic files or any other computerized electronic information.

An Introduction To The Internet

Each "Web site," or location, is made up of "pages." Those pages have been prepared by various companies, educational institutions and individuals. You can post your own page on the Web, which everyone else who visits the Web will be able to see. We will continue to refer to those who manage one collection of Web pages as a "Web site owner," whether an individual or a group.

Let's suppose there is a company named "FunkyFrog Music" that has a Web site. That site may consist of any number of pages. The pages are connected by *hyperlinks* that allow you to access another page of FunkyFrog's information with the click of a mouse. You will usually see a hyperlink appear on a Web page either as a phrase in colored text (often underlined), or as a graphic or icon.

FunkyFrog Music might have several pages of information, divided by areas of interest. Usually, companies and individuals try to normalize their Web pages into similar areas. That means when you visit FunkyFrog Music's Web site, you will see pointers, or hyperlinks, to areas highlighting their Products, Company Information, Technical Support Numbers, Files to Download, perhaps a "map" of their site, and links to other similar sites.

FunkyFrog Music may also have an FTP site where they have stored files for you to download.

Web addresses

In order that you understand what the information in a Web address represents, let's invent a Web address and break apart its components.

FunkyFrog has their own Web server Computer, so do not need an additional ISP. Our imaginary Web site is located at

http://www.FunkyFrog.com

An Introduction To The Internet

To travel the Web, you need to point yourself in the direction of the computer that contains the files you need. Let's look at the first part of the address, "http."

Http is part of the *URL*, so let's talk about that first.

URL

URL stands for "Uniform Resource Locator." It describes the "address," or physical location, of any file on the Internet.

URLs describe many different sources on the Internet. It's the first part of any Internet address you will see while using your browser, and can begin with a number of different things. The ones we'll talk about for our purposes are http:// (that means it's a World Wide Web file!) and ftp:// (File Transfer Protocol).

All the words, abbreviations or symbols that follow http:// or ftp:// describe the path that gets traveled to find each file's location wherever it may reside on the Internet.

HTTP

HTTP (HyperText Transfer Protocol) is the protocol, or method, of sending and receiving Web information from computer to computer. You'll see it as the beginning of an address for any Web site. Most browsers automatically prepend this, so you don't have to type it in for every address you want to visit.

Domain

Domain is another word for the Internet name of the computer that contains the Web site.

Suppose your Internet provider is named "Supercoolnet." You've joined Supercoolnet and use it to sign on to the Internet. The address for Supercoolnet is http://www.supercoolnet.com.

An Introduction To The Internet

"Supercoolnet.com" is the domain name.

"Supercoolnet" is the name registered as the proprietary domain, and ".com" indicates that Supercoolnet is a commercial enterprise. If Supercoolnet were a non-profit organization, it would have the suffix ".org." If it were a component of the government or military, it would end ".gov" or ".mil," respectively.

Your Home Page

If you decide to create your own Web page, your Internet provider may post it as part of their service. If so, you would create your site as a member of that particular domain.

You will be given an address or name to use as a subcategory of Supercoolnet. Pages within Supercoolnet's network are denoted by a forward slash.

If you decide to create a home page for others to visit, and you have chosen the name "musicfan", the Web address for your home page will be:

http://www.supercoolnet.com/musicfan.

All of your other pages connected to your home page will be further subcategories of this.

For instance, you may put information about your hobbies on one page, and your favorite music groups on another page within your collection.

Those pages might be

http://www.supercoolnet.com/musicfan/hobbies

and

http://www.supercoolnet.com/musicfan/rockgroups

An Introduction To The Internet

Others who use Supercoolnet as their Internet provider will also be creating pages. If the chemical corporation Morris, Inc. uses Supercoolnet, then their address would be… you guessed it:

http://www.supercoolnet.com/morris.

Accordingly, an index of the sites within Supercoolnet might be found at http:\\www.supercoolnet.com/index.html.

One way to remember how this works is to think of your own Web site (or another Web site) as the home you live in on the World Wide Web.

Think of the Web as the country you live in, and Supercoolnet as the state. Your "address" for the "home" you live in is "musicfan," and "rockgroups" and "hobbies" are rooms within that home. Morris, Inc.'s company operates out of the building in the same state called "morris." This is pretty much the way all Web pages work!

To read these pages on the Internet, you need a Web browser. A browser is a specifically designed software package that allows you to view HTML files and everything embedded in them. You may notice that most Web pages end with the extension ".html." Hyper Text Markup Language is a basic text file in ASCII with embedded characters, or *tags*, which create the different in font sizes, spacing, graphics, etc., that you see in Web pages and allows you to link them together through *hyperlinks*.

In the next chapter, we'll discuss Web sites more in depth, discover how easy it is to travel the Web, and learn about tools that help make that journey easy and enjoyable!

17
Surfing The Web

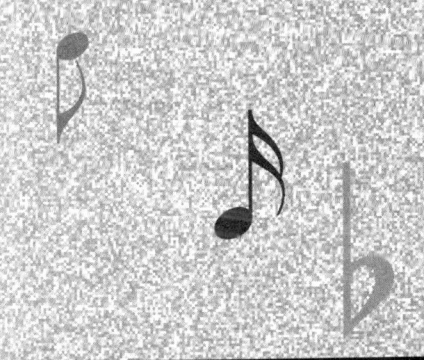

Inside Chapter 17

Search Engines	286
Plug-Ins For Your Browser	287
What's On Those Web Pages?	289
Links	291
FAQ (Frequently Asked Questions)	293
Downloading And Uploading Files On The Internet	295
Bookmarks - Saving Your Links	301

Surfing The Web

The Internet's runaway growth has opened a wealth of resources. With a recent estimate of over ten thousand Websites to visit and as many as 10 million individual Web pages, information abounds on almost any imaginable subject. This has spawned a problem for users: How to sift the information one desires from the ever-increasing chaff? No one has yet found a way to index all of these sites. Plus, new sites are added and old ones disappear daily. Indexing all of these sites would be an enormous task for any individual.

The good news is that you don't really *need* a complete index of all of these sites. It would be almost impossible for an index to keep up with the daily changes on the Web, and most sites won't pertain to your interest anyway.

Q But how do we locate what we need to find on the Web?

A search engine is one of the best tools for finding information on the Web.

17 Surfing The Web

Search Engines

Search engines are essentially research databases that store information on Websites, and contain many more locations than you could gather in a year! Even if you could gather them yourself, you'd spend all your time monitoring for sites that disappear or relocate, as well as registering new sites. Designers of search engines have done most of the research for you, saving you the headaches of keeping up with the Web's growth.

Most search engines display an initial listing of Web categories and subject headings. We'll use the very popular and well-presented Yahoo! search engine as an example. Yahoo (located at http://www.yahoo.com) lists categories for Arts and Humanities, Business, Internet and Computing, Education, Entertainment, Society and Culture and so on. Each category is further subdivided by topic and continues to refine itself into deeper and more focused topic headings.

Search engines also allow you to enter a word or phrase related to your interest. It then searches its own database to supply you with a list of Websites containing the word or phrase you are seeking, with descriptive references and hyperlinks to those Websites. Searching for the word "music" in Yahoo brings up almost 900 categories and 16,000 references. Search engines make it much easier to browse for information. You can click through a search engine's subcategories, looking for something interesting, or you can search for a specific word, phrase or concept.

Those who maintain search engines work to keep their database links updated. This is an exhaustive task, and you may find that some reference points listed in response to your search have disappeared. The message you will usually receive when this occurs is "404—URL not found." Some larger sites will intervene if you look for a page that is no longer on their server(s) and help you locate relevant information on their site.

Surfing The Web

Search engines, like all other parts of the Web, each have a Web address. The URLs (addresses) for some fine search engines are listed in alphabetical order in the table on the right.

Search engine	URL
Alta Vista	http://altavista.digital.com
Excite	http://www.excite.com
HotBot	http://www.hotbot.com
InfoSeek	http://www.infoseek.com
Lycos	http://www.lycos.com
Magellan	http://www.mckinley.com
WebCrawler	http://www.webcrawler.co
Yahoo	http://www.yahoo.com

In addition to search engines, Web "telephone" directories are also helpful. These contain "yellow pages" type directories, providing you with the Web addresses for companies and "white pages" directories for the e-mail addresses of many individuals who use the Internet.

Many search engines offer you the opportunity to reach these white pages and yellow pages at the click of a button. There are also locators that will help you seek actual home and business addresses for many individuals and companies.

Another interesting method of locating sites you enjoy is called "linking," which we'll discuss later in this chapter.

Plug-Ins For Your Browser

The World Wide Web is an amazing playground for music lovers. Many sites offer marvelous music, sound and colorful video displays for you. The combination of sound, video and graphics is known as "multimedia." Your Web browser needs some helper programs to present these home light and-sound shows to you in all their glory. Those helpers are called "plug-ins."

Surfing The Web

Plug-ins for Web browsers are small programs that plug into the browser's programming architecture, extending the browser's abilities. For example, plug-ins can bring audio and video to your browser so you can listen to music and watch film clips on the Internet.

Not all videos and music files are the same, as we've already discovered with WAV and MIDI files. There are any number of audio applications and video players; we've included some of the very best for you with this book, and all of them work with Netscape.

Many Webmasters enhance their site's pages with *streaming audio* and various types of video clips and/or animated graphics. This allows you to play sounds, enjoy background music while you work (or play), and see action films, moving cartoon graphics or icons via your browser. But without the plug-ins that make them work, you cannot hear or see these treats. You can still visit the Website, but you will miss the fireworks!

Streaming allows you to hear sound or see video as the data enters your computer instead of waiting for the entire file to download before playing

Plug-ins are usually *third-party applications*. "Third party" simply means that while a software developer (the first party) has created your browser (you being the second party), other (third-party) developers have created software that can be used by your browser to present special effects. There are plug-ins for business and pleasure, utilities such as calendars, clocks, browser accelerators, download helpers, address books and file readers, 3D and animation image viewers, and others that bring you presentations, sound and Internet radio, chat and virtual reality. The special effects we'll discuss in this book pertain mainly to music and sound with a few utilities that will make life easier for you on the Internet.

288

Surfing The Web

As browsers become more sophisticated, the basic installation might include many features originally available as plug-ins. Those plug-ins may assist you in designing a web page, chatting with friends on the Internet, listening to audio sounds or viewing multimedia clips.

However, you may arrive at a Web page that suggests you need another plug-in to take the best advantage of the site. It can be disappointing not to hear or see all there is to experience, especially when the plug-ins allow videos, sounds, 3D capabilities or even allow you to interact with the contents of the site. We hope the plug-ins on the companion CD-ROM will get you on your way to modifying your own browser environment and help you enjoy all the sparkle and excitement the Web has to offer.

And if you find yourself at a site that has a feature requiring a certain plug-in which you don't have, the site manager will almost always have a link for you to obtain that plug-in.

We'll talk about plug-ins that are especially useful to you as a musician in the following chapter.

What's On Those Web Pages?

An Imaginary Web Company: FunkyFrog Music

Though there are many types of Websites, a lot of the major companies and corporations try to keep their format fairly similar. That's a community-minded act. The Web is, in effect, a huge community, and a lot of its members try to behave like a community. You'll see examples of that on the actual sites we mention in the next chapter.

Let's start with our music software site, FunkyFrog Music, and talk a bit about what you'll find there. After navigating though our site, visiting real Websites will be more familiar to you when you start surfing on your own!

17 Surfing The Web

FunkyFrog's Website is located on this book's companion CD-ROM instead of on the Web. You can visit it by loading your browser program and selecting **File / Openfile** and selecting the default.htm in the WEBSITE directory of the CD-ROM.

FunkyFrog's Website is provided here as an example of a typical Website. Because it is not an actual Website, it can not provide all the features of real Websites. We've made it as complete and realistic as we could, but as you read through the rest of this section, there are some features discussed which you won't be able to actually use. Rather than becoming frustrated when the site or your browser doesn't perform as we've described, please follow the hypothetical example in your mind, so you'll be prepared to take advantage of all the available functions when you visit true Websites.

We've talked earlier about the imaginary company FunkyFrog Music and the Website it owns. FunkyFrog Music operates very similarly to other music and software companies, so we want to use it as an example of what you might find on a corporate software Website, because you'll probably be visiting quite a few of them!

FunkyFrog is an independent recording company and music software designer. It has several music software programs and a lot of cool music for you to enjoy, both in WAV and MIDI format.

When you first arrive at http://www.funkfrog.com, you have come to their home page. As we mentioned, the home page is the top level of any Website. Usually, you can travel to any other point on that site from the home page.

We see five or six icons at the top of the FunkyFrog Music home page, in addition to its logo and some splashy graphics and music.

FunkyFrog Music's Web page designers decided you'd enjoy visiting them more if they added some effects to their Website. So they had some wonderful graphics designed. The graphics are funky and fit right in with FunkyFrog's relaxed and friendly style.

Surfing The Web

They decided to use animated graphics, and then added some wonderful WAV files for your listening pleasure. You'll need some plug-ins to hear and see all the activity FunkyFrog provided for you! We'll imagine we've downloaded three plug-ins—a WAV file player, an animated graphic viewer and a video viewer—and installed them.

Before we start exploring FunkyFrog's collection of Web pages, let's learn a bit about how links (or hyperlinks) work.

Links

Any Website can "point" you to other related information on the Web. Rather than copy all of that additional data to every site, Web page owners provide hyperlinks to other Web pages containing that information. Just click on the link with your mouse to jump to the linked site. FunkyFrog has a page of links for you to follow.

When one Website points you towards another site, it conducts you from its own area to another collection by linking you to a file in that other collection. Those linked files can come from anywhere around the world.

Linking is a kindness! Rather than making you conduct your own exhaustive and exhausting search of the entire Web for similar information, the Website owner gives you a quick path.

The icons at FunkyFrog.com act the same as hyperlinks, or links. They do not connect you to other Websites; instead, they connect you to areas within FunkyFrog Music's Website. These other pages have been compartmentalized to offer you various services and information. Usually, these icons also have written-out hyperlinks next to them, in case your browser does not support graphics or you've chosen the option within your browser to not display graphics.

Surfing The Web

Links can be activated by clicking on descriptive text, graphics or icons (anywhere your cursor changes from a pointer to a hand). Though you see only the graphic, the "hidden" information under that graphic is another of Funky Frog's Web page addresses, or in the case of their Link page, altogether new Website addresses.

Back to FunkyFrog....

In order to demonstrate links, we've listed FunkyFrog Music's icons and the text next to them. Since the icons and text "hide" a link, we'll also write the hidden link name for you, so you know which of FunkyFrog's pages we are visiting.

Icon	Text	Hidden
PRODUCTS	Our products	funkfrog/products.html
CATALOG	Browse or order the catalog	funkfrog/catalog.html
ABOUT	Who is the Funky Frog?	funkfrog/whois.html
JOBS	Employment opportunities	funkfrog/jobs.html
FAQs	What you've asked us	funkfrog/products/faqsone.html
SUPPORT	Tech Support	funkfrog/techsupp.html
NEW	New and upcoming!	funkfrog/news.html
DOWNLOAD	Upgrades	funkfrog/download.html
ARTISTS	Our Bands	funkfrog/artists.html
LINKS	Other sites for you to enjoy	funkfrog/othersites.html

As you travel to each of these pages, you may see some "circular references." That means that links may refer to other pages within FunkyFrog's Website. Each page will also contain a link to return you to FunkyFrog's home page, thus completing the circle.

When you click on the Products icon, you'll arrive at a group of pages that advertises FunkyFrog Music's software programs and describes what they do.

Surfing The Web

You can also order or view their catalog at the Catalog icon. The catalog page (catalog.html) contains links to other pages within FunkyFrog that take you to several different categories of products, since they offer both music CDs and software.

"About FunkyFrog Music" tells you a bit about the company, including some of its history and philosophy. There are also some pages about the employees you may enjoy viewing to learn about the frogs behind the funk. Note how the addresses for the individual employee pages appear in your browser; they are one level deeper than the "About" page.

"Jobs" lets you know if there are employment opportunities at FunkyFrog Music, and how to apply if you are interested. It's a fun place to work!

FunkyFrog has a collection of FAQs, so before we visit the FAQ icon, let's find out what an FAQ is.

FAQ (Frequently Asked Questions)

FAQ is the acronym for "Frequently Asked Questions," which are groups of related questions compiled into a single file. FAQ is pronounced like the word "Fact" without the "t."

FAQs are found throughout the Internet and on many Web pages, usually in the form of a text file. A FAQ on any particular Web page usually pertains to questions about the site or its products or contents. These FAQs are usually questions that a Web page owner anticipates or has already been asked by others.

A FAQ may also pertain to a general topic. For example, a FAQ file on FunkyFrog Music's MIDI instruction program contains some informative questions and answers on just what MIDI is and how it works.

17 Surfing The Web

Back to FunkyFrog...

Now, let's get back to FunkyFrog Music and click on their FAQ icon. You'll see that they have a collection of FAQs here—one on MIDI and how it works and several that answer questions about their various software products and CDs.

Now, let's click the Home button on the FAQ page to return to the home page.

Try clicking on the Artists' icon! Here are sample WAV files of FunkyFrog's wonderful musical artists! Once you've finished this, click on "Home" again.

Now let's visit the Tech Support area by clicking on that icon. Tech Support includes links to a couple of areas, including a link to send you back to FunkyFrog Music's home page and a link to the Download area. Though you can get directly to "Downloads" from FunkyFrog Music's home page, you can also get there from the Tech Support page.

Why would you go to Tech Support first? Well, maybe you have a new product from FunkyFrog Music, and aren't sure what extras might be offered for you. Tech Support may be the place to find information on upgrades and updates for your product. It also contains a link to the FAQ pages.

The Tech Support page also provides you with addresses and telephone numbers to contact FunkyFrog Music about a question you have that you don't see answered on their Website.

This time, we wanted to go to Tech Support first, to find out what you need to download. Maybe next time we visit, though, we'll already know the file we need to acquire and how to install it, so we may decide to go to "Downloads" directly from the Home page.

Surfing The Web 17

When you click on "Downloads," you have access to the whole collection of files available for download. But what a surprise! Let's pretend you click on the first one, "Upgrade to Midi Funk 3.0 for Windows 95," all of a sudden "http://www.funkfrog.com/downloadconfiguration" has disappeared from your browser. Instead, you see "ftp://funkfrog.com/pub/upgrade/midifunk32.exe." What happened?

FunkyFrog Music has an FTP site where it stores all of its files that are available for downloading. Once you selected the file you need, FunkyFrog Music linked you to their FTP site to download that file.

We told FunkyFrog we wanted a file called "midifunk32.exe," which is an upgrade to their Funky Midi program. Clicking on that description took us to their FTP site to download the file to our hard drive.

Let's see how to download that file we were looking for, since we're at the FTP site, then go back to FunkyFrog Music.

Downloading And Uploading Files On The Internet

One of the wonderful features of the Internet and online services is that you can both *download* and *upload* sound files. A simple way to think of these features is to think of an Internet FTP repository as a "post office." Downloading a file is very much like ordering something from a company by phone or mail order, and getting a package in the mail! It simply means selecting a file you wish to have and allowing the Internet to send it directly to your hard drive.

295

Surfing The Web

Uploading is just the opposite; it can be thought of as sending a package to someone else in the mail. You select a file you wish to share with a friend or with a forum on the Internet and send that file to the location of your choice using your modem. In both cases, these files are traveling across the telephone wires to reach their destinations, rather than being carried on a postal truck. We will discuss how to do both of these things on the pages that follow.

When you choose a single file to download from the Internet, it can be in any number of formats. They include files with suffixes of EXE (executable), ZIP (PKZIP or WinZip compressed), DOC or TXT (documents) and others. When the Internet prepares to download it for you, the program's download procedure will usually suggest a filename for you. That file, whatever it is called, will have an extension of ".wav," if it is in fact a WAV file, or ".mid" for a midi file, ".txt" for a text file, and so on.

Sometimes this is harder to determine in Windows 95, because the download procedure suggests a filename, but may not indicate the extension. This is because the Windows Explorer already "knows" what kind of file is going to be downloaded and doesn't tell you what it knows!

That's a fine feature of Windows 95, but it sometimes creates confusion for new PC users. However, if you look in the example below, you'll note that, underneath the default file name, Windows 95 shows the type of file it will save the new file as. That allows you to save time by simply clicking "OK." Then the download begins.

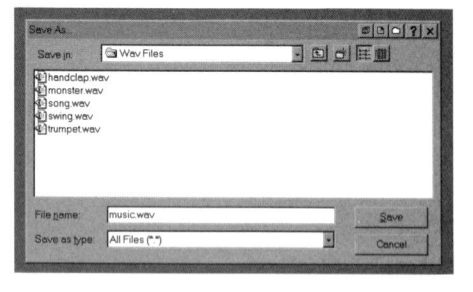

> It is important to note that some online sites contain files that have not been checked for viruses. It is always good practice to virus-check any file you download from the Internet prior to unzipping or using that file.

296

Surfing The Web

Compressed files

There is an exception to this; sometimes the selected file, no matter what the format (.wav or .mid, for example), will have an different extension of ".zip." Often files offered for downloading on the Internet are in a "zipped" (compressed) format. Compressed files occupy less space, thus they can be transferred more quickly than full-length files. After receiving a zipped file, the user simply runs an unzipping program to decompress the program and run it.

New PC users sometimes assume, once they learn how to compress files by "zipping," that all file formats get very compressed, and therefore zip every file they attach to e-mail or upload to the Internet. When a single WAV file is being uploaded, there is *some* reason to do so, but only if the file is quite large. While WAV files can be compressed somewhat, they are usually small files. The zipping process creates extra steps, so it's not necessary to zip them unless you wish to upload more than one in a single online session.

Zipping several files into one "package" enables you to send several files at once via e-mail or to upload a related collection of WAVs to an online forum, Website, or newsgroup to which you have access.

If the files you've downloaded are in zipped, or compressed, format (indicated by the ".zip" extension on the file), you can easily "unzip" them. However, I'd recommend downloading an uncompressed file or two first, and playing them, just to make sure you understand the procedure.

WinZip is a very popular utility that will help you zip and unzip files in Windows and Windows 95. The shareware version is available at www.winzip.com and on the companion CD-ROM.

17 Surfing The Web

Getting set up to use WinZip

When you install WinZip's 32-bit program for Windows 95 it places an icon on the Start Menu and one on your Desktop. That's nice, because when you click on "Start" you'll see WinZip right there waiting for you, instead of having to search through the Programs choices (although it also appears there).

We're presuming that you've installed a copy of WinZip to your hard drive and allowed it to install itself in the default manner.

If you are extracting WAV or MID files, you may wish to put them in a temporary directory to "check them out" before moving them to your C:\Windows\Media folder. So before you begin unzipping, create a folder on your C:\ drive called "Unzip" or whatever you choose. Move your zipped file (with the .zip extension) to that folder before you begin.

> WinZip for Windows 3.x installs itself into its own group by default, and you can open the program by clicking on the WinZip Group, then clicking on the WinZip icon.

Unzippingfiles

You can use a number of methods to unzip files; we're giving you our favorite one, using the imaginary wavfiles.zip file to illustrate.

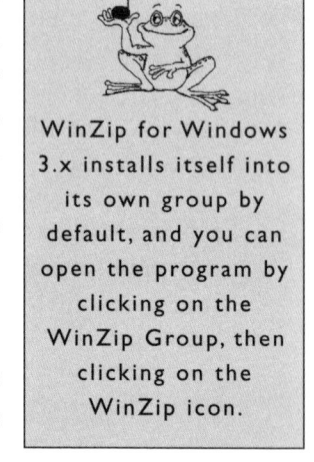

Double-click on the WinZip icon on your desktop to open it. Read the copyright message that appears, then click on "I Agree" to accept the terms and conditions. WinZip will now display its opening screen.

Click the Open folder icon and the "Open Archive" dialog box appears.

Locate the file you wish to unzip. Select your file and click so that it appears in the File name box.

Click "Open."

Now you will see the contents of the zipped file in the WinZip opening screen.

Surfing The Web

Now we'll extract the files, by clicking on the "Extract" icon.

Clicking on "Extract" opens the Extract dialog box. Select the destination directory and click the "Extract" button, and WinZip will extract the file or files from the archive by writing them to the directory of your choice.

Close WinZip!

EXCEPTION: If you use an online service (such as CompuServe or America Online) rather than an independent browser to surf the Web, the service "delivers" the files you find on that service to your hard drive. The default download folder in Windows95, which you can find using the Windows Explorer, is called "Download" and is a sub-folder located inside the CompuServe (WinCim) or America Online (AOL) folder.

Windows 3.x is the same. The directory where downloads are delivered to your hard drive can be found by locating the "Download" directory under AOL or WinCim. Use the Windows 3.1 File Manager to locate this folder.

If using an online service, you will find that there are areas in which you are permitted to upload files you've created. If you have just written a MIDI file, you may be permitted to upload it to the online music forum by locating that forum's upload icon. Once you click on that icon, the program's software asks you which file on your hard drive you wish to upload. Locate the directory on your hard drive where you've placed the file, select it, then click on "OK" or "open" (depending on the program) to upload it for others to share.

You can do the same for a newsgroup on the Internet, or you can send files to your friends by private e-mail.

Let's suppose you've found a great file or demo program at FunkyFrog Music that you'd like to share with a friend. Rather than direct your friend to FunkyFrog Music (which is another option!), you just want to attach it to an e-mail message for him or her

Surfing The Web

Most Internet providers and all online services supply the user with an e-mail inbox and outbox, which means you can both send and receive e-mail to and from other users across the Internet.

You can use this same e-mail to send files you wish to share with friends, family and business associates. With small text files you have a choice of pasting that file directly into the e-mail window or sending it as an attachment to the email. But other files, such as WAVs or formatted documents with text and graphics, cannot be pasted into the body of an e-mail message.

Most email services provide the ability to attach such files to e-mail messages, with just the click of a button. For example, an e-mail message page in America Online has a button titled "attach." This button allows you to attach a file on your hard drive to be sent along with your letter.

Once the e-mail is sent, the attachment is uploaded to a repository within America Online, and waits there to be downloaded by the recipient.

Internet e-mail works in a similar fashion. Most browser programs have a mail service contained within the browser. Check the information contained in your browser's documentation to see how to set up your e-mail. (You'll also need some information from your Internet provider in order to do this.) These browser mail programs also allow attachments.

The various providers use several types of encoding procedures for attachments; you will need to determine what your provider uses. MIME and UUE encoding are the most frequently used. The person who receives files from you via Internet mail may need a MIME or UUE decoder to view the files you have sent.

In order to use files you have sent, the recipient will need a program capable or reading those files after they have been decoded. For example, if the person to whom you have sent a WAV file does not have a program that plays WAVs, he or she will not be able to hear those files until such a program is installed.

We've finished the download now, and sent e-mail to our friend. If you don't see a way to leave the FTP site and return to http://funkfrog.com/

Surfing The Web

download.html (the download page), don't panic. Just click your browser's Back button on the top menu and you'll go to the previous page your browser displayed, the Download page in our case.

This works because your browser "remembers" the last several pages you've visited in your surfing. You may have been visiting a site earlier today before you went to FunkyFrog Music. You may be able to press that Back button enough times to return to the earlier site.

Your browser only remembers these pages for each visit. Once you've exited from your browser, and re-start the program, those links will no longer be there. There is a way to mark sites for a longer period of time. Bookmarks (in Netscape Navigator) and Favorites (in MS Internet Explorer) are quick links to sites you visit often.

Bookmarks - Saving Your Links

Once we left FunkyFrog and traveled to all of the links that FunkyFrog provided, it's time to stop for the day. Surfing the Web gets exhausting! It would have been nice if we could remember all those places we liked, because we probably are not going to remember them all tomorrow.

If you like a site, you can save that address. Not only because you may want to visit again and again, but you may have begun at a great site, followed its links, and lost your place, and now you want to get back there. A bookmark, just as the word implies, saves your place for you as you browse on.

To save a bookmark in Netscape, you can either click on **Bookmark / Add Bookmark** on the main menu or you can right-click your mouse on the page and select "Save Bookmark."

To return to that page, click **Bookmark** then select the bookmark you created for that page. The choice "Go To Bookmarks" allows you to further edit that newly saved bookmark. You can choose "Go To Bookmarks," highlight the

Surfing The Web

bookmark, then right click to edit the description or add a notation about that site, mentioning, for example, what's there, why you like this site and what you found appealing about it.

A related Website might contain more information about one of FunkyFrog's recording artists, a fan club page, for example. This page may have been created by someone other than FunkyFrog, perhaps by the artist's public relations firm, Top Hat PR. It is an excellent site to visit, and FunkyFrog knows that. This artist has also starred in some movies, so FunkyFrog's link page may connect you to some video clips on that artist as an actor. WAVs and live video of that singer's music may be available, too.

You can travel to any of those sites and return to FunkyFrog to try the others, or you can save the information about those links to visit them another day.

Top Hat Public Relations may have some great links to other bands you like, too. Soon, you're way down the road, a long distance from FunkyFrog. Remember to use those bookmarks and you'll always find your way back.

Remember earlier, we told you our FunkyFrog Music's Web page address was http://www.funkfrog.com, and that pages in that collection would always begin with those letters? Well, that doesn't mean you need to use their full address to reach their site. The main reason Netscape is the most popular browser is its ease of use. The plug-ins and bookmarks you will find on the Internet are nearly always designed to work with Netscape.

In some newer browser versions, certainly Netscape's, you no longer need to type the full Website address. We've found that (using our pretend example) instead of typing "http://www.funkfrog.com," we can just type "funkfrog." The characters "http://," "www." and ".com" are assumed! (Netscape always assumes the suffix is ".com," though, so you still need to enter the full address for organizations, government sites, etc.)

Now that we've explored a lot of what our imaginary company, Funky Frog Music, has to offer let's find out what's really out there for music lovers!

18
The Web For Musicians

Inside Chapter 18

How To Search The Net: Getting A Quick Start	305
The Companion Bookmark: Following Links And Saving Bookmarks	306
The Webring—A Community Concept	307
What's Out There For Me?	308
Magazines, newspapers and journals	308
Hardware	309
Software	310
Software upgrades for products you use	310
Audio And Multimedia—The Music Lover's Plug-ins	313
Audio Video Plug-ins	314
Apple QuickTime	314
Real Audio & Video	315
Crescendo (Plus) By Liveupdate	316
Yamaha Mid-Plug	317
Internet Phone by VocalTec	318
Live3D by Netscape	319
Shockwave by Macromedia	320
Koan by SSEYO	321
AnySearch	322
Cache Compactor	322
CYBERsitter	322
Other Types Of Software And Files	323
Artists	323
Your own Web page	324
Sound files	324
Music File Downloading	324
Making Friends On The Internet	325
Quality of Sound Files - Win Some, Lose Some	326
Research repositories	327
Going interactive	328
Some Amazing Web Sites	328
Astounding sites: A bit of everything	331

The Web For Musicians

How To Search The Net: Getting A Quick Start

Let's try an easy search to locate Websites containing the word "music." As you'll soon see, this is a broad search parameter, because "music" is such a general term. As you do more searches you'll learn how to focus your queries to receive more accurate responses. Once you've signed on to your Internet provider and loaded the Web browser, put your cursor in the "Location:" or "Go to:" box and type "www.yahoo.com" to arrive at the Yahoo search engine (most browsers automatically assume the "http://" prefix).

Note that it may take time for Yahoo! to load completely. Once it has loaded you will see a "Search" box that allows you to type in a word. Type in the word "music" and click the icon that says "Search."

In moments you will get a response from Yahoo!, bringing you thousands of places to visit that contain the word "music."

The Web For Musicians

Of course, this is far too many sites for you to visit. There are ways to refine searches, and each search engine contains instructions on how to do a more advanced search using their application.

Each of the major search engines uses a slightly different protocol, and while the returns of different engines for a specific query will overlap, one may find relevant sites missed by another. Yahoo!, for instance, focuses more on entertainment; some others are configured to search only sites of publicly-held companies, for example. Try several others to get a feel for the "personalities" of the different engines.

If you find a place you like while you are traveling, you can save that to your bookmark file by clicking on **Bookmark / Add Bookmark**. Though we've included one for you on the companion CD-ROM, you should also start your own. Later, you can combine the two bookmark files, if you like, by following Netscape's instructions for "combining bookmarks."

The Companion Bookmark: Following Links And Saving Bookmarks

In this chapter we describe what is available for you as a musician on the Web. We've included a comprehensive Netscape bookmark file on the companion CD-ROM that will take you to the far reaches of the musical Web with the click of a mouse! See Chapter one for more information.

We've divided the companion bookmarks into categories for you, such as Musical Instruments, MIDI and WAV file sites, Music Magazines and so forth. In addition, we've included what we feel to be several of the most amazing sites on the Web, under the category AMAZING. It's hard to choose

The Web For Musicians

the best of the best—there are so very many sites that are well presented and maintained and are full of informative resources and links. We selected several sites from different categories to get you on your way to enjoying the best the Web has to offer.

Using Bookmarks is not a difficult task. You can easily make a list of your own, but before you do, you may wish to try the one we've prepared for you! Besides providing quick access to great sites, our list is also an example of how one may organize bookmarks into folders and subfolders to help you easily find the site you seek. You may find some favorites of your own there; feel free to add and delete. Don't worry! If you make mistakes, you can always reinstall our original from the companion CD-ROM.

The Webring—A Community Concept

The Webring is another fantastic way to travel the Web: www.webring.org The Webring is a completely free service designed by a growing group of community-conscious Internet users from home pages all over the world. The Webring ties together sites with similar content by linking them in circular fashion: a ring. Once you are at any site in a particular "ring," you can click on a "Next" or "Previous" link to go to the next or previous site in the ring. Eventually, you will end up where you started, though it may take a while to see all the sites in the larger rings.

As well as moving to the next or previous site, you can list the next five sites in the ring and jump about the ring in a random fashion. You can also get an index of all the pages in the loop. And all of this is free!

The Sound King takes you through a series of musically related pages. Try the Webring; we think you'll like it!

15 The Web For Musicians

What's Out There For Me?

There are so many ways in which a musician will find the Internet a wonderful place to work and play, it's not easy to know where to begin. You'll find information on your favorite types of music and bands, discographies, biographies, lyrics and chords to their tunes, and sample files of their hit tunes to play. But there's much, much more! Let's see some of the wonders of the musical Web.

By installing our bookmark file you will be able to travel to all of these areas easily. You can do that right now or just read about some areas there are to visit. Let's discover what the Web offers, so that you'll have an idea of the categories of information we've included in the bookmark file or so that you can search for these areas on your own.

Whether you buy or do your research via the Web, you can find nearly limitless resources on all types of things. You can purchase music software, hardware and supplies, CDs of your favorite artists, WAV or MIDI sounds to use with business applications or as system sounds, magazines on many musical subjects, videos, souvenirs of your favorite band, sheet music, music books and instruments. Most of this same information is also available for free!

Magazines, newspapers and journals

Another way you can pass some leisurely hours on the Web is reading about your favorite subjects. There are publications on every imaginable music form: rock, pop, world music, jazz, classical and more. Computer music journals contain reviews and advice on hardware and software, and instrumental magazines explore the old, new and future of your favorite musical instrument. There are magazines on guitar building and piano tuning, dance forms and multimedia.

The Web For Musicians

Hardware

Once you've traveled to manufacturers' sites to research and shop for sound cards, CD-ROMs and other music peripherals, why would you return to those sites?

Manufacturers' pages, as you will learn, are full of other information besides what products they offer and price lists. As we demonstrated on the FunkyFrog Website, manufacturers may offer you additional technical information, FAQ pages, some fun music and enhancing upgrade files to download and links to reviews and user groups.

Many types of hardware have accompanying software called "drivers." When a manufacturer updates a driver for your hardware, they will often upload it to their Web site for you. There, you can read about changes and improvements that have been made to the drivers and learn how to download and install them. They may also provide you with an e-mail address to ask specific questions about the hardware you own.

You will need drivers to use your sound card and CD-ROM. Other musical components may have accompanying software available, too.

Many sound card manufacturers offer their own versions of WAV editors, MIDI composers and other utilities. They may or may not be as good as the other programs available, but there is a general guarantee that programs accompanying your sound card will most likely be compatible, and they are usually included with the card at no extra cost.

Some companies will even offer to contact you by e-mail whenever the software for your component is updated or when there is other information they feel may be of interest to you. Look on their Web page or check your documentation when you register for a question similar to "Do you want to be notified of upgrades?"

The Web For Musicians

We've included major hardware manufacturers' sites for you in the bookmark file on the companion CD-ROM.

Software

All kinds of software are available on the Web. We learned about some of those music programs in the software section of this book. But there's much more!

In addition to downloading music files and other information from the Internet, you can also download programs. Several general categories of software programs are available to you. Some of those categories of software are:

- Upgrades and drivers
- Utilities for programs you own
- Demo programs, such as the ones provided on the companion CD-ROM
- Browser plug-ins

Software upgrades for products you use

When you buy a software product, it is good to register it with the software company, mainly because you may be entitled to free upgrades of your product. Often, software companies make refinements to programs after their release, mainly due to feedback from users. Visiting publishers' sites for programs you own can be useful for reporting any glitches you may have discovered, obtaining technical support and acquiring "patches" or upgrades for your program.

The standard method for upgrading products has existed for many years. When you visit the Web site, usually in the Technical Support area, you may find upgrades to your version of a program. You are given the opportunity to download that patch and are given instructions as to how to install it.

But a new convention is also on the Internet—many software companies are beginning to provide "live" upgrades for your programs. This means that when you sign on to the Web and visit their site, they offer to download and install any upgrade components for you on the spot.

In addition to upgrading your programs, you may also find optional "add-ons" for your program. For example, you may find a file that, when downloaded and installed, allows you to use your current word processing software to create Web pages.

In addition to these courtesy files, many other types of software programs are offered over the Internet, ranging from simple music and text files to full-blown programs. Some are completely functional; others are demonstration programs that let you view and try out the program before purchasing.

The programs offered for you to try or to continue using fall into four monetary categories, as follows.

- Public Domain: Software anyone can use as they please; the author(s) has relinquished title and copyright.

- Freeware: Software supplied by the creator at no cost. Title and copyright for the program are retained by the author.

- Shareware: Software distributed by the author or through public channels. No fee is required to try the program, but you are requested to register with the author if you continue to use the program beyond a specified period (usually thirty days). Fee payment is on the honor system, although some demos may not work beyond a certain trial period.

- Commercialware: Software created by companies or individual authors which require monetary compensation to acquire and use. Demos may be available for a trial period or with limited functions.

These categories apply to the many working programs available on the Internet. Companies that offer programs for sale on the 'net are usually eager for you to try them out and therefore encourage you to download and install a working demonstration of their program.

Some of those products may be "crippled" in one way or another. "Crippling" is a common practice in demonstration versions of software, and the techniques are varied. Some programs allow you to use them for only a short period of time, then cease to work. Others disable one or more features of the program. In this way, software companies can demonstrate their wares and create interest without giving their product away free.

Though some plug-in developers ask you to register your product and pay the small purchase fee, their demo may be a complete working copy, with no expiration date and no crippled attributes. These developers are counting on your honesty to not use their product without reimbursing them for the development costs.

When a software product is offered as a full, working copy, registration and payment for that product usually guarantees you two important things: 1) technical support and 2) free or inexpensive upgrades of the program. It's not a bad thing to pay the creators of this software for all their hard work, either.

There are many types of programs for you to try or buy on the Web. We've provided some of these—music education software, utilities and sound files—on the companion CD-ROM and discussed them in the Software section of this book. Now let's look at another important category of musical software available for you on the Web—plug-ins for your browser, some of which can also be found on the companion CD-ROM.

Audio And Multimedia—The Music Lover's Plug-ins

Though there are many categories of plug-ins, the most exciting ones for musicians pertain to graphics, animation, audio and video, separately and combined into multimedia formats. Audio plug-ins allow you to cruise the web finding sound bites with which to play and interact. Other plug-ins allow you to set up a virtual jukebox, enjoy karaoke fun and listen to radio programs broadcast from around the world.

Animation and graphics plug-ins allow you to enjoy motion graphics from cartoon characters to stunning and hip contemporary displays.

Multimedia plug-ins bring the Web to life. You can participate in round-table interviews of performers, play interactive games, listen to streaming radio programs on every imaginable subject and hear and see a live concert of your favorite performer.

We've included some Netscape plug-ins for you on the companion CD-ROM. Music lovers will enjoy these plug-ins, as they "beef up" Netscape's capabilities to give us access to the musical sights and sounds that we'll find as we surf the Web.

You will need both a sound card and headphones or speakers to enjoy the world of audio on the Web, as well as one or several audio plug-ins for your browser.

Netscape's default player comes bundled into the browser program, and is called the "NAPlayer." It plays a very limited selection of audio files. We suggest using another player if you want enjoy all that audio on the Web.

Audio plug-ins interpret data received from an encoder/server on the Web and play it for you as music. The server is the computer equivalent of the radio station transmitter that broadcasts across the airwaves; computer radio stations broadcast in compressed digital code.

The quality of your "reception" of these sounds depends on the compression scheme used by the broadcaster and the speed of your modem. Of course, the part you can control is the modem speed—the faster your modem transmits, the better the sound quality of streamed audio is likely to be.

Let's take a look at some of the animation, audio and multimedia plug-ins available to you.

Audio Video Plug-ins

Apple QuickTime

www.quicktime.apple.com/dev/devweb.html

Apple QuickTime provides stunning multimedia presentations and is the industry standard for integrating video, sound, graphics and text. Some QuickTime movies that you will find on the Web may take some time to load, but most, because of QuickTime's "fast-start" feature, allow you to enjoy the content while it is downloading from the Website.

QuickTime has several components:

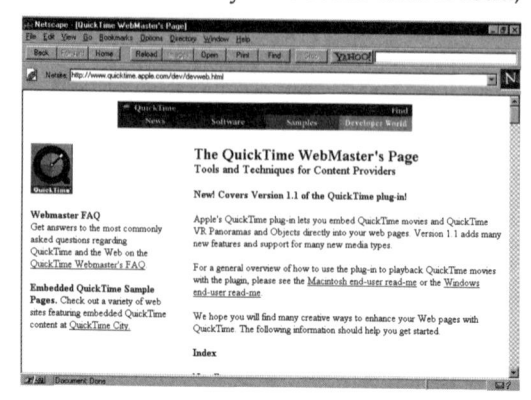

- QuickTimeVR, a virtual reality designer/reader
- QuickTimeLive for live webcasts
- QuickTimeConferencing for cross-platform video conferencing and collaboration
- QuickTime's original digital movie format

The QuickTime applets let you explore a 360 degree virtual environment; participate in live, interactive webcasts; collaborate with people across platforms, across town or across the globe; and view streaming movies incorporating video, animation, sound, text and simulated three dimensions

Real Audio & Video

www.realaudio.com

Progressive Network's RealAudio is one of the most-popular and -supported plug-ins for receiving streaming sound from the Internet. This plug-in is downloaded at roughly 1000 copies per hour. RealVideo is a recently added component to bring high-quality streaming video to you from the 'net.

RealAudio and Video support live audio events over the 'net as well as audio synchronized to video images. This creates the opportunity for live multimedia performances broadcast around the world.

When your browser encounters a RealAudio file (.RA), it automatically launches the RealAudio player and the RealAudio control Panel. You can monitor the progress of the file in the control panel, indicated by a slider bar. The easy-to-use control panel features play/pause, stop and skip buttons. You also have the option of viewing the title, author and copyright information of the file. There is also a "stay on top" feature that keeps the player window in view while you move among web pages.

The PlayerPlus is the top of the line, and six preset buttons (just like your car radio) to bring your favorite music, news or sports to you at the click of a button. A scan button is also provided, letting you browse hundreds of live online radio stations and Websites.

To supplement these features, Progressive Networks also operates www.timecast.com, a Website that acts as a directory for all live and on-demand webcasts available at any given time.

RealAudio deserves its reputation as one of the most popular Internet audio formats. The controls are easy to learn and the features are useful instead of being glitzy.

Crescendo (Plus) By Liveupdate

www.liveupdate.com/cplus.html

Crescendo was the first MIDI plug-in player for Netscape Navigator. Crescendo Plus's incorporated streaming technology and MIDI's naturally small file size makes this an efficient and fast means of hearing music on the Web.

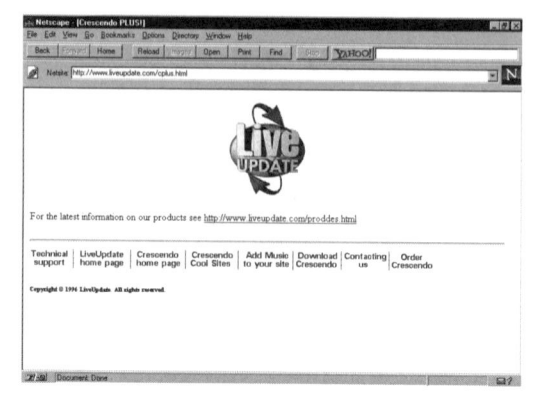

The Web For Musicians

When you reach a Website that includes MIDI music, Crescendo Plus will automatically launch its small control panel and begin playing the streamed music. The player's graphic interface has buttons for playing, stopping, fast forwarding and rewinding files.

Crescendo Plus is the streaming version of the plug-in and is available from Live Update via their Web page (for a small registration fee). Crescendo has most of the same features as the Plus applet and, besides being on the companion CD-ROM, is also available from Live Update's Website.

Yamaha Mid-Plug

www.yamaha.co.jp/english/xg/html/midhm.html

MidPlug from Yamaha reads MIDI files off the Internet. What separates this plug-in from the other MIDI players is that it's loaded with features that provide excellent playback quality and includes options to manipulate the playback.

Soft Synthesizer with 128 GM-compatible voices, eight drum kits and reverb is built into the player. It automatically launches when MIDI files are present and provides thirty-two note simultaneous polyphony.

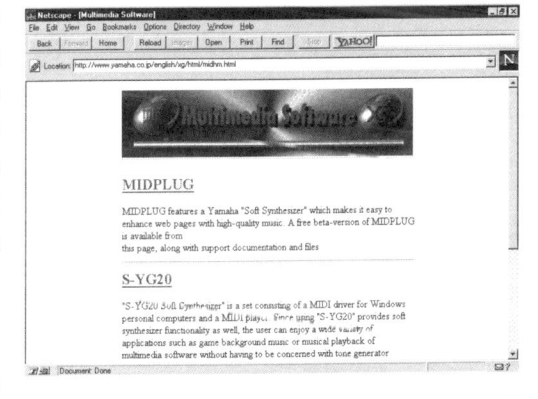

The control panel, which may be hidden if desired, has standard controls for play, pause and stop, plus tempo and pitch controls, each with a return-to-default key. Many plug-ins will play MIDI files, but MidPlug lets you do more with them.

Internet Phone by VocalTec

www.vocaltec.com

Internet Phone is the realization of real-time real-voice Internet communications. This is the plug-in that allows you to speak around the world for the price of an Internet connection.

To take full advantage of Internet Phone your computer should be equipped with a full duplex sound card (two half-duplex (standard) sound cards can also be used with proper configuration). You can use one standard sound card, but you must coordinate speaking and listening with your other party since a half-duplex card will only transport information in one direction at a time. Two half-duplex cards or one full-duplex card will allow you to listen and speak at the same time, just like any other phone.

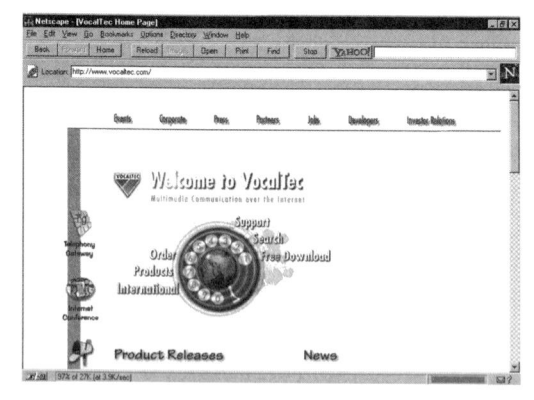

You will also need a microphone and speakers or an earphone. VocalTec recommends using an earphone or headphones to avoid acoustic feedback. This is especially true during full-duplex conversation. Otherwise, your microphone may pick up the speech emitted by the speakers and transmit it back to the sending party, creating an irritating loop for your friend and effectively blocking you out of the conversation.

Internet Phone works across platforms, so Windows and Macintosh users can speak together over the Internet. You can also take advantage of traditional phone features, including call waiting, call forwarding, caller ID, call screening and directory assistance. You can even add a voice mail box to your Web page.

The Web For Musicians

Internet Phone includes many more features than those discussed here. It's a very useful product with many convenient features that allow you to communicate around the world with your own voice in real time. The controls are quick and intuitive and many are graphically oriented.

Live3D by Netscape

home.netscape.com/comprod/products/navigator/live3d/index.html

Live3D is a virtual reality player plug-in. It's based on the industry standard Virtual Reality Modeling Language (VRML), which takes advantage of the JavaScript programming language. Virtual reality allows you to interact with objects and move around in a virtual three-dimensional environment. Any setting you can imagine can be created and posted on the Web. Although you'll only run the risk of confusing it with "real" reality if you spend way too much time with your computer, it has useful applications, is neat to play with and you can experience some interesting computer environments.

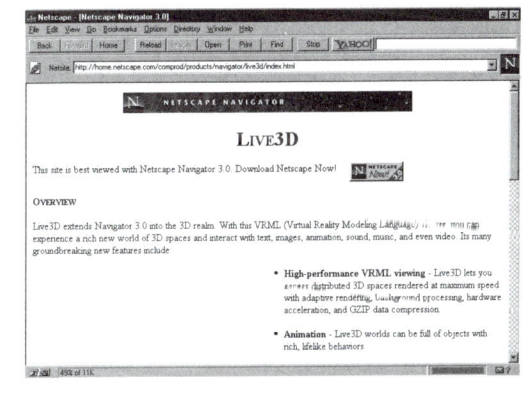

Using adaptive rendering, background processing, hardware acceleration and data compression, Live3D is built for speed, though you'll still get a smoother picture with a faster modem.

Internet virtual reality is in its infancy, but as modeling becomes more precise, data gets more compressed and modems and CPUs get faster, expect to see a lot more of it serving many more functions. San Francisco, CA, yellow pages already let your fingers walk through a virtual town, visually locating businesses and information. To get more information on Live3D you can visit www.netscape.com. From there you may track down the Cool Worlds page to experience a variety of VRML objects and environments.

Shockwave by Macromedia

www.macromedia.com/

Macromedia's Shockwave series includes some of the most widely used plug-ins available. Shockwave's audio component provides CD-quality streaming sound with compression ranging up to 176:1, more than three times as small as the nearest competitor. This provides clear sound even on modems with maximum baud rates of 14.4Kbps.

Shockwave Director allows developers to put Internet graphics into motion. The reader plug-in lets you view these presentations just as they were created, regardless of the Internet's limitations.

Director presentations can bring clickable buttons, URL links, digital video movies and sound right into your browser's window.

Koan by SSEYO

www.sseyo.com

The Koan plug-in lets you enjoy music created in collaboration between the creator and the listener. Each playback of Koan music is unique. This is possible because a Koan author creates a "chute" of possibility for each song. Each time a song is played it runs in a unique path through this chute. It is, however, constrained within the chute as configured by the author, like a ball bearing following a bobsled run.

Designers use 150 specially-constructed variable controls to produce and influence the music. It can even be configured to respond to input from the listener, meshing the music engine with the listener's perceptions and situation, making the listener a participant instead of a passive listener.

Koan is available in two flavors: "chill-out ambient" environmental sounds and "floor-shaking bass and drum" pulses of contemporary, upbeat dance music.

Koan uses MIDI file format for its technical features, speed and small file size (a one kilobyte Koan file can produce eight hours of music). Instead of downloading a prerecorded sound file, Koan transports just the music parameters. The music is then generated locally and in real time.

The 32-bit plug-in will play Koan music that is embedded on a Web page and takes 287K on your hard drive. A stand-alone player takes 477K (532K for the two combined) and will let you listen to Koan music while you browse, independent of specific pages. The stand-alone version also provides volume, pan, chorus and reverb controls.

A MIDI sound card is required to translate the information into music. Koan has already caught the eyes of many industry professionals and artists. Musician/producer Brian Eno already has released an album of Koan music.

AnySearch

www.privnet.com

AnySearch is one of the most useful plug-ins for anyone who spends much time on the Internet. You're already familiar with using search engines. You may also have discovered that different search engines are better than others for any particular search. AnySearch puts eight different search engines in Netscape's toolbar.

After you install AnySearch you'll see a new button and new window in Netscape's toolbar. Right-click on the button to see a list of available search engines. Select the engine you want to use and enter your query in the window. Then press return or left-click the button to begin the search. You no longer have to go to an engines site before you can begin a search.

Cache Compactor

http://www.nol.net/~anthonyr/Programs/CacheCompactor/index.html

CacheCompactor is a utility designed for Internet Explorer and Netscape users. The program deletes all of the files in a specified directory whenever it is run. The first time you run the program, specify the directory you want to delete (the cache directory for your browser), and then simply run the program whenever you want to clear your browsers cache.

CYBERsitter

http://www.pineoak.com

CYBERsitter from Solid Oak Software Inc. allows parents and other concerned

The Web For Musicians

individual the ability to filter (or limit) their child or children's access to any objectionable material on the Internet. Users can choose to block, block and alert, or simply alert them when access is attempted to these areas. CYBERsitter is password protected, works "behind the scenes", and is virtually impossible for a child to detect or override.

Other Types Of Software And Files

The Software section discusses a wide sampling of other music programs and utilities. Many of these are available to you on the Internet. These programs are upgraded, too, so you may wish to bookmark your favorite Web pages and schedule regular visits see what's new. As you search for information on your favorite musical artist, you will also discover that sound files abound on the Web!

Artists

Individual artist pages on the Web may have been designed by the artist's recording company, management company, a fan or by the artist. These pages contain a vast amount of information, including biographies, writings and interviews of the artist, sound bites, photographs, video clips, lyrics, chords and guitar tablature. In our bookmark file, we've classified these pages by music artists-individual, which points to pages and collections of many artists and music groups.

Besides the companies and individuals who have created their own Web pages with sound files and other musical information, many fans have dedicated their pages to their favorite musical groups. Also, there are "official home pages" for many artists, music software and hardware companies, and centralized music information on many topics. There are home pages for plug-ins for your Web browser, many of which are ideal for musicians.

The Web For Musicians

Your own Web page

There are also many sites available to help you build your own Website. You can include pages on your site offering your own sound files for downloading, to honor your favorite musical artists and to link to other sites you find enjoyable. This is also a good place to demo your own musical group for professionals and other musicians.

Sound files

In addition to sounds of individual and collected artist recordings, MIDI files are available from various individuals and companies that are arrangements of many types of music, from classical to pop.

There are also WAV files and MIDI files that can be downloaded for other uses. Some are sounds that can be used as Windows system and program sounds, others are specifically designed to work with games. We've steered you towards the gaming sites and also created a large grouping of WAV and MIDI files in our bookmarks.

You'll find that using a search engine to do simple searches on an individual artist, or on the word WAV or MIDI will bring you fantastic results! You may have to narrow your search a bit to find exactly what you are looking for. There are thousands of sound files and artist pages out on the Web, just waiting for you!

Music File Downloading

The Web is a vast resource for sound files! WAV files are large and will sometimes take a long time to download. MIDI files are smaller; if MIDI is your interest you'll be able to download more files in a shorter amount of time. You may wish to create a separate folder in which to download your

MIDI and WAV files, so that they are not scattered all over your hard drive. Additionally, this will permit you to quickly locate and listen to new MIDI and WAV files, and decide whether you wish to keep them. Trash them right away if you don't care for them—remember, your hard drive can be quickly filled by music files!

Making Friends On The Internet

You will find musical files to download on Web pages that individuals have created and in newsgroups across the Internet. Note that many of these Web pages include the e-mail address of the author, who encourages you to write and request other tunes or offer comments and questions. In this way, or by joining a newsgroup, you can make friends who share your interests and learn at the same time!

Your new friends may also know where there are live chat opportunities on the Web, or meetings of those who enjoy creating music. You can find live chats on America Online, CompuServe or other online providers by visiting their music forums and by using a search engine to search for the word "chat." Your search engine will tell you what's available on a daily basis, divided by areas of interest.

If you have Netscape's Cool-Talk plug-in installed, you will be able to easily chat with others on the Internet!

Quality of Sound Files - Win Some, Lose Some

Of course, everyone makes mistakes in choosing files that don't please—the person who uploaded the WAV files they created may not be at a creative level that pleases you. Simply delete the files that aren't up to your standards and be wary of files from that same author in the future.

Don't spam your newsgroup! "Spamming" is the act of creating an annoyance by drawing attention to oneself through repetitious behavior. It ranges from people hogging a chat room session by sending repeated (usually nonsensical or inappropriate) phrases, to those who post repeated messages to a newsgroup or other message area, sometimes with attached files. Sometimes you will find that one person has posted multiple MIDI or WAV files to a music newsgroup.

Though some may do this out of "newcomer ignorance," it's not proper to spam a newsgroup with hundreds of your own creations at a time. If you are uploading files of your own, be choosy! Pick your best works, and ask that others download them and offer opinions. If you have more than two or three, learn how to use a zipping program so that you can upload them all in a bundle attached to one message.

Those who continually spam a newsgroup are indulging themselves, and will quickly find themselves ostracized. A new participant may not know this, but one reminder from other members of the newsgroup should be adequate, and a brief apology is the appropriate response.

However, uploading amateur files can be useful for you and for others if it is handled in a respectful fashion, so don't be afraid! Even if you are a novice at creating music files, it's not wrong to upload one or two files and request that others who are more expert in the newsgroup download your files and offer their opinions and advice! It will be a good way to learn more about creating music, you will make friends and meet others who are eager to help.

The Web For Musicians

You will also find other musical authors in newsgroups and on Web pages who are devoted to creating elegant samples of your favorite band, and have chosen the perfect instrumental segment or lyrical line that you've been hoping to use as one of your system sounds.

As you become more expert in cruising the Web, and adding favorite locations to your bookmark file, you'll get to know who has files to offer that suit your own tastes and purposes.

Remember we said earlier that you need to keep an eye on your hard drive space? If you become fascinated with downloading WAV files, remember to delete the ones you don't care for as often as possible. You can quickly eat up megabytes of disk space (a single WAV file can be two megabytes

> Some tasks on the Web take time! Downloading is one, loading a movie or sound file is another. Be patient, but you don't have to wait! Open another browser window and continue working or playing while your file is loading in the background.

(more or less) depending on the content). Think of how few of those WAV files will fill up your hard disk space!

Those who spend time creating WAV files know this, so for the most part you're likely to find short files (which are also better for using as a system sound, in a document or in a chat room as a greeting).

Research repositories

Centralized music information repositories are everywhere on the Web. These are sites that contain a multitude of links and information on almost every facet of the musical Web we've mentioned.

The Web For Musicians

Going interactive

Interactive Websites allow you to participate in one way or another. Some of those we've included in the companion bookmark are karaoke sites for you to visit and interactive radio sites. There are karaoke sites for kids and grownups alike. Some Karaoke sites require Real Audio, others a MIDI jukebox. You can sing along with songs that are downloaded—the lyric sheets are provided on the site.

Other sites allow you to select a Jukebox selection of music while you work. You can access radio programs or a list of favorite songs to play while you are working or surfing the Internet.

Some Amazing Web Sites

We've organized a list for you here of some of the thousands of Web sites that appeal to musicians. We have a bigger list available for you on the companion CD-ROM that you can import into your Netscape browser!

Just run Netscape Navigator, select **Bookmarks/Go to bookmarks** and then **File/Import...** to open the Import Bookmarks dialogue box. Locate the PCMUSIC.HTM file on the companion CD-ROM and click "Open".

Author's Choice Award Sites-Some of the finest music sites the Web has to offer. We chose one site for each category. With so many fine music sites out there, it was a very difficult job!

Best comprehensive acoustic guitar site

http://www.mguitar.com
(C. F. Martin and Company)

> Features an instrument catalog, history, Martin Strings and acoustic guitar information, as well as supplies and information for building your own acoustic guitars! Wonderful.

The Web For Musicians

Best music creation software

http://www.cakewalk.com
(CAKEWALK-Home)

> Popular and easy-to-learn MIDI software and more!

Best audio links

http://www.doctoraudio.com/index.html
(Doctor Audio Links)

> Beginning of Doctor Audio-allows for graphic or non-graphic viewing. This site has links to an enormous number of musical web sites.

Best comprehensive music resource

http://www.harmony-central.com
(Harmony Central)

> This is a fantastic overall Internet resource for musicians with many, many links to other music oriented pages, new product information, instrument information, software, etc. If it has to do with music, you can probably find it here.

Best children's interactive site

http://www.kids.warnerbros.com/karaoke
(Looney Tunes Karaoke-Home)

> Karaoke Tunes for Kids! Even the youngest member of the family will enjoy this lively and fun site with favorite cartoon characters and sing-along tunes. Parents will enjoy this, too!

Best online music gear

http://www.musiciansfriend.com
(Musician's Friend Direct Mail Gear)

> Fantastic site for finding everything you need from instruments to instructional videos by your favorite music star.

Best sound file conversion

http://hem/passagen.se/fmj/fmjsoft.html

> We loved this program's graphical interface and ease of use. In addition to

The Web For Musicians

being a fine audio player and editor, you can convert almost any sound format you can think of with this very fine program. Thank you from all of us who have struggled with sound conversion over the years.

Educational public spiritedness

http://www.artdsm.com/music.html
(Piano on the Net)

> Take piano lessons online! This kind of generosity of spirit is one way the Web shows what a giving community this world can become. Congratulations!

Professional guitar design

http://www.sadowsky.com
(Sadowsky Guitars, Ltd)

> From personal knowledge I can vouch for the fine professional quality of work! Check out the raves from the professionals who have depended on Mr. Sadowsky's fine work over the years. This is a must-see site!

Community consciousness

http://www.webring.org
(The Webring: Home)

> Links are in a "ring," so that you can cycle through related Web pages and not get lost in cyberspace in the process. Congratulations to all who work so very hard to maintain these links and keep this concept going!

Sound card information and support

http://www.tbeach.com/home.htm
(Turtle Beach Home Page)

> This site has taken great pains to offer thorough information in a friendly manner, geared to professionals and newcomers alike. Plenty of support for their award-winning wavetable sound cards, fun stuff, updated drivers, FAQs and a Users' Group Forum! Check out the new professional-level Multisound Pinnacle featuring the Kurzweil Mass synthesizer, plug and play compatability and outstanding audio quality.

Best educational software

http://www.voyetra.com
(Voyetra Home Page)

>Check out this well-organized site providing music software, online technical support, press releases, demos, customer service and chances to win free prizes, including multimedia software, speakers and sound cards. Turn to Voyetra for all your music needs, whether you're learning, creating or controlling music on your Windows-based PC.

Best Windows 95 resource and education

http://www.creativelement.com/win95ann/index.html
(Windows95 Annoyances)

>Thanks! What on earth would we do without you? Fantastic tips, tricks, suggestions, links and more. The site contains a list of annoying "features" of Windows95, and workarounds for most of them. A forum for intermediate to advanced users is also sponsored.

Best Windows 95 software collection

http://www.windows95.com
(Windows95.com)

>You have to see this to believe it. 'Nuff said! Congratulations!

Astounding sites: A bit of everything

>In addition to the award winners above, this section is a great jumping-off point for those interested in getting an idea of what the Web has to offer. Consider these to be honorable mentions.

http://www.dmn.com/media
(DMN Media)

>Media site with phenomenal links to its network of music and entertainment sites. It features a free e-zine, a searchable database for your favorite artists and music chats.

http://www.iuma.com/IUMA/index_graphic.html
(IUMA, Welcome to IUMA)

>The Internet Underground Music Archive (IUMA), is an online jukebox.

The Web For Musicians

http://registration.cnet.com/Registration/1,2,,0800.html?webAbbrev=cn&from=http://www.cnet.com

Join CNET NOW! Here's the place to join CNET. Once you get to this site, click on the little red "cnet"icon to see all the wonderful things CNET has to offer you! Radio, TV, Reviews, a game center, software and tons of other great stuff!

http://www.geocities.com/Hollywood/9610/
(Madokan's Palace-Spirit of Media)

Click on the checkmark next to "Music" on this page to get to some real sound and video treats. Many wonderful tips on creating your own Web Pages and much more can be found here, as well as discussions on the spirit of media in our times.

http://musicinteractive.com
(Music Interactive)

A stunning site for musicians and music enthusiasts on the Web.

http://www.namm.com/musiclinks.html#industry
(National Association of Music Merchants)

Search for Online Music Zines, Music Industry Newsgroups and more.

http://www.gu.edu.au/gwis/qcm/staff/pdraper/pdlinx.html
(Paul Draper's Music Resources)

An honorable mention for a wonderful music search database for resources on the Web and Usenet.

http://www.wi.leidenuniv.nl/audio
(Soundcard WWW Site)

Audio related information, including software and hardware.

http://www2.utep.edu/~dgreiner/guitar.htm
(The Broken G-String)

Parent restricted, one strong language hand-slap is all. But otherwise this site is phenomenal; for guitar enthusiasts everywhere. Honorable mention.

Glossary

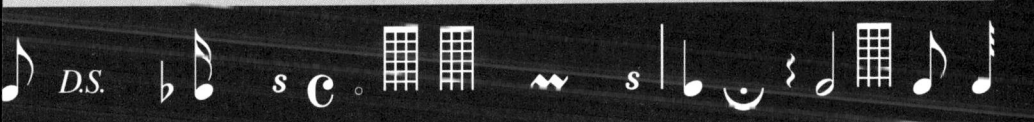

APPENDIX

Appendix A: Glossary

ADC

See analog-to-digital converter.

ADPCM

Acronym for Adaptive Delta Pulse Code Modulation, a digital audio compression format.

Aftertouc§h

A type of control data generated by pressing down on one or more keys on a synthesizer keyboard after they have reached and are resting on the keybed.

AIFF

Audio Interchange File Format: A common Macintosh audio file format. It can be mono or stereo, at sampling rates up to 48kHz. AIFF files are QuickTime compatible.

Amplitude

The amount of a signal. When this is in audio range, it is percieved as loudness.

Analog-to-digital (A/D) converter (ADC)

Any device that changes the continuous fluctuations in voltage from an analog device (such as a microphone) into digital information that can be stored or processed in a computer, sampler, digital signal processor or digital recording device.

ASCII

Text that is not formatted with HTML (see HTML). You'll also see ASCII text called "plain text" or "text documents."

Bookmark

A feature on most web browsers that let you store the addresses of web pages that you visit frequently. By using bookmarks you don't have to remember or retype your favorite web site addresses. A bookmark is also called a "hotlist" of "favorites."

Browser

Software program used to read and download HTML documents and Web files and pages.

Card

A circuit board that plugs into a slot in a computer to perform or enhance a function. Examples: graphics (video card), sound (sound card), controller functions (for hard and floppy disks) and modem.

CD-ROM

Acronym for Compact Disc—Read-Only Memory. A compact disc format that can store data other than just standard CD audio.

Channel pressure

MIDI control message, generated on controller keyboards and other keyboard instruments.

Controller keyboard

Synthesizer keyboard with the ability of being connected to a computer via a MIDI interface for the purpose of translating music to software programs within the computer and playback of musical compositions.

DAC

See digital-to-analog converter.

Appendix A: Glossary

Daughterboard

A small circuit board that can be attached to a larger one (the motherboard), giving it new capabilities.

Decibel

A unit of measurement used to indicate audio power level.

Digital

Using computer-type binary arithmetic operations.

Digital-to-analog converter (DAC)

A device that changes the sample words put out by a digital audio device into analog fluctuations in voltage that can be sent to a mixer or amplifier. All digital synthesizers, samplers and effects devices have DACs (rhymes with fax) at their outputs to create audio signals.

Domain

A registered top-level World Wide Web address, such as "Funkyfrog.com."

Downloading

The act of moving pictures, programs, files, etc., from a web site or online service to your computer. Downloading is the opposite of uploading.

DSP

Digital Signal Processing: Broadly speaking, all changes in sound that are produced within a digital audio device, other than changes caused by simple cutting and pasting of sections of a waveform, are created through DSP.

Echo

A discrete repetition of a sound, as opposed to reverberation, which is a continuous wash of closely spaced, non-discrete echoing sound.

Effects

Any form of audio signal processing—reverb, delay, chorusing, etc.

E-mail

Abbreviation for "electronic" mail. A method of communicating with other users over the Internet. Also refers to the messages themselves that are sent on a network using a computer.

Emoticons

Text symbols representing emotions that are used in e-mail or chat rooms. Most emoticons are read sideways, so ":)" represents being happy and ":(" represents being sad.

External viewer

See Helper application

FAQ

Acronym for Frequently Asked Questions: A text file that lists and answers commonly asked questions on a particular topic. FAQ files are important sources of information about the Internet.

FM

See frequency modulation.

FM synthesis

A technique in which frequency modulation (FM) is used to create complex audio waveforms. See frequency modulation.

Appendix A: Glossary

Frequency modulation (FM)

A change in the frequency (pitch) of a signal. At low modulation rates, FM is perceived as vibrato or some type of trill, depending on the shape of the modulating waveform.

FTP

Acronym for File Transfer Protocol: An easy method of transferring files between computers on the Internet.

Gain

The amount of boost or attenuation of a signal.

General MIDI (GM)

A set of requirements for MIDI devices aimed at ensuring consistent playback performance on all instruments bearing the GM logo. Some of the requirements include 24-voice polyphony and a standardized group (and location) of sounds.

Helper application (Helper app)

Programs that you can link to different file types and commands. These programs launch automatically when you access a linked file through a browser.

Hertz (Hz)

Measurement unit of frequency. One Hz equals one cycle per second. The frequency range of human hearing is from 20Hz to 20kHz (20,000Hz).

Hits

The number of times a specific file is accessed at a Web site.

Home page

This is the main page of a Web site, usually the first one sees at the site.

HTML

Acronym for HyperText Markup Language: The standard programming language used to create Web pages. These codes tell a browser how to display the text, hyperlinks, graphics and attached media of the document. HTML documents are essentially text documents with embedded tags that contain the codes for formatting, graphics, etc. Also called "hypertext."

HTTP

Acronym for HyperText Transfer Protocol: A protocol used to transmit and link Web pages. It's the standard language used by Web browsers and servers to communicate with each other.

Hyperlink

A reference in an HTML document (word, picture or button) that when clicked, takes you to another Web page or another part of the current page. Same as "link."

Interface

A linkage between two things. A user interface is the system of controls with which the user controls a device. Two devices are said to be interfaced when their operations are linked electronically.

Internet

An interconnected group of worldwide computer networks using standard computer formats to exchange information and other data.

Appendix A: Glossary

Internet Service Provider (ISP)

Companies that provide connections to the Internet, usually for a monthly or hourly fee. ISPs provide only a direct Internet connection. They do not provide instructions or interest catalogs to help you navigate through the Internet.

IRQ

Interrupt Request level: In IBM-PCs, a setting given to peripheral devices like sound cards and CD-ROM drives that identifies them to the computer's CPU. When the peripheral needs to communicate with the CPU, it will send an interrupt with that value. Problems will result if two or more peripherals are set to the same IRQ value.

Java

Programming language for embedding small applications called "Java applets" into Web pages. Java allows Web developers to write programs that will run on any computer with a Java-capable browser (i.e., Netscape or Internet Explorer).

Java applets

Small programs written in Java that are sent over the Internet and normally run inside a Web browser window. Most Java applets are currently used for minor functions like simple animations.

Kbps

Acronym for kilobits per second: Refers to the speed at which data is transferred over a line. One kilobit equals 1000 bits so a 28.8Kbps modem transfers data at a rate of 28,800 bits per second.

kHz

Kilohertz (thousands of Hertz). See Hertz.

Kilobyte (Kb)

Literally, a thousand bytes. In practice, a kilobyte generally contains 1,024 bytes.

Maintain

To regularly update a WWW site.

Mapper

A device that translates MIDI data from one form to another in real time.

Megabyte (Mb)

Linguistically speaking, a million bytes. In practice, a megabyte often contains 1,024 kilobytes.

Memory

A system or device for storing information — in the case of musical devices, information about patches, sequences, waveforms, and so on.

MIDI

Acronym for Musical Instrument Digital Interface, a standardized specification for the types of control signals that can be sent from one electronic music device to another.

MIDI Out/Thru

A MIDI output port that can be configured either to transmit MIDI messages generated within the unit (Out) or to retransmit messages received at the MIDI In (Thru).

MIDI thru

Hardware connection found on the back panels of many synthesizers, that duplicates whatever data is arriving at the MIDI in jack.

Millisecond (ms)

One one-thousandth (0.001) of a second.

Appendix A: Glossary

Mixer
A device that adds two or more audio signals together.

Modem
A device that allows computer information to be sent over a telephone line.

Mod wheel
A controller, normally mounted at the left end of the keyboard and played with the left hand, that is used for modulation. It is typically set up to add vibrato. See vibrato.

Mono mode
One of the basic reception modes of MIDI devices. In mono mode, an instrument responds monophonically to all notes arriving over a specific MIDI channel.

Monophonic
Capable of producing only one note at a time.

Multimedia
Combining and using several types of media, including graphics, audio and video, into one resource or program file. A powerful means of communicating information.

Multitimbral
Capable of making more than one tone color (timbre) at the same time. A typical multitimbral tone generator can play, for example, the brass, piano and violin parts all at once.

Page
One HTML-based document that you can view using a browser (also called a Web page).

Pitch-bend
A shift in a note's pitch, usually in small increments, caused by the movement of a pitch-bend wheel or lever; also, the MIDI data used to create such a shift.

Plug-in
A software program that acts as an extension to a larger program to add new features.

Polyphonic
Capable of producing more than one note at a time. All synthesizers place a limit on how many voices of polyphony are available. General MIDI-compliant synthesizers are required to provide at least 24 voices of polyphony.

Polyphony
The ability to produce multiple voices (notes) simultaneously.

Protocol
Specification of rules and procedures governing the transfer of information with data connections on networks. Unfortunately, there is still no uniform standard, thus different protocols exist alongside one another and must take each other into account.

RAM
Acronym for Random Access Memory: RAM is used for storing user-programmed patch parameter settings in synthesizers, and sample waveforms in samplers. A constant source of power (usually a long-lasting battery) is required for RAM to maintain its contents when power is switched off.

Real time
Occurring at the same time as other, usually human, activities. In real-time sequence

Appendix A: Glossary

recording, timing information is encoded along with the note data by analyzing the timing of the input. In real-time editing, changes in parameter settings can be heard immediately, without the need to play a new note or wait for computational processes to be completed.

Reverb

A digital signal process that produces a continuous wash of echoing sound, simulating an acoustic space such as a concert hall.

ROM

Acronym for Read-Only Memory: A type of data storage whose contents cannot be altered by the user. An instrument's operating system, and in some cases its waveforms and factory presets, are stored in ROM. Compare with RAM.

Sample

A digitally recorded representation of a sound. Also, a single word of the data that makes up such a recording. Also, to make a digital recording.

Sampler

An instrument that records and plays back samples, usually by allowing them to be distributed across a keyboard and played back at various pitches.

Sampling

The process of encoding an analog signal into digital form by reading (sampling) its level at precisely spaced intervals of time. See sample, sampling rate.

Sampling rate

The number of samples taken per second.

Scrub

To move backward and forward through an audio waveform under manual control, in order to find a precise point in the wave for editing purposes.

SCSI

Acronym for Small Computer Systems Interface: High-speed communications protocol that allows computers, samplers, and disk drives to communicate with one another. Pronounced "scuzzy."

Sequence

Set of music performance commands (notes and controller data) stored in a sequencer.

Sequencer

A device or program that records and plays back user-determined sets of music performance commands, usually in the form of MIDI data. Most sequencers also allow the data to be edited in various ways, and stored on disk.

Sine wave

A signal put out by an oscillator in which the voltage or equivalent rises and falls in a smooth and symmetric manner. Sometimes used to modulate other waveforms to produce vibrato and tremolo.

Smiley

See Emoticons.

Appendix A: Glossary

SMPTE time code

An acronym for the timing reference signal developed by the Society of Motion Picture & Television Engineers and used for synchronizing film and videotape to audio tape and software-based playback systems. Pronounced "simp-tee."

SND

Sound resource. A Macintosh audio file format.

Split keyboard

A single keyboard divided electronically to act as if it were two or more separate ones. The output of each note range is routed into a separate signal path in the keyboard's internal sound-producing circuitry, or transmitted over one or more separate MIDI channels. Applications include playing a bass sound with the left hand while playing a piano sound with the right.

Sustain pedal

Electronic equivalent of a piano damper pedal, which allows a struck or played note to ring beyond the time in which it would normally die or decay when a key is lifted.

Synthesizer

A musical instrument that generates sound electronically and is designed according to certain principles developed in the 1960s. Sounds can be programmed by the user.

TCP/IP

Acronym for Transmission Control Protocol/Internet Protocol: Standard protocol for wide area networks (WAN).

Terminal

Combination of monitor and keyboard.

Timbre

(tam-ber) The color of sound; tone color that defines the sound of a particular instrument.

Touch-sensitive

Equipped with a sensing mechanism that responds to variations in key velocity or pressure by sending out a corresponding control signal.

Tremolo

A periodic change in amplitude with a periodicity of less than 20Hz. Similar to vibrato.

Upload

The act of moving pictures, programs, files, etc., to a web site or online service from your computer. Uploading is the opposite of downloading.

URL

Acronym for Uniform Resource Locator: Address system used in the WWW that can reference any type of file on the Internet. A Web browser can locate that file because this address is unique to each page. A typical Web URL looks like this: http://www.funkyfrog.com.

User

A user can be assigned rights and be administered in an account, or user account. The user logs on to the network by means of a password.

Velocity sensitivity

A type of touch sensitivity in which the keyboard measures how fast each key is descending. Compare with pressure sensitivity.

340

Appendix A: Glossary

Vibrato

A periodic change in frequency with a periodicity of less than 20Hz. Similar to tremolo.

VOC

File extension specifying the Creative Labs Sound Blaster audio format.

WAV

Windows audio file format. Usually encountered as FILENAME.WAV.

Waveform

Signal, either sampled (digitally recorded) or periodic, being generated by an oscillator. Also, the graphic representation of this signal, as on a computer screen. Each waveform has its own unique harmonic content.

Wavetable

A set of numbers stored in memory and used to generate a waveform. The wavetable synth on a soundcard typically plays sounds whose digital representations have been stored in a wavetable.

Web

Abbreviation for World Wide Web (see World Wide Web)

Web page

Refers to one document on the Web. A web page can include a combination of text, pictures, video and sound.

Web site

A collection of web pages maintained by a business, institution, individual, organization, etc.

Webmaster

A person responsible for administering a WWW site.

Wheel

A controller, normally mounted at the left end of the keyboard and played with the left hand, that is used for pitch-bending or modulation.

World Wide Web (WWW)

A network of hypertext documents on the Internet that can be navigated with a browser and are connected through hyperlinks.

Index

Symbols

3DLEDCD 263

A

AnySearch 322
Apple QuickTime 314–315
Assigning sounds 27
Audio codecs 213–217
Audio video plug-ins 314–323
Autoeject 262
AWave for Windows 95 215–217

B

Bookmarks 301–302, 306–307

C

CacheCompactor 322
Cakewalk 244–246
CD-ROM drive types 135–138
    CD-ROM playback-only drive 135–136
    Multi-disk CD-ROM drive 136–137
    Recordable CD-ROM drive 136
    SCSI 138
CD-ROM drives 133–139
    CD-ROM playback-only drive 135–136
    Data access time 134
    Data transfer rate 135
    Drive speed 134–135
    External 134
    Installing 156
    Internal 134
    Multi-disk CD-ROM drive 136–137
    Optimizing performance 138–139
    Recordable CD-ROM drive 136
    SCSI drives 138
    Types 135–138
CD-ROM playback-only drive 135–136

CD-ROM player 64
CD32Bit 263
CDWizzard CD Audio Player 263
CMF 52
Common questions 17–30
Companion CD-ROM 5–13, 22, 201–229
    _MUSIC 12
    3D LED 8
    3DLEDCD 263
    Autoeject 262
    AutoEject for Windows 95 8
    AWAVe 7
    AWave for Windows 95 215–217
    Basic Music Theory 11
    Cakewalk 12, 244–246
    CD 32-bit 9
    CD Wizzard 9
    CD32Bit 263
    CDWizzard CD Audio Player 263
    Contents 6–13
    Cool Edit 7
    Digital Orchestrator Plus for
        Windows© 3.1 and 95 247
    DR. Worm's Master Chord Music Theory ... 261
    Drum Trax 7
    DrumTrax for MIDI 247
    Ear Power 10–11, 261
    GoldWave 8, 219–220
    Guitar Workshop 10–11, 262
    Harmony Assistant 8, 248
    Kaleidoscope 264–265
    Kaleidoscope 95 11
    MIDI & WAV programs 7–8
    Mozart 11
    MOZART the Music Processor 248
    Music Chord 10–11
    Pat's Music Theory 260–261
    Sound Play 8, 264
    Tune It 11
    Tune It! 262
    Virtual Web Site 9–10
    Voyetra Technologies' Demo 12–13

343

Index

WavAudit For Windows 95 264
Wave Audit 8
Wind Chimes 265
Conversion program 23
Converting sound 37–38
Cool Edit 96 202–204
Crescendo 316–317
CYBERsitter 322–323

D

Data access time 134
Data transfer rate 135
Digital Orchestrator Plus
  for Windows© 3.1 and 95 247
Digital sampling
  Wavetable synthesis 39–41
Digital sampling rate 43–45
Digital sampling resolution 44–45
Digital Signal Processing 18
Digitized sound 37–41
Direct recording sources 42–43
Downloading 23
DR. Worm's Master Chord
  Music Theory 261
Drivers (sound cards) 65–66
DrumTrax for MIDI 247
DSP 18

E

Ear Power 261
Electronic keyboard 63
Exercises
  Assigning system sounds 27
External CD-ROM drives 134

F

FAQ (Frequently Asked Questions)
.... 293–295
FAQs 17–30
File Transfer Protocol 277
Finding sounds 20–21
  Companion CD-ROM 22
  Voices 22

Windows 3.x 21–22
Windows 95 20–21
FM synthesis 38
Frequency Modulation (FM) synthesis 36
Frequently Asked Questions (FAQs) ....
.... 17–30

G

General MIDI 234–237
  See also MIDI
  MIDI patches 235–237
Glossary 334
GoldWave 219–220
Guitar Workshop 262

H

Hardware (finding on the Internet) ....
.... 309–310
Hardware installation 143–166
  Basic considerations 145
  CD-ROM drive 156
  Cleaning your computer 150–151
  Components 151–152
  Installation and kids 146–147
  Keyboard (music) 157–166
  Microphone 156–157
  Music hardware 153–157
  Registration forms 152–153
  Sound card 154–155
  Speaker 156–157
  Technical support 144
  Tools needed 147–150
  Warranties 152–153
  Workspace preparation 150
Hardware maintenance 143–166
  Technical support 144
Harmony Assistant 248
Headphones 19, 63, 127–128
Hertz (Hz) 35

Index

I

Indirect recording sources 42–43
Installing hardware 143–166
  See also Hardware installation
Installing music hardware 153–157
  See also Music hardware installation
Internal CD-ROM drives 134
Internet 271–282
  Artist pages 323
  Bookmarks 301–302, 306–307
  Components of the Internet 272–277
  Connecting 277–282
  Downloading files 295–301
  FAQ (Frequently Asked Questions) 293–295
  File Transfer Protocol 277
  Hardware (finding) 309–310
  Journals 308
  Links 291–293, 301–302, 306–307
  Magazines 308
  Mailing lists 274
  Making friends 325
  Music files 324–325
  Netiquette 274–277
  Newsgroups 274
  Newspapers 308
  Online services 278
  Plug-Ins 287–289, 313–314
  Search engines 286–287
  Software (finding) 310–312
  Sound files 324
  Surfing 285
  Uploading files 295–301
  Web addresses 279–282
  Web site examples 328–332
  Webring 307
  Websites (finding) 305–332
  World Wide Web 278–279
  Your own page 324
Internet Phone 318–319

K

Kaleidoscope 264–265

Keyboard (music)
  See also Music keyboard
  Installing 157–166
Koan 321–322

L

Links 291–293, 301–302, 306–307
Live3D 319–320

M

Mailing lists 274
Maintaining hardware 143–166
Microphone 64
  Installing 156–157
Microphones 129–130
MID files
  Windows 95 Media Player 175–177
MIDI 50, 54–55, 233–248
  Defined 233
  General MIDI 234–237
  General MIDI patches 235–237
  Sound cards 95
  SysEx MIDI information 237–239
  Using 239–241, 241–248
MIDI Adapters 115–116
MidPlug 317
MOD 50–51
Moving Pictures Experts Group 52
MOZART the Music Processor 248
MPEG 52
Multi-disk CD-ROM drive 136–137
Multimedia files 20
Multimedia packages 64–65
Music equipment
  Shopping for equipment 75–83
Music files
  Finding on the Internet 324–325
Music hardware 61–66
  CD-ROM player 64
  Electronic keyboard 63
  Headphones 63
  Microphone 64
  Multimedia packages 64–65
  Sound card 62

345

Index

Speakers 63
Synthesizer 63
Music hardware installation **153–157**
   CD-ROM drives 156
   Keyboard 157–166
   Microphone 156–157
   Sound card 154–155
   Speakers 156–157
Music keyboards **105–116**
   AC power 106
   Acoustic action 111
   Basic features 105–113
   Built-in sounds 108
   Buying a keyboard 105–116
   Channel pressure 110
   Full-sized keys 106
   Key range transposition 110
   MIDI 107–108
   MIDI Adapters 115–116
   Modulation pedal 109
   Modulation wheel 109
   Multitimbral capability 111
   Octave range 106
   Pitch wheel 110
   Polyphony 107
   Standalone capability 112–113
   Sustain pedal 106
   Touch sensitivity/response 106
   Trying before buying 113–115

N

Netiquette 274–277
Newsgroups 274

O

Online services 278

P

Pat's Music Theory 260–261
PC speaker 19, 62
PC Systems Sounds 26

Plug-ins **287–289, 313–314**
   AnySearch 322
   Apple QuickTime 314–315
   Audio video plug-ins 314–323
   CacheCompactor 322
   Crescendo 316–317
   CYBERsitter 322–323
   Internet Phone 318–319
   Koan 321–322
   Live3D 319–320
   MidPlug 317
   RealAudio 315–316
   Shockwave 320

R

RealAudio **315–316**
Recordable CD-ROM drive **136**
RMI sound files
   Windows 95 Media Player 175–177
ROL **52**

S

Samples **55–56**
Sampling **55–56**
   Sound cards 96
SCSI CD-ROM drive **138**
Search engines **286–287**
Shockwave **320**
SND **52**
Software (finding on the Internet) ......
.... **310–312**
Sound **33–45**
   See also Sound files
   Converting 37–38
   Defined 17
   Digital sampling rate 43–45
   Digital sampling resolution 44–45
   Digitized sound 37–41
   Facts about sound 33–45
   FM synthesis 38
   Hearing sound 34
   How it travels 34–35
   Measuring 35

Index

Quality 42–43
Syntheses 36
Synthesizers 36
Wavetable synthesis 38–41
Sound card drivers **65–66**
Sound cards **18, 62, 72–75, 87–102**
Capabilities 95–100
Development 88
Drivers 65–66
Features 89–91
Installing 154–155
MIDI capability 95
Sampling capability 96
Shopping for a sound card 72–75
Software 19
Sound Blaster compatibles 79–83
Tips on buying 100–102
Uses 91–94
Wavetable add-on card 97–98
Wavetable synthesis compatibility ... 96–97
Sound facts **33–45**
How sound travels 34–35
Sound file types **49–56**
CMF 52
MIDI 50, 54–55
MOD 50–51
MPEG 52
ROL 52
SND 52
ULAW 51
VOC 51–52
WAV 49, 54–55
Sound files **23**
Adding effects 189–191
Changing formats (Audio Codecs) 213–217
Combining 205–207
Combining and overlaying 220–221
Combining two files 194
Converting sound files 217–220
Cut and paste files 195–196
Cutting sound files 191–197
Dead air 221–222
Editing 189–193
Fades 224–225
Finding on the Internet 324
Identifying 24
Inserting in a document 255–257

Linking in a document 257–259
Mixing 196–197
Noise 223
Overlaying 208–210
Overlaying and combining 220–221
Quality of Internet sound files ... 326–328
Stereo recording 210–212
Types 24
Types of sound files 49–56
Unwanted noise 223
Using 26
Sound Play **264**
Sound quality **42–45**
Sound system **69–84**
Building a sound system 69–84
Compatibility issues 71
Music equipment 75–83
System requirements 70
Sounds
Assigning to events 27
Companion CD-ROM 22
Inserting in a document 255–257
Linking in a document 257–259
Windows 3.x 21–22
Windows 95 20–21
Windows 95 system sound scheme 254–255
Sounds and system events **252–253**
Speakers **19, 63**
Acoustics 125
Adapters 121–123
Built-in speakers 119
Buying 119–125
Connections 126–127
External speakers 120
Getting the best sound 125–128
Headphones 127–128
Home stereo speakers 120–121
Installing 156–157
Positioning 126
Stereo recording **210–212**
Surfing the Internet **285–302**
Syntheses **36**
Frequency Modulation (FM) 36
Wavetable synthesis 36
Synthesizers **36, 63, 105–116**
See also Music keyboards
SysEx MIDI information **237–239**

347

Index

System events 252–253
System sounds 27–28, 254–255

T

Tune It! 262

U

ULAW 51

V

VOC 51–52
Voices
    Adding to your PC 22

W

WAV files 49, 54–56
    Combining audio clip 181–185
    Creating a voice recording 185–186
    Recording from a VCR or stereo 187–189
WAV sounds 172–175
    Windows 95 Sound Recorder 172–175
WavAudit For Windows 95 264
Wavetable 56
Wavetable add-on card 97–98
Wavetable daughter cards 97
Wavetable synthesis 36, 38–41
    Digital sampling 39–41
    Sound cards compatibility 96–97
Wavetable upgrade cards 97
Web addresses 279–282
Webring 307
Website examples 328–332
Wind Chimes 265
Windows 3.x
    Sound system requirements 70
    Sounds 21–22
Windows 95
    Sound system requirements 70
    Sounds 20–21
Windows 95 CD Player 178–181
Windows 95 Media Player 175–177

Windows 95 Sound Recorder 172–175
Windows 95 sound utilities 171–198
    Windows 95 CD Player 178–181
    Windows 95 Media Player 175–177
    Windows 95 Sound Recorder 172–175
Windows 95 system sound schemes ....
.... 254–255
World Wide Web 278–279
    See also Internet
    Finding websites 305–332

PC catalog

Order Toll Free 1-800-451-4319
Books and Software

Includes CD-ROM with Sample Programs

Abacus

To order direct call Toll Free 1-800-451-4319

In US and Canada add $5.00 shipping and handling. Foreign orders add $13.00 per item.
Michigan residents add 6% sales tax.

Developers Series books are for professional software dovelopers who require in-depth technical information and programming techniques.

PC Intern—6th Edition
The Encyclopedia of System Programming

Now in its 6th Edition, more than 500,000 programmers worldwide rely on the authoritative and eminently understandable information in this one-of-a-kind volume. You'll find hundreds of practical, working examples written in assembly language, C++, Pascal and Visual Basic—all professional programming techniques which you can use in your own programs. PC INTERN is a literal encyclopedia for the PC programmer. PC INTERN clearly describes the aspects of programming under all versions of DOS as well as interfacing with Windows.

Includes CD-ROM with Sample Programs

Some of the topics include:
- Memory organization on the PC
- Writing resident TSR programs
- Programming graphic and video cards
- Using extended and expanded memory
- Handling interrupts in different languages
- Networking programming NetBIOS and IPX/SPX
- Win95 virtual memory and common controls
- IRQs—programming interrupt controllers
- Understanding DOS structures and function
- Using protected mode, DOS extenders and DPMI/VCPI multiplexer
- Programming techniques for CD-ROM drives
- Programming Sound Blaster and compatibles

The companion CD-ROM transforms PC INTERN from a book into an interactive reference. You can search, navigate and view the entire text of the book and have instant access to information using hypertext links. Also included on the CD-ROM are hundreds of pages of additional programming tables and hard-to-find material.

Author: Michael Tischer and Bruno Jennrich
Order Item: #B304
ISBN: 1-55755-304-1
SRP: $69.95 US/$99.95 CAN
with companion CD-ROM

To order direct call Toll Free 1-800-451-4319

In US and Canada add $5.00 shipping and handling. Foreign orders add $13.00 per item.
Michigan residents add 6% sales tax.

**Productivity Series books are for users who want
to become more productive with their PC.**

Upgrading and Maintaining Your PC
New 4th Edition

Buying a personal computer is a major investment. Today's ever-changing technology requires that you continue to upgrade if you want to maintain a state of the art system. Innovative developments in hardware and software drive your need for more speed, better hardware, and larger capacities. **Upgrading and Maintaining Your PC** gives you the knowledge and skills that help you upgrade or maintain your system. You'll save time and money by being able to perform your own maintenance and repairs.

New! Win95 Upgrade Info Included

How to upgrade, repair, maintain and more:
- Hard drives, Memory and Battery Replacement
- Sound & Video Cards, CD-ROM's
- Pentium Powerhouses 60 - 133 *MHz,* overdrive processor
- Large Capacity Hard Drives
- Quad Speed CD-ROM Drives
- Sound Cards - 64-bit and Wave Table
- Modems/Fax Cards, ISDN
- AMD, Cyrix, AMI and Intel Processors
- Operating Systems - DOS 6.22, Novell DOS, IBM PC DOS 6.3, OS/2 Warp & Windows 3.1 to Windows 95

On the CD-ROM!

System Sleuth Analyzer from Dariana ($99.95 value) - A toolbox of valuable PC diagnostic aids rolled into a single, easy-to-use software utility. It lets you explore exacting details of your PC without fear of accidental, unrecoverable modifications to a particular subsystem.

Cyrix Upgrade Compatibility Test - Run "Cyrix's" own test to see if you can upgrade with one of their new 486 chips!

Intel's Pentium Chip Test - calculate the now famous "math problem" on your own system!

Authors: H. Veddeler & U. Schueller
Order Item:#B300
ISBN: 1-55755-300-9
Suggested retail price: $34.95 US / $46.95 CAN with CD-ROM

To order direct call Toll Free 1-800-451-4319

In US and Canada add $5.00 shipping and handling. Foreign orders add $13.00 per item.
Michigan residents add 6% sales tax.

Software

ZIP KIT

Learn to Use the World's Most Popular Data Compression Programs!

Start Using WinZip and nine other fully functional evaluation versions of the most popular data compression shareware in the universe today.

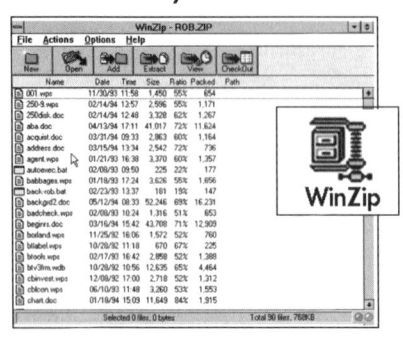

This Windows-based utility makes unlocking the treasures of the information superhighway a breeze. Zip and unzip. Drag-and-drop. Virus scanning support.

Graphic & Video Utilities

Special graphic and video programs in the **ZIP KIT** will help you work with dozens of different formats.

Learn to convert and compress numerous graphic formats with unique image processing software: ART, BMP, DIB, GIF, IFF, ICO, LBM, MSP, PCX, RLE, TIF, WPG, CUT, EXE, HRZ, IMG, JPG, MAC, PIC, RAS, TGA, and TXT.

Discover the world of compressed video files: FLI, AVI, MPG, FLC, and MCI.

ZIP KIT
Item #S287
ISBN 1-55755-290-8
UPC 0 90869 55290 1

SRP: $34.95 US/ $46.95 CAN

To order direct call Toll Free 1-800-451-4319

In US and Canada add $5.00 shipping and handling. Foreign orders add $13.00 per item.
Michigan residents add 6% sales tax.

Beginner's Series
easy learning for everyone

Paint Shop Pro for Beginners
"no experience required"

Paint Shop Pro is an award-winning graphics application and one of the most popular shareware products in the world. This beginner's book takes a first-time users approach to learning and working with Paint Shop Pro 3.12 for Windows 95 and Windows 3.X. you'll discover what plug-ins and filters are, how to create special effects and then onto working with your very first image.

Author Scott Slaughter takes a "how-to" approach to the book and illustrates the steps involved in doing things like fixing a treasured photo, adding color, converting images to any of the 30 different formats available and why. Paint Shop Pro is an ideal utility for creating the kind of GIF files required of the Internet. In addition you'll learn how to perform screen captures and numerous tips & tricks used by the pros.

CD-ROM Included

Other topics include:

- Working with image files
- Zooming, cropping, and moving images
- Paint tool techniques like airbrushing and flood fill
- Learn to use select tools such as the clone brush, lasso, and magic wand
- Working with color palettes
- Deformations and special effects
- Retouching photos

The companion CD-ROM includes a fully-functional evaluation version of Paint Shop Pro 3.12 for Windows 95 and Windows 3.X.

Author: Scott Slaughter
Item #: B319
ISBN: 1-55755-319-X
SRP: $19.95 US/26.95 CAN
   with CD-ROM

Order Direct Toll Free 1-800-451-4319

In US and Canada add $5.00 shipping and handling. Foreign orders add $13.00 per item.
Michigan residents add 6% sales tax.

Productivity Series books are for users who want
to become more productive with their PC.

Your Family Tree
Using Your PC

Your Family Tree is a beginners guide to researching, organizing and sharing your family's heritage with relatives and friends. If you want to trace your family roots, get started by using this book and companion CD-ROM.

Author Jim Oldfield, Jr. shows how to get started tracing your roots using his expert, easy-to-follow steps and your personal computer. An experienced genealogist, Jim has produced three family history books of his own, and now you can too.

You'll learn how to gather facts and information, transfer them to popular genealogy programs, add illustrations, use your word processor or desktop publisher to produce reports, share the info in a meaningful way and keep up with 'newer' family additions.

Topics discussed include:
- Researching on the Internet
- Creating a Web site for your family pages
- Starting your own newsletter or association
- Adding photos and sound to your family tree
- Using conversion programs to publish data on the Web
- Using software like- Family Tree, Family Origins and more

CD-ROM INCLUDED!

On the CD-ROM-

The companion CD-ROM has various family pedigree forms for collecting family information, sample family data that shows you 'hands-on' how to get started, family photos and a collection of the most popular shareware for genealogy and illustrations.

Author: Jim Oldfield, Jr.
Order Item #B310
ISBN: 1-55755-310-6

Suggested Retail Price
$25.95 US/$34.95 CAN
CD-ROM Included

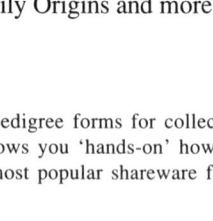

To order direct call Toll Free 1-800-451-4319

In US & Canada Add $5.00 Shipping and Handling
Foreign Orders Add $13.00 per item. Michigan residents add 6% sales tax.

Software

Pilot's Shop
for Microsoft Flight Simulator
Aircraft, Scenery & Utilities

Pilot's Shop is a new CD-ROM collection of the world's best add-ons for Microsoft Flight Simulator. This new CD-ROM instantly makes flying even more authentic and exciting as you travel virtually anywhere.

New Planes—fly new powerful and classic planes form the past.

Fly new and modified planes to new locations, plan detailed flights, make precision landings and build your own sceneries using sophisticated tools.

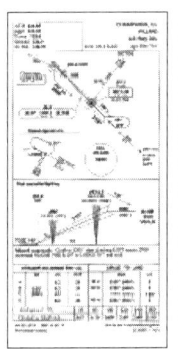

Flight Planners and Approach Plates—plot and print your own graphical maps and step-by-step plans with waypoints help you plan short flights or transoceanic trips and realistic precision instrument landings

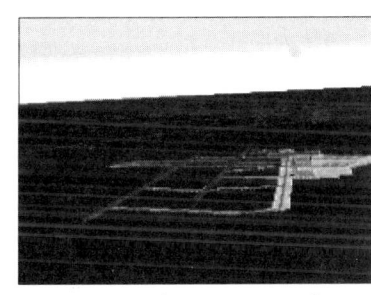

New Impressive Scenery— fly to new destinations—exciting Las Vegas, adventurous Grand Tetons, exotic Hong Kong, lovely France, Canada, Scotland, Switzerland, Vietnam and more!

Pilot's Shop
Item #S308
ISBN 1-55755-308-4
UPC 0 90869 55308 3

SRP: 29.95 USA/$39.95 CAN

To order direct call Toll Free 1-800-451-4319

In US and Canada add $5.00 shipping and handling. Foreign orders add $13.00 per item. Michigan residents add 6% sales tax.

About The Companion CD-ROM

The CD-ROM included with this guide contains some of the best shareware and evaluation software for music and CD-ROM usage.

To run the CD in Windows 3.X:

Select **Run...**" from the **File** pull-down menu located at the top left corner of your screen (this is the Microsoft Windows' Program Manager screen).

Type **D:\MENU.EXE** (where 'D' is the device letter assigned to your CD-ROM drive) and click OK. Click OK again and the MENU program will be loaded.

To run the CD-ROM in Windows 95, click the **Start** button, select **Run...**, type **D:\MENU.EXE** (where 'D' is the device letter assigned to your CD-ROM drive). Click OK and the MENU program will be loaded.

With a little exploration on your part, you'll discover some great music tools, utilities, music and much more to help you with music on your PC.

Be sure to check out Funky Frog Productions 'Virtual Web Site' on the companion CD to see an example of what you can do.

See Chapter 1 for more information about this CD-ROM